Leading With Courage

A CAREER-LONG GUIDE FOR IDEALISTIC WOMEN

DR. JODI VANDENBERG-DAVES

To my children, Allison, Sylvia, and Brad, and all the rising generations. Thank you for inspiring me in all the ways that you do good work, show up with love, and dream a better world.

TABLE OF CONTENTS

INTRODUCTION

WOMEN IN TODAY'S WORKPLACES

Crisis and Opportunities for Courage

I'VE SPENT MOST OF MY CAREER working with idealistic young people, especially women. I wrote this book because I want a better world for them, and for my grown children, two Millennial women and a Gen Z son. I continue to be inspired by the social-justice visionaries who filled my college classrooms for years, and who now show up as coaching clients and in professional learning spaces. I admire and learn from the idealism and vision of Millennials and Gen Z. I rejoice in their resilience when it shines through. And I worry about them because they are facing a hard moment.

I especially want young women with bold, progressive ideas to find meaning, balance, and the freedom to do work that feeds them. I want them to leverage their talents and claim their leadership. I want them to feel empowered in the face of discriminatory systems while building caring, inclusive communities to ground them through the crises of our times. And I want justice-oriented women who have been in the workplace for a while to also take up more space, step into their power, and build connections across generations as transformational leaders and mentors, ready to lead with courage while finding joy and impact at work.

We can do this. We can nurture this kind of vision and leadership across generations and identities. As a historian, I ground myself in the awareness that women have been transforming institutions throughout the centu-

WOMEN IN TODAY'S WORKPLACES

ries. Women have been brilliant, resourceful, and persistent, even in very harsh times and circumstances. We still are!

No matter your age or identity, if you resonate with the idea of courageous, progressive leadership at any age and through any position, I'm excited to invite you on the journey of *Leading with Courage*.

The premise of this book is simple: social-justice-minded women, leading from anywhere, can find empowerment and meaning through their values, while contributing to a more humane and just world. *Leading With Courage* goes beyond the success memoirs and transactional frameworks of corporate leaders and offers "leadership for the rest of us," a workplace self-help guide for the collectively minded.

One of the lessons of this book is that we don't need to look very far to find our mentors and heroes. The women leaders who inspire me, some of whom shared their stories for this book, often work and live in places like my medium-sized midwestern city home. Many are mothers; all have faced personal, professional, and systemic challenges, from sexism and racism to being misunderstood. Yet they've done beautiful, life-affirming work over the long haul, guided by pro-social values. Their work builds communities, not just companies or organizations. They use their workplace platforms to create crucibles of innovation and spaces for decency, diversity, and social justice.

It's getting so very much harder under a second Trump administration. But pro-social values can't be legislated away. Workplaces remain the everyday spaces where we show up and try to make a difference in the world. How and where we work, the relationships we build, and the projects we pursue, all can have an impact.

Thanks in part to the people who have been pushing for fairness at work in so many capacities across so many sectors over decades, many workplaces do provide mechanisms within them to make change. We can make meaning out of the hours we spend earning a living. We can contribute to human growth, reduce inequities, and improve our communities and our world. The oral history journeys spotlighted in this book offer us some inspiration for how to do this. Throughout the book, you'll find reflection questions and actionable advice to help you actualize empowered, inclusive leadership from wherever you are.

But before we get there, let's be sure we understand the context, so we can use knowledge as power to understand and transform our workplaces as we're empowering ourselves.

GENERATIONS AT WORK IN OUR HISTORICAL MOMENT

What's at stake for younger generations? Entirely too much. Millennial workers, now the largest generation in the workforce, and Gen Z coming right behind them, are more likely than previous generations to care about an organization's actual commitment to values like diversity and inclusion. They're more likely to be alert to inequities and skeptical of established institutions. This attitude both reflects and fuels broader changes in the culture, including the lived experiences of these generations themselves, who are far more racially and ethnically diverse than their predecessors. Only 51% of members of Gen Z are white, compared to 55% of Millennials, 60% of Gen X, and 72% of Baby Boomers, and significant percentages report facing discrimination at work related to their backgrounds or identities.[1]

Significant portions of these generations are committed to racial justice, work-life balance, mental health support in the workplace, and sustainability. And they want their employers to be committed, too. Younger professionals often ask about diversity and inclusion in their job interviews, reject jobs that don't align with their values, and leave employers for similar reasons.[2]

One of the young women I interviewed for this book, a graduate student in social work, said, "From my perspective, at least, one of the core values of social work across the board is to advocate for social justice and human rights. And yet somehow, so many of us continue to get our social work degrees and licenses and stuff and then just continue to perpetuate the same stuff." Peyton did not want to be part of that, but at the time of our interview, she wasn't sure how she would translate her own values about social work into workplace settings and overcome some of the negative histories of social work. We need the talents of big-thinking, idealistic and ambitious women like Peyton, and yet we are too often failing them. When their voices don't get heard or amplified, or when critical opportunities to mentor them and encourage their critical questions are lost, we are all losing out.

The outright hostile, punitive, and fear-inducing "anti-DEI" tactics of the second Trump administration reflect longer patterns of inequality that make young women's paths harder. In the 2020s alone we've seen more evidence of massive economic inequities and endemic issues of racism and sexism, unprecedented political dysfunction, all in the midst of a climate crisis and in the wake of a global pandemic. Reactionary movements and executive orders against DEI create fear and harassment in the workplace, as many employers abandon support of women, BIPOC people, LGBTQ+ workers, and people with disabilities.

At the same time, things are getting less secure for those entering their professional paths. We're experiencing the decline of the middle class and the slow creep of work hours for professionals. Many young people are discouraged from pursuing college degrees due to the debt crisis and stagnant or declining investments in higher education. They have real concerns about jobs disappearing with the AI revolution. Their economic precarity as a generation, more pronounced for young people of color, people with disabilities, women, and other marginalized groups, is real. And so is their anxiety. Indeed, not just in the U.S. but globally, almost half of people aged 18-24 reported a deterioration in their mental health in the second year of the pandemic a trend that represents a continuation of mental health decline in the young since the Great Recession. These young people also frequently report that they have trouble relating and connecting to others.[3]

Publicly funded institutions and nonprofits, more likely than corporate workplaces to be headed by women, are being squeezed by an austerity-focused "do more with less" set of public policies that create overwork, burnout, and demoralization, not to mention a public safety crisis for many in caring, service, and educational work, such as healthcare and K-12 schools. These are fields disproportionately occupied by women. We need to be real about these obstacles, especially if we are to have valuable conversations across generations.

POSITIONAL LEADERS STILL DON'T QUITE "LOOK LIKE US,"
And there are reasons for that

Meanwhile, it is a thrill to have my daughters and son see women, BIPOC and LGBTQ+ people become more visible in formal leadership roles in ways I rarely saw at their age. But the long feminist and anti-racist project of disrupting the norm of who's in charge is still yielding many unsatisfying results. In spite of important and undeniable progress, white men, usually straight, cisgender, Christian and from class-privileged backgrounds, continue to occupy a very disproportionate share of formal leadership positions, wealth and power, and people still too often assume white men to be "natural leaders."[4]

McKinsey's 2024 "Women in the Workplace" report, for example, found positional leadership progress for women continuing in spite of the pandemic and other crises, but at a slow pace. Women now occupy about 29% of C-suite seats a gain from 17% in 2015 but early promotions still lag. The pipeline to formal leadership is leaky. For every 100 men promoted to manager, only 81 women are, and numbers are much lower for Black women (54 for every 100 men) and Latinas (65 for every 100 men).[5]

The broken rung on the ladder to advancement is often the first one on the pathway to manager roles. In fact, women of color have higher aspirations for the C-suite than white women do, and yet they are more likely to be judged harshly, discouraged, harassed, and passed over for leadership roles. Gender-non-conforming workers face significant challenges as well. Eighty-two percent of transgender employees report experiencing workplace discrimination or harassment at some point in their lives, including being denied promotion.[6]

Inflexible workplaces, covert and overt sexist and racist discrimination, sexual harassment, pay gaps, the "caregiver penalty" for mothers and other caregivers, and other barriers to advancement and leadership too often silence women's voices and hinder their careers, including for women who don't necessarily aspire to formal leadership roles.

LEARNING FROM WOMEN:
Values-Driven Leadership At Every Level and in Every Generation

The problems can seem overwhelming, but inspiration can always be found. As a historian, I put my faith not only in the inventiveness and brilliance of young people, but also in stories and in intergenerational wisdom. Generations of women have both struggled and triumphed in the workplace, and we have so much to learn from one another. Too often, we lose track of a piece of the larger picture, of the patterns of women's problem-solving, self-advocacy, mentorship, and institutional change toward more just, expansive, forward-thinking, and innovative workplaces.

And too often, we narrow the conversation about empowering women in the workplace to a specific idea of "leadership." We tend to think of women leaders only as CEOs, corner office holders, and coastal elites, the ones who write the most popular leadership books. In fact, women's leadership is everywhere, at lots of levels of organization, spanning workplace, community, and family life. And it always has been.

We do need to advance women into formal leadership roles, and to learn from the women who have occupied those roles. We need this not just because it's long past time to have more women's voices at the table, but also because advancing women often helps advance social change, especially when the women who are advancing are intentional about progressive values such as inclusion, belonging, anti-racism, feminism, and LGBTQ+ and disability justice.

But viewing leadership as present in any position reveals deeper insights into transformation. By focusing on women's stories of resourcefulness and resilience, we begin to understand why people increasingly value women's leadership. These journeys are complex and multifaceted, marked by struggle and beauty. In each generation, even as they survive discrimination, discouragement, and sometimes harassment, idealistic women chip away at problematic workplace cultures. They advocate for themselves, break down barriers, and bridge gaps between hierarchy, workplace, and community, challenging old norms and amplifying new voices.

NOT JUST ANY WOMEN LEADERS

Few leadership books for women talk about social justice values, instead turning values discussions into vague concepts like "integrity" or "grit." But what our institutions need most are not just any women leaders. Indeed, some women leaders are racial harassers, as Minda Harts has shown in disturbing and sobering detail in her book, *The Memo: What Women of Color Need to Know to Secure a Seat at the Table*.[7] In addition to more male and white allies, some of whom are social justice leaders themselves, we need women leaders of all backgrounds and nonbinary leaders too who lead with courage, who can learn to thrive and self-advocate while also developing a practice of leadership connected to justice.

Anyone, regardless of gender and other identity, can be a transformational leader in the workplace. Indeed, a number of women I interviewed cited values-driven white men as excellent mentors and champions for them in the workplace. But there is a reason to focus on women as the teachers here. Research shows that women, especially women of color or women who struggle with other forms of intersectional discrimination, are more likely to raise questions about the hierarchies and unethical practices that tend to not only hold back even the most race- and class-privileged women, but especially hold back a variety of less privileged people, including LGBTQ+ people, immigrants, and men of color. Women tend to see workplace rules and norms from the perspective of people for whom those rules were not made. Women of color are especially likely to be underrepresented in professional workplaces, and find themselves having to "code-switch" their behavior to accommodate white-dominated workplaces and modes of communication that are different from the circles they move in outside of work.[8] People tend to experience women leaders as more likely to bring to work the values that help more people around them thrive, which in and of itself is a social good.

Half of Americans specifically say they want to work for female leaders, whom they see as more "purpose-driven" and more likely to set up structures to address employees' needs that are, at their core, about gender equity and other forms of equity. Survey respondents to an online Harris poll considered female-led organizations more likely to have childcare and to attend to equal pay. Employees at female-led companies are more likely to have "engaged, inspired, and satisfied employees than male-led firms," and several studies show women-led companies outperforming male-led ones.[9]

Moreover, history shows the value of collaborative leadership styles for social transformation. Though not all women are collaborative leaders, these skills are generally part of women's socialization. In the workplace, many women can and do develop relationship-orientation, network-building, collaboration and compromise as practices that can foster transformational change. For example, women are more likely than men to consider multiple perspectives when making a decision.[10] Often, it's women who do the work of bringing others up with them, whether or not they have an extensive framework and vocabulary for inclusivity and equity.

ADVICE TO WOMEN?

There are lots of reasons to be skeptical of "advice literature" for working women. One semester, when teaching my "Women and Leadership" class, my older daughter sent me an article titled "All Career Advice to Women is a Form of Gaslighting." To wit, we will always be writing advice to women about how to alter themselves to fit into existing structures, until the structures themselves are different. Women are expected to expend their energy on all this adaptation WHILE they're also working hard to accomplish their actual work. There is an alarming amount of truth to this.

The advice literature directed at women is beset by deficit models (you should be more confident and more assertive), by a bias toward CEOs and celebrities, and by a focus on individualism: here's how YOU can succeed within existing systems that often have a winner-take-all model. Though newer books by women of color are helping to disrupt the assumed whiteness of "success in the workplace" advice literature (see, for example, work by Minda Harts),[11] there is still a long way to go toward making our understanding of women's workplace issues more intersectional, and really showing the way toward making our workplaces spaces to advance racial, gender, and other forms of social justice.

In this book, I can't promise to transcend that inherent tension between acknowledging how harshly women are judged and how entrenched inequality is in our institutions and just telling women to go for it anyway.

But I can promise to treat the subject of women's empowerment and leadership from the perspective of a diverse array of women deeply committed to values of equity, inclusion, and justice whose stories show how resilience works over the long arc of a life and a career.

THE VOICES IN THIS BOOK

This book is grounded in deep oral history research that illuminates how diverse women progress through various stages of their careers by leveraging their values, and how generational experiences shape those journeys. Sixteen women generously shared their journeys with me through in-depth oral history interviews. Portions of my own story are included here, too, along with the insights of numerous women who provided short reflections on specific topics, and of the many women whose stories I have heard or witnessed over my decades in academia and my nonprofit and consulting work.

The women I interviewed in-depth are a diverse group. All reside in or have deep connections to a small city/regional economy in the Upper Midwest. But they vary by race and ethnicity (seven women of color, including Black, indigenous, Asian American and Latina, and nine white women); by age (with ages ranging from 24 to 61 at the time of interview); by sexual orientation (I did not ask for this information, but three self-identified as queer or bisexual); and by industry/type of work. Nine of the 16 had experience with or worked in the corporate world at the time of our interview. Beyond the corporate setting, interviewees had experience in, or worked at the time, in nonprofits, education, government, and independent consulting. To protect the interviewees' identities, I have changed names and, in a few cases, other identifying details.

These women only speak for themselves, and do not represent all kinds of diversity. This book has limitations and biases. Though certainly not all the women whom I interviewed for this project were where they wanted to be in their careers at the time they shared their stories, they were in strong enough places in their working lives to be willing to tell their stories. If I emphasize resilience through obstacles and have stories to back up that perspective in this book, I also acknowledge that many women along the way gave up on the professional workplace or on their dreams of advancement within it, because it failed them too many times.[12] Moreover, there are some costs we don't always share publicly, and stories always have omissions, mine included.

Additionally, though I have always been a huge proponent of collective organizing, including via unions, the reality is that few professional workplaces are equipped with these vital channels for collective change. In our individualistic professional cultures, too often, we tend to need to fight our battles on our own, while hopefully having a network of mentors, advisors, and people who "have our backs" as we move through these systems. In the stories I collected, it's mentoring, relationships, ad hoc coalitions, and the inspiration of role models that often form the thread of collectivism.

On a related note, while there is variation in the careers of the women I've interviewed, the book does focus on what we might call "professional workplaces." I put this term in quotations because the professional workplace and the credentials required to access it are constantly changing.[13] I think of "professional" work as often, though not always, requiring a college degree, and promising (if not always delivering) some upward mobility potential beyond direct service. Much more needs to be written about the changing class dimensions of the professional workplace.

I also hope to see more books in the future written by and directed at male allies in the workplace, and more research into how we can leverage the leadership strengths of nonbinary leaders at every level. Women shouldn't have to do it alone, and we can all make more common cause around gender-inclusive courageous leadership. Indeed, I long for the day when the many workshops I facilitate on women and leadership include and even focus on the role of men and all genders.[14] As women, we can and should advise one another, but throughout this book, I suggest ways that other people can also help.

Limitations notwithstanding, what you will find in this book is a larger framework and an injection of honesty about the lives of real-life women, through the lens of context, history, career stages, and intergenerational connections.

LEADING WITH COURAGE:
Mapping Career Journeys

The book is organized into three sections that correspond to career journeys. Everyone's journey will be different, of course, and sometimes career shifts mean repeating "steps" or experiences. But general patterns are notable.

Part I explores themes of "Establishing Credibility: Empowerment Through Your Voice and Values." In this career chapter, which often spans through the late twenties or early thirties, many women complete their education and find their first professional jobs, while also establishing their values and developing their curiosity about the kinds of problems and issues they want to work on. This is a time of figuring out our boundaries, working to build confidence and credibility, and developing competence and transferable skills, while also trying to challenge systems in which we have relatively little power. In this chapter of career, we search out spaces of belonging, finding them, sometimes losing them, and having to re-find them again, as we navigate the world of work. We often think hard about what authority and power mean to us, as we watch other people wear those identities, and wonder about the pros and cons of seeking out formal leadership roles.

The second section, "Mid-Career: Balancing Acts and Barriers, Resilience and Leadership," focuses on issues common to women who are a decade or more into the professional world, through their early-to-mid-fifties or so. This is often a period of expanded networks, and hopefully expanded influence. It's also a time of high risk for obstacles of sexism and other "isms" in the workplace as we seek advancement and use our voices on issues that matter to us. Often, we take on caregiving responsibilities. Indeed, college-educated women have their first child on average, seven years later than women without college degrees, and by the end of this mid-career stage, it's not uncommon for women to be taking on elder care responsibilities.[15] One of the consequences of caregiving is that other people are relying on our paychecks and our career stability, and we have complex risk assessments with respect to making career changes. For many women, work responsibilities expand along with caregiving roles.

And yet, this is often a time of hitting our stride and knowing our worth, of feeling the empowerment that goes with gaining competence, knowledge, and often confidence. Many of us try on formal leadership roles, change careers, and experience the satisfactions of using our voices and bringing our values to the workplace. We may become the mentors we needed when we were younger and may take pride (and likely experience some frustrations too) in trying to open the door for others and make our workplaces more diverse and inclusive. This is a time of juggling acts and a requisite high energy and investment in careers, and often other commitments too.

The third and final section of the book explores "Adapting, Leaving a Legacy, and Building Bridges Across Generations." Late career is a time of expansive networks and deep institutional or industry knowledge, a time to take stock of how to shore up our most crucial contributions to the work that has driven our careers. We may have assumed some level of formal leadership role by this time, and we may be able to influence change and do transformative work in our workplaces. We may also be experiencing ageism. We may have risen as far as we're going to rise in formal power, but perhaps we're giving our talents to projects outside of our organizations. Hopefully we are leaning into being lifelong learners, and reaching out to generations behind us, while also continuing to look forward toward greater self-definition in the contributions we want to make in the final years of working life.

Just as there are throughlines in everyone's individual journeys, there's a continuity and a set of precepts that grounds the stories of women who continue to find ways to thrive at work while lifting up others and advancing pro-social values. Indeed, those throughlines illuminate the possibilities for values-based leadership to be a mainstay in our democracy through the community building, empowerment, and even justice-making that can happen at work.

What emerges from women's stories of surviving, thriving, and using their voices for social impact are several key themes:

THE THROUGHLINES

- ▸ **PEOPLE:** The people you work with matter so much, often more than institutions or even high-minded missions. Everyone will teach you something. People can make or break our experiences of our everyday lives at work. At the same time, you need to lean on YOUR people, including your loved ones outside of your workplace.

- ▸ **CONTEXT:** Pay attention to the context of your workplace and understand yourself and your journey in relation to that context. Seeing things as part of larger patterns will help you avoid taking things personally, and you can better navigate institutions.

- ▸ **BOUNDARIES:** Healthy distancing and continual reflection and pivoting when necessary are vital to your success and your ability to make change.

- ▸ **AUTHENTICITY:** Being intentional about how you "show up" in the workplace, while being observant, helps you find your spaces of authenticity, even when compromises are necessary.

▶ **ADVOCACY, INCLUSION, AND SOLIDARITY:** Commit yourself to the life-affirming value of creating spaces of belonging and inclusion, working collectively with others. Push to improve the spaces where you and your coworkers labor, knowing that your working conditions are often connected to the quality of service you can provide to clients, students, patients, or constituents. This is well known in spaces like education and healthcare, but it's true in other areas as well.

▶ **LEARNING AND HUMILITY:** Commit to lifelong learning, humility, and curiosity. This makes it possible to ask critical questions and to make your best contributions while finding new ways to build coalitions.

▶ **SELF-COMPASSION WITH YOUR HUMILITY:** What Anne Lamott said about writing is equally true of social justice work: "Perfectionism is the voice of the oppressor, the enemy of the people." Combine self-compassion, self-advocacy, AND advocacy for others. Recognize that when perfectionism or self-criticism hold you back, you are also probably holding back gifts the world needs. You must make the work your own, and adopt a growth mentality about yourself, so you can give your best gifts.

▶ **ENTREPRENEURSHIP:** Be entrepreneurial with respect to your own career. Think ahead, seek out new opportunities and places for you to do your work. When you do this, you're setting an example for others to ask new questions, innovate, and empower themselves.

▶ **RECOGNIZE CYCLES:** Over our entire career, our relationship to our work cycles along axes such as empowerment/disempowerment, confidence/self-doubt, balance and equilibrium/imbalance and challenge; safety and stretch. The demands of the workplace will challenge our groundedness at many points. And because we will hopefully always be growing, we won't arrive and stay at a place of empowerment, confidence, and balance. Keep strategizing to right the ship, growing wiser and more resilient.

▶ **TAKE THE LONG VIEW:** It helps a great deal to take the long view, both historically and in terms of your career journey. Opportunities in particular institutions and fields vary over time, in sometimes dramatic ways in our era of constant change and institutional disruption.

▶ **NURTURE HABITS OF SELF-REFLECTION:** The leaders who inspire me most are the ones with established habits of reflection. They ask often: what's working and what's not? Which battles are worth fighting right now, and do I have the energy to fight them? What's my relationship to this work and to my larger purpose? They think ahead to the legacies they want to leave behind, not just with their careers overall, but even with individual projects and the presence they convey at work. They also strive to stay grounded in their values and a sense of the possibilities for joy in doing work that matters.

As you read the stories and interwoven research insights in *Leading With Courage*, I invite you to pause regularly and practice those habits of self-reflection. And I invite you to continually think about how you can use the book's collective wisdom to build deeper and broader connections, to create understanding, inclusivity, solidarity, and community in your work. It will make you more resilient and empowered, and it will contribute to more humane systems, strengthening the platform of your workplace as a space to make social change.

Leading with courage happens at all levels and all stages of career. It's a practice, and we all practice it imperfectly. It works best when we acknowledge our vulnerability and humanness, leading with humility, but also with confidence in our own values and gifts. And it works best when we de-center individual leadership and build toward all we can accomplish at work in the spirit of community.

TAKING STOCK OF YOUR PLACE
ON THE JOURNEY

As we begin, no matter your age or career stage, I invite you to consider the following questions:

▶ Where are you on your journey, in relation to career chapters as well as in relation to the change happening around you? Where are others with whom you work?

▶ What developmental tasks or turning points are you facing in your career?

▶ How will you continue to empower yourself, and right the ship if you've become disempowered?

▶ How will you, or have you, use(d) your voice to live your values, regardless of how much formal power you have, what kinds of change you're facing, and what stage of career shapes your journey?

▶ How can you participate in projects and coalitions that will leave a legacy, no matter what stage of career you happen to occupy right now?

▶ What does leading with courage mean to you?

PART I
ESTABLISHING CREDIBILITY

Empowerment Through Your Voice and Values

CHAPTER 1

OPENING DOORS

IN THE FIRST DECADE or so of adulthood and professional life, values-driven women test their mettle, learn from their environments, and hopefully find their voices and figure out what lights them up. There's an energy, a sense of forward movement. You usually know that this place you started is not where you want to end up, but you're building your scaffolding to get to whatever that next level might look like for you.

You're imagining and learning to occupy spaces where you can learn and do work that feels meaningful. You're learning who you are and what matters to you, while testing yourself and your values in different environments, beginning to understand your contexts. You're likely completing some stage of formal education, perhaps confronting post-college feelings of lostness, likely getting a first "real" professional job at some point, and then learning what its possibilities and limitations are.

In this stage, you're working hard to build both your credibility and your confidence. You're hopefully envisioning some roles you might try and some problems you want to work on. You're likely doing some job hopping, perhaps exploring more than one industry. This stage is about building competence and transferable skills. Ideally, you're also seeking mentoring, learning from the stories of older women, and older people in general, as well as your same-age peers. Hopefully you're also taking seriously the value of what you already know and how you can mentor others. You're using your voice, trying to raise critical questions where you can, and building confidence and authority as you learn and contribute.

When I asked Lee, now in her early 60s, about any "getting in the door" struggles she might have faced in her youth as a content writer and strategist in the healthcare field, she said she just did not remember those struggles. This was because "people opened doors for me." While her career was not without obstacles, especially in later chapters, as a young woman Lee walked through those doors. She enjoyed a fairly steady movement into positions that offered her opportunities for growth and contributions. From the beginning she found mentoring and ways to feed her entrepreneurial spirit, both as a solopreneur and later in various positions that led to increasing opportunities for advancement and impact.

Even when Lee was a freelancer, not ensconced in one organization, mentors showed up. A woman copywriter Lee knew had left her job at an agency, taking one of the bigger clients with her. She needed a copywriter and reached out to Lee. The older woman, who had founded her own agency, said to Lee, "You can do this. You can write." She coached Lee through the process of creative brainstorming, ideation, winnowing ideas. "We did some knockout creative work for a client which she had at that time." Together they put together a mailing to promote Lee's work to other people in the community.

This built Lee's confidence. Before long, a chief marketing officer at a hospital, who'd heard Lee was freelancing, "offered me a newsletter job for older adults, which got parlayed into other opportunities." In her field, Lee found both women and men who "opened doors and took chances" and who helped her find her niche and grow her passion in the field of healthcare education and content strategy. At the time of our interview, she was a content development manager in multimedia for a well-known large employer.

On the other end of the continuum, a college administrator in her mid-40s, Jessica, responded to my query about establishing credibility with, "Honestly it was impossible." In her early years designing an academic program, she said, "The only thing that gave me any credibility is that I was a workhorse, and I had the evidence of it." Jessica grew an academic program from 22 to 85 students in a few years. Even then, she recalled, "I constantly got told, 'You're a baby,'"(a way of reinforcing rank by age) "or 'I remember you when you were in your first year,'" as colleagues reminded her of a time when they held a higher status than she did.

Gatekeeping can take harsher forms too, of course, as happened to one of my interviewees, Mai, when she was young in her career. Like so many women (disproportionately women in their 20s and 30s and women of color), Mai experienced sexual harassment as a young Hmong woman starting out in her career. The harassment took up significant emotional energy and closed off options within her organization. Like most women who face sexual harassment, Mai ended up leaving that employer to move on and look for other work. She was in her early 40s at the time of our interview and was experiencing a much more positive work environment where she could grow.

These women are all talented. They are also varied in some of their privileges around race, sexual orientation, and generation. (For example, Lee is white, Jessica is white but identifies as queer, and disabled, and Mai is a Hmong woman.) In these early stages of career, it can be hard to tease out what is happening to us and why, especially when we consider the vagaries of personalities and luck on top of patterns of discrimination or marginalization. What we can see, though, is that work environments and culture, and individual people, matter so much in creating contexts that can allow young women to thrive, or not. Institutional norms can range from enforcement of hierarchy, gatekeeping, and cultures of constant proof of competency, or even harassment, to cultures of support, humility on the part of leaders, and an emphasis on growing individuals for the greater good of the work. People with more authority, clout, and experience can both protect young women and help them grow and shine.

Even if you do not encounter problematic gatekeepers, early career, and higher education on the way there, can sometimes feel like a proving ground. It can feel hard to get older people to take you seriously. Those feelings can connect to being female and can be amplified by other dimensions of your identity, such as your country of origin, gender presentation, race, or sexual orientation. Still, you may find spaces that welcome young people and take a developmental, collegial attitude. Many workplaces contain both patterns but lean toward one or the other approach. And individual managers can make a huge difference.

It helps to take the long view, even at early stages of your career. It helps to root into your values, seeing yourself as a lifelong changemaker who is going to be trying out different positions, platforms, and contexts in your work, and learning as you go, sometimes being empowered, sometimes finding that a situation doesn't work for you.

Know that you can use this stage of your education and career, regardless of where you study or work, to grow professionally while opening doors for yourself AND others. No matter where you are, you can do this. Think of each work or educational experience as a platform for your growth and the development of your voice on behalf of your values, as well as a place to make a contribution to the organization and to a larger cause.

EDUCATION AND EARLY WORK
AS TRAINING GROUNDS

This book focuses more on the professional work world than on education, but education as a social space matters a great deal. If you're still a college student or even a high school student, you should do what feminist writer and poet Adrienne Rich said back in the 1970s: "claim" your education. Don't just "receive" it.[16] Go after those internships and leadership experiences, and ask the hard questions, within and beyond the classroom. Find ways to collaborate, consider where you can use your voice. In these ways, you'll learn how systems work, and how you can sometimes challenge the status quo. Learn how to plug in and contribute. And listen and observe.

Everyone has something to teach you. You can learn to identify and navigate institutional cultures, develop coping skills, find your people, and make an impact from spaces that might not seem like you have much power, even as a student. And you can lean into all forms of learning in the academic space. Of course, if you didn't do this as a student, it's never too late to do this kind of learning.

Early jobs, college, and graduate school showed up in my interviews as places of learning and trying out values and voice, and also as spaces of conditioning around gender and other systems. If you are still pursuing higher education, or if you're reflecting back on that life stage, it's important to realize that our college and possibly graduate school experiences and our pre-professional jobs offer us opportunities to test our values and sometimes to grow into leaders. Growing up does a lot of this too, but for our purposes, let's briefly consider work and education.

WORK AS SOCIALIZATION

Early work can also be a space separate from the social worlds of schooling, and can help young women envision career possibilities, as happened for one of my interviewees, Nina, whose high school job as a pharmacy tech fed her college dreams because she could see herself in a role like that. But many jobs to which young women have access are less inspiring. By the time women enter professional workplaces, many have had a slew of sex-typed and/or low-status jobs under their belt, e.g., waitress, cashier, certified nursing assistant. Jobs they may have worked in high school or through college often reinforce a long cultural history of perceiving women to be more "compliant, cheerful and noncompetitive," and the preferred gender for deploying "niceness" for everything from soothing irritated customers on the phone to calming a frustrated boss or feuding coworkers.[17]

The restaurant industry has especially high rates of sexual harassment, and even in the absence of harassment, often contributes to objectifying women.[18] One of my students once told me that she experimented with wearing makeup or not wearing makeup as a server; her tips were astronomically higher when she spent her own money and time applying makeup. Indeed, research shows that women servers who are perceived as attractive earn more tips while perceived attractiveness doesn't impact the tips of male servers.[19]

Rosalind, one of my interviewees, was a bartender during her college years in the early 2000s. She remembers, "I experienced racism in that patrons didn't want me to serve them because of my color." Rosalind, a young Black woman working in a predominantly white community, leaned on her family's teachings: she might not be able to avoid racism, but she had choices in how to handle it. "And I handled it with grace." She says she allowed someone else to serve these customers and didn't "take it on as an immediate threat," rather just stepping "to the side." She continued her work, she explains, "and through doing so, those patrons watched and listened and actually apologized and came and said that I taught them that what they believed wasn't true, and that it wasn't fair. And they apologized for treating me that way. But sometimes people need space, because people come to the table with a preconceived notion of what's going on, and it's not right. Some people (not everyone) but some are able to see that they were wrong, and they make it right."

If everyone worked to make it right, our workplaces and communities would be far more equitable than they are, but Rosalind's story of being a young Black woman bartender in a predominantly white community reminds us of the wisdom it's possible to bring to negative workplace experiences, even when we're young. Rosalind was learning leadership, through presence, perseverance, and resilience, while navigating obstacles of race and gender in her service position. When you learn the skills to cope with the obstacles you might face, you too are developing leadership skills that will benefit you as well as others whom you will mentor and lead along your career journey.

EDUCATIONAL SPACES:
Learning To Use Your Voice

For women already inclined to raise some critical questions about inequality in systems, educational spaces--even in high school sometimes--can also be training grounds for navigating complex institutions and pushing the needle to try to change them. Consistent with national trends in which high school girls are more likely than boys to be involved in school clubs beyond the realm of sports, my own daughters both led social justice organizations in high school: Environmental Club for one (including an unsuccessful though instructive lesson in trying to institute school recycling) and Gay-Straight Alliance for the other.[20] Both daughters collaborated with me in organizing a very visible support picket for their teachers when they did a "sick out" to go to the state capitol to protest their loss of labor rights under the then-new governor of Wisconsin, Scott Walker in 2011. Legions of high school students have become active in the last decade and a half, on issues like DACA and gun violence, Black Lives Matter, and the environment, learning powerful advocacy lessons along the way. This wave is powerful, though high school activism is not new; just ask the Civil Rights activists of the 1950s and 60s.

At the college level, opportunities for student involvement expand. These educational spaces can host massive personal growth, as we gain knowledge and skills to realize the dreams that brought us there. My interviewee Nina, for example, took her difficult experiences and translated them into activism. She worked to transform the institution that offered her the empowering potential of learning while also marginalizing her. Nina found being a Black student on a predominantly white college campus very challenging. For example, she realized that if she arrived early to class, the white students still coming in the door often wouldn't sit by her. "I used to hate it when I would go into a class and no one would sit next to me, maybe for many reasons, maybe someone just wanted a different seat. But a lot of times because you're the only person that looks like you, you think that it's because I'm Black."

Nina developed a technique of arriving late and putting herself in control of whom she would sit by (a tip she later shared with the younger students of color she mentored as part of her job on a university campus). In college, Nina became president of the Black Student Unity club, growing as a leader, learning new advocacy skills, and pushing her institution to confront white supremacy wherever it showed up. Regular meetings of this student organization also "helped me survive," she says. Conversations beyond the meetings continued, and Nina enjoyed opportunities to "not even have a conversation," but "just to breathe, and go do something fun" with the Black Student Unity club members.

Remembering her college experiences, Peyton, a young white woman who identifies as a lesbian and disabled, recounted that, "I had professors who were really uncomfortable with me speaking up about gay and trans issues and who have called me in for private meetings and insisted that I need to apologize for creating an uncomfortable environment." But Peyton didn't stop. She chose a field of study where she could more easily raise her voice and test out her ideas. She developed that voice and took her social justice values into her pursuit of graduate training as a social worker.

As Nina's and Peyton's stories remind us, college campuses are complex spaces. While they can be crucibles for growing awareness of diversity and the possibilities for social justice, they can also be frustrating places. The expansive worldviews and vocabulary for social change can lead students to expect a lot from them, intellectually and in terms of career prospects, making discrimination and marginalization on the basis of their identities particularly disillusioning.

Over my years as a professor, I knew of many women students who endured sexual assault or sexual harassment on campus. Being housed in a gender studies department, my colleagues and I probably heard more than the average faculty member did of the heartbreaking stories of how these traumas impacted students' health, and their emotional and academic lives. As with other difficult experiences, sexual assault and harassment galvanized organizing and protests on the part of some students. One of my students started an empowerment organization related to sexual violence and later organized a long-standing picket to protest the university's handling of a case of sexual harassment by a professor.

As college has become more expensive and less supported through public policy, many students miss out on opportunities for campus involvement, whether by not enrolling in the first place, or by needing to work part-time or full-time jobs (10% of full-time college students also work full-time jobs), in addition to sometimes caring for family members.[21] Many don't complete college, of course, and new research shows that women more than men cite financial considerations as a key reason for considering exiting college.[22] Nevertheless, like the workplaces students may already be experiencing while in school, and like the workplaces they'll enter after college, college can be a crucible of development, often full of its own triumphs.

Annie's story illustrates these patterns well. She began her studies at a tribal college with an emphasis on environmental studies but later transferred into a predominately white four-year college where she pursued a liberal arts degree. She was what colleges call a "non-traditional" student: older than most of her peers, and parenting children with special needs. Annie's journey was not easy. It included numerous medical and financial crises and the need to juggle work, parenting and school while holding multiple marginalized identities. But in her short time on her new college campus, she focused on improving the climate for student parents. She also undertook a first-of-its-kind activist project to address the ways that institutional furniture choices for classroom desks created educational barriers to larger-sized bodies, including pregnant people, tall football players, and anyone with a large body.

Annie also was an active journalist for the student paper, reporting on the institution's response to Trump-era changes in Title IX, informing students about the frightening consequences of having the federal government narrow the definition of sexual assault, and empowering them to be informed resisters. She documented student protests against the murder of George Floyd, and against all institutionalized racism, in the immediate aftermath of the police killing that galvanized the nation. And, having built her skills at the on-campus paper, she began working off-campus at an independent, community-based newspaper on projects like giving voice to Black youth advocates in the community.

Both Annie and Morgan, age 26 at the time of our interview (and identifying as white and queer), benefited from and contributed to a campus culture that nurtured and celebrated activism. Morgan looked back at her time in college as a time of empowerment when she felt "social justice driven," because, she explained, "we're constantly having those conversations in school and with other students about social justice. And it was really empowering; you were constantly learning. I just felt so young and like I can do anything, like the world is my oyster."

I can relate to Morgan's feeling that college opens up a world. In the mid-1980s, as a first-generation college student, higher education offered me a vast sense of the life of the mind and its possibilities, and ways to consider a life of working on social justice. My undergraduate education in the 1980s, anchored in the study of history, was transformative for me. It provided me with a deep sense of the sweep of humanity's exploits and triumphs and gave me a vocabulary to understand myself and my world. It shaped the trajectory of my emerging social consciousness, as the daughter of a union electrician who always fought for the underdog and a resilient, resourceful, hard-working mother. Gradually, I came to learn a lot more about who the underdogs were and how people could work together to challenge oppressive systems. On a campus with disproportionately wealthy students (where I first learned the term "trust fund"), I also came to terms with my class identity as a first-generation college student, at a time when that population was not identified and supported the way students are today.

Some out-of-placeness notwithstanding, I thrived on learning, especially as a way to make sense of the world through history. I was a kid from a working-class family who did not leave college with a mountain of debt. Both my parents sacrificed greatly for me to pursue college, but I also benefited from white privilege and generational privilege. I was supported by better public policy than today's too often debt-ridden generations of learners.[23] Though I was not yet an activist in college, I was enthralled with the study of activists, in the history of the labor movement, movements for civil rights and racial and gender justice.

I remember, around this time, my dad telling me about how he had responded to some of his fellow electricians who did not support the National Football League strike of 1982 because the players were already rich. He had told them, "There are little old ladies cleaning toilets who think YOU make too much money." For my dad, solidarity meant supporting workers trying to have a voice and improve their workplaces, regardless of the things that separated workers.

Through study in college, I connected my own family background, labor history in particular, to the long, fraught, but still inspiring history of solidarity as an ongoing struggle for workplace justice, economic justice, and sometimes, racial and gender justice, too. I also came to see my mom's scrimping and saving as part of her contribution to the work of creating family dignity and survival that had an equally long history. Looking back, I can see that I was beginning a journey then as a story collector, and eventually a scholar, of these movements. This was part of my own leadership journey as a thought leader and future activist.

Although it is hard to predict our futures, college students and early career professionals are wise to start identifying and owning the patterns of their own activism and leadership and mining their stories for how they developed the values that drive them to speak up. We are making choices about how to use our voices when we are young, and we can find support as we continue to do that in life after college.

Gina, who identifies as Latina and is now in her mid-30s, credited her college education with teaching her how to be a leader in the future through a different kind of journey. Gina had grown up in foster care and was a single mom while in college. One of her professors, who had also been a single mom while in college, provided accommodation and support that were pivotal to Gina's own success. This greatly shaped Gina's sense of what people with authority could do for others, and how instrumental supportive people, like her professors, could be in helping people accomplish their goals and take pride in their work. Gina brought her son to class "many times and [this professor] would entertain him sometimes while I was taking a test, things like that. It was really cool to have that support throughout college. And when I graduated college, it was just like this cornerstone of accomplishments in my life... At that time, there was nobody in my family who had even graduated from high school. And so, to have graduated from college was huge." Gina's struggles and the support she received helped her see how humanity can show up in big institutions, how the individual needs of people can come first, an ethic she would use in her own future leadership roles.

When students are supported well, or even when they figure out against so many odds how to carve out a space for themselves, as Nina did, a college education can develop critical thinking and a sense of their connections to the larger world. College can create spaces for questioning in and out of class, accessing mentors and role models, and connecting to student organizations where students can develop skills, experience, and links to community or campus-based projects that advance social change. It can provide avenues for leadership, teaching young women how to navigate their worlds with strength and drive, to seek out and provide help, and to become changemakers. They can thrive. And sometimes they can transform their surroundings.

Women in graduate school face a similar mixture of profound opportunities for empowerment and high risks of running into power structures that can set them back on their heels. With respect to empowerment, graduate students have unique opportunities to dig into learning, growing their sense of purpose, a budding professional identity, and often a connection to a cohort and perhaps a future professional network. We can experience this growth with less struggle and more joy and empowerment, when people support us at critical moments, and when we lean into embodying the values we want to represent and advocate for in our future careers.

Erin, in her early 30s, recalled the hardest struggle of her two-year master's program in Student Affairs was her own perfectionism. But meaningful connections and mentoring lifted her up. She spoke glowingly of a summer internship at a historically women's college where she felt "strongly mentored" for a few months. Her supervisor gave her lots of autonomy, and other people on campus were eager to connect with her. "There was an investment in me," she says, and that helped her see how she might grow professionally. She also took part in exciting conversations about how the college should approach admission of and language around trans and nonbinary students. The institution's historical commitment to providing a space for women was in tension with that same commitment's "legacy of inclusion." The latter, says Erin, "won out," and this inspired her. She could see an institution "not using a legacy to be a gatekeeper around what can and cannot happen in the future." In the meantime, she developed a student mentorship program, an initiative she says helped her develop a lens for future endeavors. Indeed, at the time of our interview she ran a leadership program in her corporate workplace, and worked to integrate education and reflection on diversity, inclusion, and equity.

Erin's work is a reminder that even students can accomplish institutional change. Especially with the right support, students can find their niches of contributions, and even create programs, as Erin did. Advocating for something new or getting in on the ground floor of creating something new can expand the space for the values that matter to you and build significant transferable skills. When I advised students in internships, I always told them: consider how you can help this organization build its capacity in the time you are there, even if just a semester. And consider what skills, accomplishments, and contacts you want to see on your resume when the internship is complete.

On the other hand, graduate programs come with particular kinds of vulnerability. Graduate and professional schools are explicitly about career preparation and socialization into professional norms and networks. Students are often economically dependent on their departments for support during their graduate studies, such as through graduate assistantships, and they depend on those same professors for future references within sometimes tight specialized professional circles.

In addition, as one study of the prevalence of experiences of interpersonal violence in graduate and law school noted, these students tend to be more isolated than undergraduates, increasing their vulnerability to serious problems like harassment. The study authors noted, "We find higher rates of sexual harassment among lesbian, gay, bisexual, transgender, queer, intersex, or asexual (LGBTQ+) women and multiracial students and higher rates of coercion and stalking among women."[24] Lengthy professional training in fields like medicine, law, and Ph.D. programs can ensnare students in years of troubling relationships and departmental cultures.

When Sue, in her late 30s at the time of our interview, was in her residency for medical school, for example, she heard a male preceptor tell another woman student that she should wear her hair more like Sue. Sue (who was white and straight) hated having women compared to each other based on their appearance and was chilled by this incident. Even more disturbing, Sue herself was sexually harassed by another male preceptor, a man who asked for a ride home one night and then began groping her while she was driving.

Recounting this incident years later, Sue still second-guessed herself (a common self-blame reaction to sexual assault, in a culture that too often blames victims). She still wondered, why hadn't she listened to the male friend who gently tried to dissuade her from giving this man a ride home? She had called that friend when she got home, and cried on the phone, telling him what had happened. Years later, she continued to wonder how she had "put myself" in such a situation. Something similar had happened before, she said. But now, at age 29, she'd expected "a certain level of accomplishment, right? I would think that I'm no longer at that level of subjectivity like I was at 19 or 20 when the manager of the bar I was working at who owns it, put his hands down my pants, right? Like all of the things that, when you look back" at them, "I just kind of shook it off." Or tried to, at any rate: the experience, she says, still "affects me now, but I do not talk about it. I haven't spoken about this since that evening."

Sue, already in a formal leadership role when I spoke to her, had high aspirations for senior leadership roles in her field, and had many opportunities to move forward thus far in her trajectory. But the reality of sexual harassment made her anxious about her future: "My only concern is that, when I do try to get to the next level, right, or as I continue moving on those kinds of experiences won't sideline me or won't roadblock me."

Sue's story is a reminder to everyone in higher education that when we work to dismantle the systems that allow sexual assault and harassment to happen to students, we're helping prevent the long-term impact of such experiences, which can sap women's talents, energy, and confidence in their careers. Prolific research shows the connections between sexual harassment experiences and challenges with self-esteem and confidence. Moreover, whether it's in a graduate program, college, or in a workplace, it's also worth noting that some studies have shown "that negative effects extend to witnesses, workgroups, and entire organizations."[25]

Though I was very fortunate to avoid sexual harassment or sexual assault during my graduate education, I did learn a lot about the sometimes-demeaning ways people can exercise power in the ivory tower, and how I wanted to cope with that. In the late 1980s and 90s, I was working my way through the byzantine system of Ph.D. training, following the passion that college had ignited for me by studying the grand canvas of history. I was on my way to change the world through education, using teaching as a vehicle for social justice. I struggled with some disillusion, and a LOT of anxiety, as I discovered that Ph.D. programs are not just about learning. They also condition us toward over-performing and guardedness, knowing we are always in a proving ground, even as we are grossly underpaid, often while accumulating student loan debt. A first-generation college student with very little background in the world of higher education and its professional norms, I was finding that I was also being socialized into a profession, one that I now recognize is as replete with gatekeeping and hierarchy as it is with grand purpose and social impact.

In my second year, for example, the graduate faculty decided (perhaps in spite of what I now imagine must have been some strong but insufficient opposition from the less controlling members of the faculty), that every graduate student would be independently evaluated by someone who did not know them, had never had them in their classroom, and was totally outside their field of study.

I was specializing in twentieth-century U.S. women's history and social history more generally, but my evaluation was in the hands of a historian of medieval Europe, who reviewed my still meager portfolio of historical writing. The gentleman wrote in my file that although I could probably be a decent teacher, in his esteemed opinion, I would "never be a scholar." Looking back, and knowing academia the way I do now, I realize this could have been a way for him to slam my field of study: U.S. women's history as a whole. Just as I have seen some version of this again and again in the academic world over the years: women who study women, people of color who study race, people who push the boundaries of knowledge as established by straight, cisgender white men are often told their work is not "real" history, philosophy, management, etc. Of course, there was probably a lot of equal opportunity suffering that resulted from this project as well. I wonder who else was told what they could "never" be by someone who barely knew them, and I can only imagine what kind of bizarre competitiveness prompted the whole exercise of cross-evaluation of one another's students in the first place.

The medievalist's critique could have been devastating for me. I was sensitive, insecure, often bewildered and intimidated on my journey to an advanced degree. But as I've found to be true often for my story and those of others, one person's pivotally important discouragement is another person's "whatever." We find our power at odd moments in our lives. Youth and hope can sometimes protect us from slights, while at other times when we're young, we feel like baby birds who want to rush back to the nest.

At that particular time, focused on learning and becoming a great teacher, I was not particularly worried about making my name in the research world. I was well supported by my peers, filled with my own sense of purpose, and extremely lucky to not have to work with professors who harassed, bullied, or blocked my way forward. I more or less shook off the medievalist's arrogant critique and decided to prove the self-appointed evaluator of my entire future career wrong (a coping tactic that I now recognize is common among so many women professionals, and which came up often in the stories I collected for this book).

Fortunately, I learned about belonging as well as gatekeeping during graduate school, and I took the lessons learned in college into activism. In spite of my raging anxiety, in many ways I did thrive in graduate school. Part of it was that I just loved learning and considered it a privilege to study in such depth about the history of humanity. When things got hard, I thought, no one can take this away from me, all this knowledge that I'm soaking up.

I also set myself up for future career success by writing a prize-winning article for a major journal. A contest for "the best" research article by a graduate student in the huge field of U.S. history is not something I would ever have thought to enter. But a professor from college, Dr. Emily Rosenberg, had stayed in touch, and she encouraged me to submit my article on the impact of programming for women and girls at the YMCA during the early twentieth century. It turns out, only 28 people applied across the country. The odds that one of them was me, and that I would win, were slim. I wonder how many of those other entrants had someone in their corner, saying, why not you? You should try. And if you are reading this as someone who could nudge a woman to try, consider yourself nudged to be that voice of advocacy.

Like Nina and the other undergraduates I profiled above, I found my people in graduate school. My peers gave me companionship, solidarity, and great advice. Finding limited mentoring from my graduate professors (I was mostly just pretty afraid of them), I benefited greatly from a culture of peer support and mentoring. My friend Louise, for example, said something that stuck with me for decades: "Jodi, no one thing you do is going to wreck it for you." Maybe this would have been obvious to some, but my perfectionist self-needed to hear it, and I was lucky to have a friend who knew just what to say.

Like the activist undergraduates I would later teach and mentor, I bonded with my people through the work of trying to make academic spaces more equitable, growing from the seeds of the possibilities of activism that had been planted in college, and before that, by my family. For me, this meant working with a fellow graduate student to strategize about expanding Ph.D. training access to students of color, during a decade when the needle was finally moving a bit in racially diversifying graduate programs.[26] Together we researched best practices for recruitment and retention and shared them with the faculty.

I also got political in the streets, such as marching for racial justice in the wake of the Rodney King beating and subsequent exoneration of the offending officers in 1991. For my own support and solidarity, I joined a newly formed "Women with a Past" group of grad students studying women's history. And to promote fairness all around within the profession I was entering, I joined my fellow graduate students who were organizing a graduate student union in the early 1990s. The effort failed, but I learned valuable lessons about how to transfer to new contexts the solidarity I had grown up honoring. I learned that, in spite of the upward class mobility I was pursuing through higher education, I too, was a laborer in the "knowledge factory," and we all needed labor rights.[27]

With the exception of co-leading recruitment efforts with my fellow graduate student, I didn't "lead" any of these efforts. And I'm not sure I would have considered myself an activist, an uncertainty I have often seen among young women, who think of activism as something lofty and leaderly. I mostly followed and joined in solidarity with people who often sacrificed progress toward their degrees to do things like organize unions, imagine new political parties (as some did at that time), or risk more than I did organizing and marching in social justice causes. But through participating, I learned about changemaking and about using my voice with others.

Years later I would revisit the labor activism lessons when I agreed to be a faculty representative for a burgeoning union movement in 2010 and 2011. Wisconsin Governor Scott Walker crushed our efforts, and state employee unions more broadly, but our continual protests around the state created new kinds of solidarity. And I like to think of it as just one piece of a struggle for labor rights that is ongoing. Within my profession, I would spend the next several decades trying to mitigate patterns of privilege and hierarchy by co-creating spaces of community, belonging, encouragement, collaborations and advocacy for fairness.

One of the gifts (and challenges) of our current historical moment is the intensity and penetrating nature of the questions people are asking about all our institutions, including educational institutions that train people for their professional futures. As in the 1990s, graduate student organizing around issues of livable wages is on the rise again today.[28] And like students at the high school and college levels, graduate students are taking on topics like the racial assumptions of established curricula, demanding more diversity in what students read and learn.[29] As graduate students and emerging professionals, there can be a greater opportunity to question the credentialing processes of the fields in which they intend to practice.

My oldest daughter began a two-year, online master's program in social work in Minneapolis in the fall of 2020, as the city and nation were reeling from the murder of George Floyd and ensuing demands for police reform or abolition. My daughter was paying for her education with her own money and was frustrated that the pandemic made for subpar internship opportunities and exhausting classes on Zoom. This probably contributed to the many critical questions she and her peers were asking of the program. Why, she wondered, was the first year of the program primarily theory courses, with no skill-building? Why was the course she took on diversity and racial justice not a prerequisite for the program, and then fully integrated into the curriculum? My daughter had an excellent grounding in these topics from her undergraduate degree and her own activism and wanted to see them fully integrated in the context of learning professional problem-solving in social work.

As the year progressed, and the nation watched the trial of Derek Chauvin for the murder of George Floyd, and Winston Smith was murdered in nearby Bloomington, Minnesota by federal agents in that same week, new questions emerged. My daughter wondered, why did her grad program and its courses continue to feel like business as usual when the opportunities to learn about and practice social work were in the streets? The educational system did not seem to be meeting the moment.

One MSW grad, who had completed this program in 2019, stayed involved in my daughter's grad program. This alum prodded her former professors to include more reading on racism and racial justice as well as ableism and disability justice. Thanks to her activism, my daughter and her cohort saw the results on the syllabi for the classes she took. Wanting still more (a broader vision for what social work could do) some of these MSW students developed their own reading group on abolitionism, envisioning a society that met peoples' needs instead of imprisoning them.

My daughter and her peers were also thinking deeply about what it means to prepare people to be social workers, especially at a moment when the country was beginning to consider dispatching more social workers and fewer police officers to handle the emotional pain of the systems that made so many people's lives so hard. Was a two-year graduate degree really needed for this professional credentialing process, and if so, what should that degree look like? Considering the debt load of so many students coming out of their undergraduate degrees, pursuing graduate education is more financially risky than ever, especially for historically low-paid and over-whelmingly female fields like social work. The field is 81% female, and yet men in the field still earn more on average than women, people of color are underrepresented and have higher debt loads than their white peers.[30] Continuing to require two years of graduate education to certify social workers almost certainly means perpetuating racial, class, and gender inequity.

This new cohort of MSW graduates is shaking up their professions, sometimes before they even get their first jobs. The students in my daughter's grad program weren't the only ones asking these questions. In 2023 the National Association of Social Workers went on record objecting to the current state of licensing exams for the field due to problems of bias, after review of data revealed potential biases in these exams, which limited the credentialing opportunities of certain groups. The NASW said that data revealed "significant disparities in pass rates for prospective social workers of color, older adults, and those who speak English as a second language."[31] Younger social workers like my daughter will soon be sitting at the tables where credentialing decisions are made. Their questioning provides a reminder of finding the means of advocacy long before we may take on any formal leadership roles in the workplace.

HONORING YOUR QUESTIONS

If you are still a student, at any level, when you're reading this, my advice to you is to honor your questions, and insist on finding a place for them. Find out where to take your questions and concerns, which levers of power make sense to push on. You might take your ideas and concerns to your professors, to Student Affairs staff, to the head of your graduate program, to your graduate student union, if you have one, or to more highly placed administrators at your institution. Get together with others who can help. Connect your urgent questions to coalitions and movements beyond the curriculum and the university. Use your time in school to cultivate an understanding that social justice work can happen within institutions, programs, and systems, and change is often more impactful when it involves coalition building and reaches beyond the confines of campus into communities.

Later, as you move into your career, you can join the professional associations that guide the practices and credentialing of your field. You don't have to wait until you're more established to bring your voice to the table. Your profession or industry, whatever it is, needs the voices of young people to accelerate change.

Though I've been talking a lot about activism, not everyone can be an activist, and almost no one can stay consistently in the fray at every stage and chapter of education, career, and life. For one thing, people with marginalized identities risk more by speaking up, since they tend to have a tenuous place in situations where they are "othered," whether it's the only person of color on a work team, or the only woman in a graduate-level Physics program.

In addition, part of taking the long view in imagining and pursuing a career path that allows you to live your values is practicing self-compassion and understanding that your capacities will fluctuate over time. Your mental and physical health will likely vary over time. Self-care, as well as leaning into and participating in community care are essential for the long haul. Your sense of safety in particular spaces will also vary as you move into different environments in school, work, and community.

Because personal lives are complicated, too, sometimes your need for a job and a paycheck and keeping your head down may be your most appropriate survival strategy. Also, your personal life will wax and wane in terms of both its demands and the joys of that life that you want to be sure to experience. Work is just a part of life. Hopefully, life is long, and we can't be firing on all cylinders and being fully present "public" selves all the time. Take breaks often. Nurture yourself and the people you love, recharge, and keep doing the work in your own way and at your own pace.

But when and if you're able to, take up space and kick open the door for others. Use this practice for the rest of your career. If you're having to fight for a place for yourself at any level of education, know that you're not alone, that there are people around who can empathize and help. And know that you'll be learning how to do that in professional spaces. If you're not aware that others are fighting (e.g., if you're still learning about your white or class background privilege, or other identities), please ramp up the learning so you can be a better ally throughout your career. And if you work in one of those educational contexts, you can build a bridge to the students by honoring those questions and challenges.

REFLECTING ON YOUR
EDUCATION & EARLY CAREER STORY

▶ In addition to your family background, how have your experiences with education and workplaces as a young adult shaped your sense of possibilities as well as limitations?

▶ How do you think early work experiences conditioned you around gender, race, and other systems of inequality?

▶ What critical questions kept showing up for you at any stage of your education?

▶ Were you able to use your voice to challenge the status quo while you were a student? If not, what prevented you from doing so? If so, what did that experience teach you, and does it represent some continuity in how you're approaching your workplace through your values in the current stage of your journey?

▶ What questions have emerged for you about "business as usual" in the profession or field you're entering or in which you have been working for a while?

▶ What are the actual core competencies of key positions in your profession or role? What do people really need to know to do the job? Are there any arbitrary barriers to participation? How can you be part of eliminating barriers to participation in your profession, so that you can add diversity, and in the process, contribute to the transformational possibilities of whatever work you do?

▶ What did you learn about using your voice on your educational journey, for yourself and/or on behalf of other people and causes?

▶ What core competencies did you develop through early work, any activism you have done, and your educational experiences?

▶ How does the story of your youth and early adulthood lead you to consider some roles that you tend to play in situations, and that you would like to continue to play? For example, are you, or did you start to become, a storyteller, a critical questioner, an emerging policy wonk, a community builder?

▶ How have your youth and young adult experiences impacted your early career experiences?

▶ If you are long past this stage of life and career, how can you help young women identify their strengths, not just in a traditional business-skill sense, but as emerging thought leaders and changemakers?

CHAPTER 2

UNDERSTANDING PROFESSIONAL CONTEXTS

CARRYING YOUR ASPIRATIONS and the skills you learned in school, you may enter professional spaces wondering if there is a place for you, hoping the work will align with your values, and aiming to make a difference.

If only more of the workplaces these young people are entering were more ready for them. Thankfully, transformation IS happening, even in the face of hostile and powerful backlash. Creative advocates for equitable workplaces haven't abandoned their values, in spite of a punitive environment. There are visionary leaders in many organizations, and more roadmaps and attention to creating better work environments than were around in my era of early career. As you enter your early career, it's helpful to understand the patterns, the landscape of typical work environments, because knowledge of context is a piece of empowerment.

The stories of most of the women I interviewed reflected an awareness, including at quite early stages of their careers, of some of the inequities around them. Morgan, who had thrived on social justice conversations and experiences in college, was 26 at the time of our interview. She had recently transitioned from nonprofit work at Planned Parenthood, into a corporate setting, where she was discouraged to see "so many male leaders" and so few female leaders. She explained that it made her feel "aware of my gender," which might keep her from being "considered for that role one day."

Morgan also noted that, though her job combines analytics and administrative tasks, her supervisor gives her male colleague, in the same position, more of the analytical work, leaving her with the administrative tasks, even though she is more interested in analytics. This seems to reflect a general bias in which men are imagined to be more adept with all things mathematical, despite strong evidence to the contrary.[32]

Erin, in her early thirties at the time of our interview and working in a mission-oriented company, in a position and an environment she genuinely enjoyed, nevertheless looked skeptically at gendered communication around leadership. She noticed how the first woman leader on the senior leadership team at her company was introduced. The CEO used adjectives like "approachable and friendly," to describe her, rather than emphasizing the critical competencies that had earned her that leadership role. Erin was troubled by the way this woman's qualifications were undermined.

Given the well-established expectations that women leaders demonstrate their "niceness" as well as their competence, these kinds of introductions are not surprising, but they are disturbing. An opportunity was missed here to make visible the actual competencies that made this woman a good fit for a leadership role. This issue connects to the ways that women's expertise is more frequently erased by inequity in use of titles to refer to credentialed women. For example, a recent study of medical doctors found that men introduced women doctors with their titles only 49% of the time, while they introduced men with their titles 72% of the time.[33]

Early career experiences can also caution women about issues of workplace climate. Laura, a woman of color in her mid-forties at the time of our interview, remembers noticing disparate treatment of women, especially women of color early in her first full-time professional position after graduate school. She saw a woman of color colleague, a "Latina with Indigenous identities" lose her job in part because she was outspoken about racism. "She had gotten a lot of blowback from students and then also from the faculty... The feedback was always, 'She tries to make each class a diversity class.' And that was seen as a negative thing by students, that was seen as a negative thing by faculty. She had been given feedback, she didn't change, this kind of thing. And then my second year, she was not retained. She didn't get tenure."

Laura says, "I remember sort of seeing her experience as a little bit of a cautionary tale." Though Laura is clear-eyed about continuing problems of racism and exclusion in academia, she does see a hopeful sign of progress in the way things have changed in the past decade or so "because that is not feedback that would be given today in any department. And if it were, you'd be in big trouble." When she was a little more established in her career, Laura went on to found a campus group specifically for women of color, creating community and belonging through her own innovation and initiative.

In many workplace environments, including all of the examples above, good work is possible, even when you're young or new. But it does help to situate your particular situation in that larger context.

BOYS' CLUBS

Large organizations such as corporations, national nonprofits, and institutions of higher education were very often started and developed primarily by white men and still operate under many of their rules and professional norms established before the influx of more women, people of color, people with disabilities, and LGBTQ+ people. They may have changed their mission statements and their policies and may have mentoring programs for women and people of color and anti-discrimination policies for LGBTQ+ people, and perhaps even lots of great, transformational leaders. But white, heteronormative, patriarchal norms or unwritten rules may still shape organizational culture, including how different kinds of leadership are recognized and rewarded. People often subscribe to a myth of meritocracy, the notion that people who get ahead do so simply by hard work, and in many organizations, there is little space to talk about how structural inequalities and bias make some people's paths more difficult.

The more male-dominated your workplace, the more likely you are to experience male-activated types of institutional sexism, including homophobic, racist, or ageist intersected sexism. Jessica Bennett's practical and satirical book, *Feminist Fight Club*, lampoons (while offering advice about) the types of men you may encounter in such spaces: the "manterrupter," (whose role is obvious), the "bro-priator," who takes credit for your idea, the "mansplainer," the "undermine-her" and more. The terms are funny, but, as Bennett clearly reminds us , the problems are real. Sexual harassment is also more likely to occur in heavily numerically male organizations.[34]

There are gradations of male-dominated environments. What's been called "masculinity contest cultures" are probably the most toxic. These spaces operate with cultural norms of "show no weakness" and "work-first." Women and people of color are especially at risk for emotional and career damage in such spaces. As the researchers who identified this pattern explained:

> Organizations that score high on masculinity contest culture tend to have toxic leaders who abuse and bully others to protect their own egos; low psychological safety such that employees do not feel accepted or respected, feeling unsafe to express themselves, take risks, or share new ideas; low work/family support among leaders, discouraging work-life balance; sexist climates where women experience either hostility or patronizing behavior; harassment and bullying, including sexual harassment, racial harassment, social humiliation and physical intimidation; higher rates of burnout and turnover; and higher rates of illness and depression among both male and female employees.[35]

Beware of these places. Especially when you're just starting out in your career, trying to survive in, much less change, one of these environments may not be where your energy and your limited power should be going. You can learn from it, of course. And later, when you're in a more empowered role, you can be aware that many of the women you've been working with may have had to survive these environments and may bring those scars with them. If you see any of these behaviors going on in a new job, it might be time to polish off your resume while you are still in the early testing ground of your professional life.

These kinds of organizations also tend to have gender-skewed leadership levels, in which women have difficulty moving beyond middle management, and in which they face special challenges. In the late 2000s, I led a training on career advancement through my university's Small Business Development Center, in which most enrollees worked as lower-middle managers for a very large retail chain. By the end of the day, these women seemed to be seething with newfound understanding about how little power they had when they actually thought about it, particularly in gendered terms. They understood more clearly that they too often took the heat from "below" (their direct reports) for implementing decisions made at upper-management tables to which they were not invited. Indeed, women in middle management often face these frustrations across industries, as they are more likely than men to be in positions of low visibility and limited power, with lack of access to senior levels of management and the related decision-making tables. Meanwhile their organizations often adhere to masculine ideas of what a true senior level looks like.[36]

Indeed, a kind of mask-like, depersonalizing masculinity that implicitly devalues what's been culturally defined as feminine can show up in lots of workplaces, as can whiteness as a cultural value. There is often a parallel between this kind of depersonalization and rigidity and what Dr. Jenny Newsum-Vazquez calls "low-trust workplaces," in which "friction" (such as challenging questions about processes) "can result in harmful responses and reactions."[37] Back in 1999, Tema Okun laid out a critique of how a sort of whitewashed professionalism can look at work, with unspoken rules that are not just about monolithic dress standards, but also about a "culture of urgency" (endemic to so many organizations in our internet age), perfectionism, quantity over quality, presumed objectivity, and defensiveness. Okun has a more nuanced website exploring all of these issues that should be required reading.[38]

The decades of research on male-dominated environments (usually with white men in charge) suggests that we should also be on the lookout for workplaces where masculinity is a kind of impervious norm, often intersecting with whiteness. I outline several features of this here:

EXTRA-MASCULINE WORKPLACE CULTURES

▶ **EMOTIONS ARE SEEN AS "INAPPROPRIATE,"** with the possible exception of male anger. Hyper-rational, instrumental, transactional communication is the norm from leaders. Feminized communication, often conducted by women, is marginalized. For example: Effusive, positive language, thoughtful and carefully worded emails and conversations meant to soften challenging feedback, and the exclamation points that women leaders laboriously add to their emails to make sure people know they're "nice."

▶ **EMOTIONAL LABOR IS DELEGATED TO WOMEN, PEOPLE OF COLOR, AND OTHER MARGINALIZED GROUPS.**

▶ **CONNECTED TO THE SUPPRESSION OF EMOTION AND THE TRANSACTIONAL, NON-TRANSPARENT NATURE OF DECISION MAKING, WOMEN AND PEOPLE OF COLOR ARE OFTEN LEFT TO CLEAN UP THE EMOTIONAL MESSES,** while also invisibly providing support and encouragement to employees. They are doing the daily work of retaining the workforce by making them feel individually valued. For example, second-in-command women (e.g. associate directors) are the ones who handle messy conflicts brought to leadership by department heads. Or it's women middle managers who provide customized individual support to their team when personal issues impact their ability to do their work; these same middle managers organize the sending of flowers for personal losses, as well as the celebrations and gatherings that mark special occasions, and create the fabric of workplace culture.

▶ **INFORMATION IS MORE LIKELY TO BE HOARDED RATHER THAN SHARED:** the culture lacks transparency.

▶ **HIERARCHY IMPEDES THE FLOW OF IDEAS AND INFORMATION.** Employees in general, and mid-level managers in particular, are hindered in their ability to make decisions about their units.

▶ **PEOPLE'S PERSONAL LIVES AND COMMUNITY COMMITMENTS AND AFFILIATIONS ARE RARELY ACKNOWLEDGED;** accommodation for life needs may be nonexistent, minimal, and/or grudging.

▶ **FEEDBACK MECHANISMS ARE MINIMAL;** everything passes through hierarchy; those at the top rarely receive feedback from "below."

▶ **INDIVIDUALISM AND THE MYTH OF MERITOCRACY ARE THE UNSPOKEN NORMS OF THE CULTURE,** as evidenced in performance reviews, the makeup of leadership, and other indicators.

With all of the cautions I'm inserting here, the fact is that there are also organizations led largely by white men in which it's entirely possible to do good work, and even to thrive. Indeed, these organizations may be good places to work, to earn money for a while, and to grow. Tina, now a nonprofit director, started out at a pharmaceutical company, an experience that she says did not align with her values or long-term goals. But right out of college in 2001, she just needed a job: "I was very unsure of myself. I really just took it because I needed to pay off student loan debt and I was tired of waitressing three jobs." Looking back, she says, it was a very difficult environment for her because the goals of a pharmaceutical company felt very out of alignment with her values. "I believe in socialized medicine," she said, and here she was working for a for-profit company that opposed that idea, and that had very homogenous leadership. She said she "would never work there again. And I would never send anybody to work there again."

At the same time, Tina said she was very thankful for her experience there. "During the 11 years I was there I had fantastic leaders," she said, "people who developed me and coached me. They are the reason I am the leader I am today." The company, Tina estimated, was 95% white, and "there were no women in leadership." But she had what she understood as an unusually "positive male mentor experience" thanks to three men of color who, she said, "developed me and coached me and protected me." Tina is white, and these men "were in the minority," but perhaps they understood (in ways that their white colleagues did not) how important it was to help lift people up. Tina isn't sure, she says, "But for some reason I got lucky."

The leadership lessons were powerful for Tina. Her supervisor gave her a significant stretch assignment but set her up for success and insulated her from any mistakes she might make while learning to manage a huge and complex set of tasks and relationships.

> He put me in charge of a national project and granted me complete free rein to manage it as I felt fit. He didn't micromanage me, he coached me, and mentored me, and helped me, he really let me do it the way I needed to do it. And when I messed up... I was young it was my first job. And there are things that I did that I really messed up on just because I didn't know. And the intention was not bad. And I also saw him take the heat for that. Never pointed to me... If there was a mistake, he took full responsibility.

Tina says this was "a huge leadership example to me at a young age. That when you're responsible for a team, if they are not performing, it's a reflection on your leadership, not on them. They didn't have the tools and support that they needed. That is the first time I really felt empowered. When I was given that confidence by my leader and found a huge project where I could really mold and shape it in the way that I wanted to. I was completely supported in a very loyal protective way."

Mary also experienced positive male mentoring early in her career, from a supervisor she says she'll always remember. Describing herself as a verbal processor, Mary remembers going to his office to talk one day, and he said: "'I figured out, Mary, that you just need someone to listen to you as you process the problem. And then ask questions and help you figure it out.' And I thought, yes that's what I need... That whole idea of being able to work for someone that took that time to figure me out and figure out what best helps me do my job. And then support me in that and in many, many other ways... I always felt safe, always felt that he was respectful and honoring." This man, says Mary, "had a passion for treating people well. When I think of that equitable piece, I think of him and how he led and so many women [who worked with him] would have told you that they felt respected, they felt heard, and they felt safe."

Rosalind, who experienced racism while bartending in a mostly white town, consistently found ways to thrive at work in predominantly white environments in the professional world. A big believer in the idea that "you can curate and create your career within an organization," Rosalind worked at an architectural design firm for years in her early career, as a client advocate and software trainer. She said she experienced this company as "a family organization, where the people you work with become your second family, very tight knit." When she moved on to work for a large healthcare organization, she said the experience was similar. She found that the organization was "very good at providing opportunities for self-development; if you seek to do it." And she did. She suggested that developing yourself and your contributions in an organization "comes back to perspective. It comes back to your own belief in yourself and how you choose to see things."

That said, as Rosalind knows and helps others understand in her current leadership consulting work, there is ample research on the extensive challenges many women of color face in white workplace environments, and not all of them are survivable, much less friendly. As Ruchika T. Malhotra recalled in an article in *Harvard Business Review*, "I saw up close how the rules were different for my white peers. The white men and women who got promoted despite underperforming, the male leaders who only hired attractive white women. I was left out of meetings, social gatherings, and inside jokes, and I never saw anyone who looked like me." Malhotra found patterns of racial gaslighting among women of color who tried to seek redress from racism at work, and explored in depth the toxicity of accumulation of microaggressions. She quotes Danielle Jenkins Henry, licensed marriage family therapist associate (LMFTA) and founder of Dream Life Out Loud, a psychotherapy practice for Black women with advice for such situations: "'You don't have to keep going in there and taking abuse,' Jenkins Henry says. Many women of color feel like they have to 'go in there and fight,' especially if they're the first in their family to have a corporate career." But Jenkins Henry insists "'there are parts of yourself that you have to protect' and it's okay for you to not battle it out in a workplace; 'you can fight a different battle.'"[39]

Sometimes women find they need to leave an employer or even an industry. Sometimes, luck and effective self-advocacy prevail, or good allyship and/or leadership help, and things shift toward more breathing room. Lee, for example, went through a period of time in her work in healthcare, where old boy networks were an inhibiting factor in a division where she worked: "that golf course gathering mentality where there's an inner circle, usually men, who feel really comfortable together, who are getting together at the local bars, and at the local meat raffle."

Although Lee is white and was a well-established and highly skilled professional in her mid-fifties at the time, she was still hindered in her ability to establish her professional presence in this context. On a team that was about 80% male, "Every Wednesday night the entire team went to the local VFW for the meat raffle and beer, to talk about sports and how the

Packers were doing and about their golf game. It was almost excruciatingly difficult to plug in. I would go, but to try to figure out how to plug into the conversation and become part of the group. The more part of the group you are the more people think of you... It wasn't like I lost opportunities, but I definitely felt on the outside of that group."

Thankfully, leadership changes resulted in the dispersal of this group. In her organization, Lee said, those networks tend to get broken up, in part because of frequent reorganization of units in a dynamic corporate environment. So, "that old boy network has been put in their place." Lee continued to move forward and landed in increasingly rewarding positions in the company.

When you're still establishing yourself and building your confidence, it can be easy to see and worry about the deficits of an organization if you don't see leaders who look like you, But the stories of the women I interviewed remind us that, while you should never ignore your gut telling you that you're being excluded, slighted, or bullied, it's also important to notice when you are being supported and mentored. It may be possible to take advantage of the growth opportunities of that experience, absorb lessons of leadership that you can take forward in your career, build positive and constructive relationships, and learn how to be a values-driven and inclusive leader who helps others grow.

"WOMEN'S WORK"

More difficult contexts to figure out than the "boys' clubs" are the ones in which women are running the show. Many young idealistic women find work in human services, at nonprofits, or in some healthcare fields like nursing and public health. In some of these workplaces, women leaders are very visible, at least at the local level and in smaller nonprofits.[40] Everyday sexism from male colleagues may be less apparent, but this does not mean sexism, racism, homophobia, or ableism aren't part of the larger picture.

Underfunding of social services in the U.S., at a time of very high need and income inequality, shapes patterns in which supervisors work. They are often too overburdened with crisis management and writing the next grant proposal to save their funding streams to have time to deeply mentor and develop employees. Our society has designated areas like reproductive health, human services of all kinds as areas for women to congregate and often to perform significant emotional labor.[41] In these fields a disproportionately female workforce struggles against policies and systems that make it hard for people to get vital services.

Depending on the community, leadership in the helping and education fields is often disproportionately white as well, and women of color and racial justice advocates of any background may struggle with unconscious bias and problematic systems as they try to bring about racial justice through their work. Many educational settings (like elementary education) and human services occupations (like social work) are numerically dominated by white women, who may approach people of color (students, "clients," fellow employees, etc.) with unconscious biases. Those same systems often treat communities of color as supplicants whose behavior needs to be regulated in order to have basic needs met. Examples range from the many practices that support a school-to-prison pipeline, to credentialing and leadership barriers for people of color in nonprofit and helping professions.[42]

Across differences of race and background, people in these female-dominated fields often face the daily frustration of being unable to provide people with the help they need. These issues have become all the more pronounced in an era of what some have called the "hollow state," as social safety net programs have been defunded and people of color continue to disproportionately face the more punitive faces of government, such as over-policing and police brutality. The extreme politicization around women's reproductive rights, and indeed the extreme curtailing of these rights, also shapes the context. This means that no matter what social service field you enter and who you are, you can't help but notice that needs often overwhelm the availability of services and often the emotional capacity of staff and supervisors.

For example, in 2018 and 2019, shortly before COVID-19 and the overturning of *Roe v. Wade*, which left abortion rights in severe jeopardy, or nonexistent in many states, Morgan worked for Planned Parenthood as a recent college graduate. In some ways, she loved the work. She was passionate about the organization's mission and felt she was making a difference, even though her role was not quite what she expected: "It was really empowering to help," she said. "A lot of people shared their stories, and it was especially empowering scheduling abortion procedures... I felt like I was helping this person, you know, advocate for themselves and make a really important decision in their life. Granted I was just a small piece of the puzzle by scheduling the appointment, but that felt really great." Morgan also loved the people she worked with. Like so many Millennials, Morgan was interested in working in places where people can be themselves, and that's what she found in the nonprofit world.

But the frontline work took its toll, and she quickly burned out. Her work involved fielding 70-80 phone calls a day, and after a while, "it was just saddening." She was dealing with people in intense situations, including physical abuse. Morgan remembers telling one man how much his girlfriend's abortion procedure would cost and hearing him mutter something about how throwing her down the stairs would be easier. "I remember crying a lot after work," she said.

The pace of the work was intense, dictated by the scarcity of resources in the nonprofit world. Morgan blamed herself for being too sensitive and said she probably needed some therapy to help her set better boundaries.

But organizations can also step up to help people like Morgan set those boundaries, whether via supervisors trained in supporting employees in these high emotional labor contexts, or concrete investments in employee wellness. By 2022, the National Council of Nonprofits was touting initiatives, often in the form of low-cost or cost-neutral solutions, to support a critically stressed-out workforce and recruit and retain employees. Examples include instituting a "nonprofit day of rest," a four-day work week, and "organizational pause" periods where staff took a break from the immediacy of emails and other relentless tasks.[43] Of course, nonprofits staffed by women and existing in a context of growing wealth inequality and divestments in the public good could do so much more for their employees if they had more resources themselves.

Olivia, a public health professional in her early thirties, working in a county health department during the height of the pandemic, shared how these stresses impacted her work and her ability to set boundaries when I interviewed her in early 2021. A public health specialist in a rural county health department, Olivia was well supported at work overall, having received excellent mentoring and supervisor backing. But she recognized that the mostly female workforce of public health involved its practitioners in significant emotional labor, and the pandemic dramatically heightened the burdens of this work.

For example, with contact tracing added to other public health duties, stress and burnout were common. "A lot of us feel that personal responsibility," Olivia said, "like if I don't get this person to stay home, they're going to go out and get other people sick, [but] they can't afford to be off of work, and what can I do to help them? It's horrible, to tell someone, hey you have to quarantine and you're self-employed. So, no you really can't get paid. And I had to keep reminding myself and our staff, this is not our fault... We are just one piece of the puzzle. I have to keep reminding myself of that, but it feels bad."

Organizing to try to address many systemic problems laid bare by the pandemic is work often done by coalitions of nonprofits and government entities. It's women like Olivia who often lead this work, along with many grassroots organizations, like the kind that Nina helped found, which focused on empowering Black residents in a predominantly white community. Referring to the challenges of launching and sustaining this small nonprofit while holding down her other job, Nina noted that it's the "emotional labor and logistical labor that keeps things going and makes things possible," she said, and Black women, like her often took on a disproportionate share with minimal credit.

Olivia observed that in the disproportionately female field of public health in general, "I feel like I need to be the cleanup crew or take on all the problems that other people aren't taking on. I'm involved in a lot of coalition work and things like that. Sometimes I think, if I wasn't doing this work, would it even be happening? ... And would the people who have power necessarily even care?" Olivia saw the gender dynamics in the ways that her paid work extended into community care. "Even the work that goes into coordinating a coalition and bringing people to the table... you don't really see too many men doing that. And it's like, are we just the cleanup crew?" Olivia lamented the burnout she saw in areas like social work and healthcare. Since the abatement of the pandemic, some of the crisis work has lessened, but the Great Resignation means that employees that remain in high emotional labor fields like healthcare, government social service, or nonprofit work are often severely overburdened due to staffing shortages.

Even beyond the explicitly "helping" world of social services and nonprofits, the corporate world can contain similar gendered patterns. In customer service, public relations, and human resources, women's "be nice" training puts them on the front lines of conflict management, while often giving them limited opportunities to influence organizational policies that lead to the patterns of conflict and customer dissatisfaction. Lower-middle management in general is full of women who have to implement decisions made by a higher layer of management, usually skewed male. In 2022, for example, McKinsey reported that in corporate America, 27% of "manager" roles (below the senior level) were occupied by white women, and 14% by women of color. Four levels up, in the C-Suite, these percentages dropped to 21% and 5% respectively.[44]

On the other hand, female-dominated fields can have their perks. In her first professional job with her Master of Public Health degree in hand, while Olivia was facing the aforementioned challenges of public health work in the pandemic, she felt "very, very valued" within her own unit. As is so often the case, the feeling of being valued came from her supervisor, who, Olivia says "was very much an advocate for me and really asked for me to get raises... Originally my position was part time; she pushed to get it full time." The supervisor also nominated Olivia for an emerging community leader award a few years later. "I thought that I'm just whoever, working as a government employee. But it was empowering to know that my skills were even worthy of that."

That same supervisor, Olivia says, was a powerful advocate for the undervalued field of public health, and Olivia was inspired by that advocacy. On top of that, her supervisor created an environment that helped Olivia develop a variety of skills and interact in diverse spaces beyond the office, such as when she went to the state capitol and learned how to testify and advocate with lawmakers. Olivia also performed health needs assessment, planned and implemented programs, and became a mentor to emerging public health professionals, all rewarding and resume-building opportunities and skills that would facilitate her next transition.

Lee's generally positive experiences in spaces or divisions that skewed more female might be understood in the context of the flexibility of communications fields where many levels of leadership (if not always the top ones) are female, and where some of the strengths of typically female socialization can yield rewards. For example, a story in *The Atlantic* by Olga Khazan investigated the perks of a career in public relations for women, which included good pay, the opportunity to learn a variety of skills, to take on exciting work assignments, to collaborate, to enjoy a sense of security because of the many opportunities in the field, and to advance in their careers.[45] Lee noted that, "the field of healthcare communication tends to draw humans who are more open minded, higher EQ [emotional quotient], probably. I wouldn't say it was heavily female, but it was at least 60% in our communication division."

Over her 10 years in one organization, creating healthcare content, Lee thrived. "The woman who hired me just sort of saw this spark of passion for the product, saw me as an important voice for the product." Her two supervisors during those ten years were "friends as much as supervisors," and "growth was pretty organic. In both of those cases, I was just sort of reaching out for more," and her managers supported her. "I mean both of them were managers that did not feel that they had to be the smartest one in the room and did not feel threatened. There was not even a whisper of feeling threatened by what I could bring to the table, just sheer support and kind of backstop helping through hurdles... At one point I was struggling with one of our internal clients. I had a difficult one that was really micromanaging everything that our company put in front of her. I got a lot of really good coaching about how I could get that client's needs met but also holding our ground for the brand and using good communication practices. That era was pretty dreamy."

ASSESSING YOUR EARLY CAREER WORKPLACE CONTEXTS

▶ How much space is/was there in your workplace to be your authentic self and advance your ambitions and values?

▶ Can you/could you work with others to create more space?

▶ What messages are/were being sent in your workplace or industry about the possibility of creating the kind of work-life balance you desire?

▶ Is/was your workplace promoting discussion around and addressing issues like burnout, racism, sexism, and other problematic systems?

▶ What is/was the gender and racial makeup of formal leadership? Are/were there any "out" LGBTQ+ people here? Are/were there immigrants, people with disabilities, people of color, trans and nonbinary people, and diverse women in leadership roles?

▶ What messages are/were sent about the organization's willingness to make space for people who want to bring diversity, equity and inclusion values to whatever work comprises this organization's stated purpose?

▶ Who is inspiring you/who inspired you? How can/did you learn from the people who are approaching their work with joy and enthusiasm? How can/did you initiate a connection?

▶ Even if you only played a small part, what conversations and projects have you felt privileged to participate in and contribute to?

▶ When (if at all) did you have the resources, you needed to do the work that felt vital to you? And if so, who and what situations and systems provided them?

▶ In what situations did you have a sense of possibilities? And if so, where did this come from?

CHAPTER 3

FINDING YOUR WAY

Leveraging Voice and Values
To Build Confidence

WORKING FROM A CORE SET of progressive values isn't always straight-forward, especially when you're starting out in your career and learning the landscape of an organization or a field. Intertwined with issues of gender, race, sexual orientation, and other categories through which people can be marginalized at work, being young can itself be a challenge. You'll have moments of clarity, but also moments of confusion, and of compromise. It's all a building process: of skills, awareness, and potentially community, around shared principles that make our workplaces more inclusive and help them serve people better.

The stories shared with me in my research contain hopeful lessons about how speaking up in service to your values and your self-worth can also be instrumental to building confidence. Using your voice helps you get grounded in the kind of presence you want to cultivate at work, and to eventually find the kind of organizations where you can thrive as a growing professional.

Early in your career, you might not have the confidence, not to mention the sense of security in a professional work world you've barely begun to access, to ask for what you want from the get-go. One of my former students, Brianna, noted that when she was first interviewing for jobs, she "just wanted to get my foot in the door." But as her experience grew, so did her confidence as a job seeker. "When I first interviewed with [a healthcare union], I worked for," Brianna told me, "I mentioned my interest and passion for gender equity work, and how I believe unions could help to enhance the work lives of folks by negotiating around gender, race, ethnicity, and LGBTQIA rights." But, she says, "I did not at the time specifically ask about what the organization was committed to, because my online research told me that they were progressive and committed to social justice work."

Brianna added, "I also did not ask because of the power dynamic in that space that made me, a recent college grad, feel unable to push back and ask those questions so I could get my foot in the door. At this specific interview I was one of 15 other potential candidates, who were put through a five-hour interview process involving Q+As in front of the group, extensive role playing, and then a personal interview process with a panel of interviewers."

Brianna was enthusiastic about her new job but later became disillusioned in this organization: She saw a "consistent pattern of terminating the Black folks on staff with no transparency as to why they were being let go or pushed out. In addition, they displayed a lack of diversity within hiring practices, which prompted the staff union to push back together." Still in her mid-20s, Brianna, a white woman, already brings a deep sense of authenticity, personal boundaries, and values to her work. She continued, "The org hired more BIPOC folks, but would then show them a lack of support in learning their new role, leading to a similar issue of turnover. Additionally, there was an issue of the new young women on staff being picked out by a member of the leadership team for special mentorship that was inappropriate and created a hazardous work environment."

She did find that she "loved the core aspect of the work," and wanted to stay in the world of unions, just not at this particular union. Brianna learned to use job interviews not just to sell skills, but also to vet potential employers.

When I interviewed elsewhere, I always asked about workplace culture, diversity within leadership, and if there was a staff union. I am at a place in my professional development where I understand my worth and the quality of my work, so I need to make sure I am also interviewing the organizations I have applied to. From the handful of places I have interviewed with, these few questions were incredibly helpful in gauging which org was the best fit for me at the moment. I have recently moved to Chicago to work with a smaller union that so far doesn't display any of the issues previously seen at my last workplace.

Brianna may move again, because her broader lens on what she wants in an organization has her longing for the best possible workplace. She shared that,

There was a union I interviewed with that was seemingly perfect: run by women, committed (on their job posting) to working for gender equity in their communities, and worked incredibly hard at creating a safe space for their staff to avoid burnout, have time to take care of their families, and ensure they were supported in their position. This union was too far from my family at the moment so I couldn't accept the job, but I really appreciated seeing their clear stance on gender in their job description.

Brianna's proactive and intentional approach to interviewing for positions allowed her to see what was possible and helped her envision the kind of organization she wanted to work for, even if she couldn't get there right away.

Peyton, who had sometimes been discouraged in college when she spoke her mind, also used a thoughtful, boundary-setting approach to post-college work opportunities. She did not hesitate to quit a post-college job in disability services when she felt the organization was being hypocritical and not keeping staff safe during the pandemic.

> I was working in Homeless Outreach at the time, and I have really severe and debilitating OCD... COVID has been kind of a perfect storm for OCD, if you know how that works. And so I voiced to my manager that I was especially worried because this was at the beginning of the pandemic when they wouldn't let anybody come into the office, but they wanted me to go down to like help people in person in small rooms [working one on one with clients in person] and just be okay with it, kind of sacrifice myself to it to make it easier for them. And I wasn't comfortable with that.

This conversation did not go well. "I was told by the director of the company that I needed to get a little bit tougher if I wanted to keep working there," Peyton said. She tendered her resignation instead. She found the experience liberating, noting, "I think my most empowering moments have always been when I've decided that I get to choose myself in my professional life and in my personal life."

Practicing integrity around core values can have some short-term costs, but it can also strengthen us, helping us build a strong sense of professional identity. Mary, whom I interviewed when she was in her early 60s, remembered that "in my very first job, I was asked to lie, like a little white lie, and I couldn't do it." It was hard to tell her boss that she refused to tell this lie. But "making that little statement kind of helped because then later on taking a stand against someone else that wanted me to lie about something, it helps me to figure out what those values are. When it's a little thing, it helps you then when it's a bigger thing."

Sometimes, we forge our professional identities in our early careers through resistance to systems, grounded in assertion of our values. Ronda, for example, an Associate County Administrator in her mid-50s when we spoke, recalled the way an early job challenged her integrity. She says, "I didn't even think about systems being imperfect until I was in my late 20s." That was when, she says, "I realized I needed to quit my first, I'm going to use air quotes, 'real job' in the DA's [district attorney's] office as a victim witness coordinator." It was about values for Ronda. "I remember the exact moment when I said to myself, you've got to find a different job or do something else, or you're going to get fired."

Ronda recalled that a girl who had been sexually abused by her uncle over a span of years was "brought to the attention of law enforcement a long time after it stopped." She said that "the attorney handling the case asked me about asking her to do a sexual assault exam." Ronda knew such an exam only yielded results when abuse was ongoing or quite recent, which was not the case here. Moreover, the tests are "very invasive. And the victim was still a child, probably 13 or 14 years old. And with sexual trauma on top of it."

Ronda protested, "'What's the purpose of doing it?' Basically, he told me I had to do it anyway. I called a friend of mine who is a nurse and said, 'Help me understand. Am I wrong? Is this going to tell us anything?' 'Nope. Not going to tell us anything.' I went back, said again, 'I'm not going to do this. It's not going to tell us anything. We would just be re-traumatizing her.'" But Ronda's supervisor would not back down.

> I left the office, went to my office. And I remember this distinctly because it's the only time I've ever done this in my life. I slammed the door... I was probably 27... I was just so angry and so frustrated and thinking, I can't do this. I can't tell people who I work with every day, I'm not going to do what you asked me to do. I'm not going to re-traumatize people. That goes against my values, right?

The refusal to have an exam done on this girl was, Ronda says, "a defining moment in my life, [acknowledging that] things are imperfect, the system is imperfect. I can't be part of it. But I also didn't know at that time other things I could do to maybe make it better. I didn't have those skills." She credits this incident with inspiring her to go to graduate school in social work. In that field, she developed the skills to change systems from within, and is now a county administrator, a space from which she works to empower both public sector employees (disproportionately women) and entire communities.

Although quitting a job, as Ronda did, may be the appropriate path, it's obviously not for everyone. We need our jobs for our paychecks, for one thing, and not everyone feels they can make such a move, even in an unsatisfactory situation. Often, you can find ways to thrive in your early career, in spite of the barriers. You can work with the strengths and resources of your organization and with your mentors. Understanding context and the situations of older workers around you can help. Believe it or not, they may be struggling with their own insecurity, a sense that their contributing roles may be in jeopardy. Sometimes this is why young people get the message that older people just want to hang onto their "in charge" roles and defend "the way we've always done things here." And to be fair, sometimes they do, and this can create significant obstacles.

Rosalind, in her mid-40s at the time of our interview, observed that, "Particularly when you're young, you're kind of a new, or a younger hot off the press kind of person, colleague, employee. And you might be a threat to those who have been in the room for a while." Rosalind wisely points out that if you step back, you might be able to see "how much fear there is around, 'Well, you're going to take my job,' 'you're going to make me look bad', 'Do you realize how long I've been here?' those types of things."

I asked Rosalind how she thought young people should address this issue. She advised, from her own experience, "learning when to speak up and when to just let it go, and have a side conversation with a challenger," or, if you are emotionally able to do so, be direct in saying "that was not right, and now I'm very upset." You might, she says, "go back to your desk, write an email and then delete it, and just have those tools to navigate what's happening." It depends on the situation, your own emotional capacity, and the overall support you have, or do not have in your context.

For Rosalind, methods of challenging authority might have looked different at various points in her career than for many white women. She says, "Being a Black woman, a leader, I had to really reflect on how I show up and why. There are certain stereotypes around making people feel uncomfortable, being intimidating, being loud, being boisterous. There's a lot of different stereotypes around what Black women are, and how interesting it is reflecting on how very conscious I had become in order to lower my voice, in order to be very aware of who's in the room and how I'm showing up" She added, "And then there's instances where I've definitely not spoken up when I should have, due to feeling that I would intimidate or I would be too loud, or those types of things, that are very real when you're trying to grow and figure out and navigate the corporate world, or navigating the world in general."

As for not speaking up publicly sometimes, I don't know anyone who doesn't have regrets about not raising their voice at a particular moment when they saw something wrong. In fact, though, Rosalind's "side conversation with a challenger," a quiet form of leadership that most people don't see, can be a very effective form of fostering change. It can protect you from stereotype-based pushback while avoiding the defensiveness of public "call outs." The truth is, sometimes we're just too flustered, surprised, or fearful to find the words, or the courage. We step back, take a breath, regroup, and hopefully find another way to tackle the larger problems that came up in a particular moment at work.

Rosalind's reflections are also a good reminder that people have different risk assessments based on their identities when they speak up or don't speak up at given moments. And that we don't always lose our moment just because we can't find the right thing to say in a meeting. Private post-meeting conversations can both create less shame and more opportunity for relation-based education and forward movement. The fact that speaking up is often riskier for women of color than white women is another reason to consider the importance of allyship in creating change in the workplace, something we'll explore further in the next section.

Learning how you're going to use your voice takes time and practice, including some trial and error. And if you're reading this as a more established professional, you can find ways to support young women. To borrow again from the wise insights of Jenny Vazquez-Newsum, imagine if the women in the examples above had worked at organizations that intentionally leveraged the fresh perspectives of young people, of new employees in general, as a way to learn about improving the effectiveness of the organization? Or, in her words, "Imagine if, when someone new joins an organization, they are asked to share what has worked and not worked during their first months in the position, regardless of how big, small, or critical the observation is. Imagine what they might notice that someone else might have dismissed as 'just how it is.'"[46]

Young women can consider what room there might be in their organization to ask critical questions and can learn from these experiences.

People, connections, solidarity, mentoring, being grounded in your values, authenticity, and self-awareness—these magic ingredients lift us up throughout our careers, and the early career stage is no exception. As the above examples suggest, confidence in ourselves can be linked to setting boundaries at work and finding ways to speak up in service to our values and integrity. Sometimes this even involves strategic quitting, taking our life lessons with us to our next position.

If we're going to be advocates for others and our values, we also have to continually nurture our own confidence. And it's no secret that confidence for women, and even more so for women who hold additional marginalized identities beyond being female, can be a struggle.

RELATIONSHIPS, CHALLENGES, AND CONTEXTS TO HELP YOU GROW

The truth is, we all need to figure out a way to use our voices with kindness and authority. And like many ideals we pursue (confidence and poise, mastery of a desired skill, a sense of belonging and being in the right place at the right time) we often need to keep working, and reworking, at them as life changes. Nothing is permanent about a perfect fit between confidence and role or task; we all have highs and lows, and when we take on new challenges, and new roles, we're going to have to re-energize our confidence in a new setting, with new people, or in relationship to a set of tasks we might never have done before.

That said, the good news is that confidence does tend to grow over time for most of us. One study that included thousands of women and men in corporate America finds that the gender confidence gap is highest for people under age 25, with men asserting significantly more confidence than women. By age 40, that gender gap in confidence closes, and indeed, that's something to leverage for mid-career women. And by age 60, on average, women corporate leaders report feeling more confident than men in their age cohort. The researchers reported: "According to our data, men gain just 8.5 percentile points in confidence from age 25 to their 60+ years. Women, on the other hand, gain 29 percentile points."[47] Confidence grows because we stretch ourselves, and learn to acknowledge what is working, to look around us and see the evidence that people think we're capable.

People who are in our corner can of course help us build confidence, as Olivia's supportive supervisor story from the previous chapter illustrates well. But as important as support and recognition are, especially for undervalued "women's work" in areas like human services and education, it's also incredibly valuable to cultivate your own ability to step back and look at what's happening and how it informs your journey. And it's important to recognize when people are placing trust in you, and place that trust back on yourself.

Madeline, now in her 60s, is a leading advocate for inclusive healthcare, serving in an executive role in the hospital where she works. In her early career, she remembers, "I wasn't sure I was as adept at nursing." She had "a pretty critical nursing instructor along the way," and spent "those first couple of years" on the job growing her confidence. The confidence issues, she said, were related "not just to nursing, but really to myself as an individual and as a woman."

At the same time, Madeline was open to assignments that offered opportunities for growth, especially when she was asked to take on leadership roles. "What I would do is think, 'Oh, okay, I think I can do that because they came to me.'" That "self-awareness" served her well, and she "kept getting assignments to do other things." That, she says, is "how my professional path just started moving and I started to reflect on that myself. And saying, 'Oh, they're giving me more to do as I'm taking on more. How do I do that authentically?'"

This question—"how can I do this authentically"—is beautiful and necessary. Unless you're starting your own business, nonprofit, or grassroots organization, you didn't create the workplace systems you're navigating and within which you're trying to empower yourself and others, while also paying your bills with your income. But you can tap into your values and authenticity to make your role your own.

Madeline got herself promoted early in her career and kept moving forward. As an Indigenous woman, her work is underpinned by her devotion to making healthcare more culturally sensitive and the healthcare workplace more inclusive. These are commitments she has nurtured extensively, in part through her work with the Native American Nurses Association, and her state's Center for Nursing Diversity Committee, which sustain and inspire her beyond the borders of her workplace. But before she had fully found her way into how she would do this work, she noticed the possibilities she was accessing. And she checked in with her authenticity so that she could move forward in her own way within systems other people designed.

Authenticity feeds innovation and aids our ability to grow into formal leadership roles, even when we're young. Nina grew her confidence by being challenged during the COVID-19 pandemic in a new role for her, as an assistant director of a pre-college program. She took on this role in her mid-20s, and she would continue to serve in this leadership position while pursuing her master's degree and adapting to the pandemic. Nina remembered how excited she was when she was offered the position. "When I got it, I was just like, 'What? Are you sure? Me? That's fabulous.'" Nina had a deep affection for this program from her involvement during her own undergraduate experience just a few years earlier.

Just one year into this position, when the pandemic hit, a summer program that had been in person suddenly had to be online. The program was having a hard time hitting its enrollment targets, and the staff was struggling to figure out how to provide the level of impactful programming for students that they had managed in the past. Nina says that the whole preparatory period and the summer itself were "chaotic." But the problem-solving along the way helped her grow. For example, the team decided to deliver care packages with surprise items (including school supplies and board games) to the students all summer, making them feel special in ways that compensated for the lack of an in-person experience. And staff sent students recipes and ingredients to make food from the countries the program explored each week in their summer curriculum, as well as books by authors from those countries.

The results made Nina feel genuinely proud. The program ended with highlights like a virtual talent show, and a student-directed video in which the students shared the powerful impact of the summer program. Nina remembers thinking, "Oh, you noticed what I was trying to do there. And it was very empowering because it was like every student had something good to say... We knew that the program was making a difference in people's lives." At the time of our interview, a year past this challenging summer, Nina said, "Slowly but surely I find myself stepping more into what my purpose will be" in the leadership position she was pleased to occupy. The work, she said, "genuinely feeds my soul."

BUILDING CONFIDENCE IN SPITE OF THE BARRIERS

As Nina's story illustrates, confidence often truly must be gained by rising to challenges, sometimes challenges we would never have chosen. For me, growing my confidence in key domains took many years. And I would find over time that having confidence in one domain helped carry me into others. I knew from early on in my climb to the Ph.D. in History that I could understand the material I was studying. And I amassed a growing body of evidence that I could write my way into opportunities, graduate school, fellowships, job interviews, and eventually publications. Other pieces of my professional work, like becoming a skilled teacher, took much longer. Most of us have confidence in parts of what we have to offer, and much less certainty that we know how to say things, in the crucial moment, that we'll say the right things, that we'll be taken seriously and made to feel that we belong.

Like most of us, I can point to key people who said just the right things at the right moment to keep me moving. Encouraging words from people I trusted helped show me what was possible. One professor told me during my freshman year that I was a natural writer. Another, my history professor, Dr. Norm Rosenberg, said, when I told him about my K-12 teacher aspirations, "I'd love to have you teaching my kids, but you have what it takes to go for the Ph.D." Both were men, incidentally, as was the person I eventually married, who was always rooting for me to take my career as far as I wanted it to go.

Like my interviewees, my confidence grew, but it still had to swim up-stream sometimes. And this had a lot to do with being a woman in one of the many careers in which male-centered ideas, and men disproportion-ately occupying powerful positions, were still the norm. Even when we study inequality in great depth, as I have, that doesn't mean we become equipped with superpowers to "fix" these problems. Indeed, it was only in the past several years that I thought more deeply about a corrosive aspect of sexism in academia that had no doubt impacted my confidence throughout. For years, I had been able to trace back to college the impres-sion I got from some of my male friends that I wasn't so much smart as I was a goody two-shoes hard worker.

But it wasn't until 2018, during the Brett Kavanaugh hearings, that something about academia bubbled up for me: not its permissiveness for celebrated male abusers, which in some ways was old news, but the way it rewards a certain "know-it-all" masculinity over women's knowledge. The horror stories of sexual abuse I heard at that moment, from women I'd known for years, somehow contributed profoundly to a heightened aware-ness of sexism and power in my own experience more generally in my work.

When I mentioned to a man I knew that I was really angry about Ka-vanaugh, this man was dismissive, in an arrogant way. And it made me fu-rious, not just at him, but at every man who had ever assumed a casual air of entitlement to "Knowledge" with a capital K, while subtly questioning mine, and questioning the validity of what I knew about, including the way male power works. I want to reiterate that I have studied gender my entire career, and there were still ways in which this didn't sink in for me until I was in my early 50s.

So, it makes sense that when I was fresh out of my Ph.D. program, my confidence in my teaching abilities, the capacity to handle all that "Knowledge" properly was still very shaky. Still, I was excited about the potential impact I could make as an educator, and eager to share the knowledge I had spent seven years acquiring through intense study. And I had a belief in what I had to contribute underneath it all. I was offered a one-year job teaching History at my alma mater for a miniscule amount of pay. I negotiated hard for a better salary, which I didn't get. Even after I started teaching, I took a while to sign the contract, arguing (with my late 20s boldness, moral clarity and more than a little self-righteousness) that this kind of pay was not only unfair to me, but was cheapening the work of the entire profession. That shaky confidence in my professional abilities somehow co-existed with a core belief in the value of my work and my skills. Years after this gig ended, I carried a note from the department chair in one of my course textbooks, which read "Jodi, the Provost is still waiting for you to sign your contract." It reminded me that I had stood up for myself, even though I lost.

Sometime during that one-year stint, when the college's alumni magazine wanted to do a story on how I had returned to the alma mater to teach in the department where I got my degree, I said no. I felt I was being exploited, making far less than what a single student paid to attend that institution. Though I've stood up for myself and others many times since then, the fact that I did this at age 29, in such a relatively undiplomatic way, still surprises me.

As my story suggests, women's confidence challenges need to be understood in the context of gendered messages and other systemic messages about race, disability, immigration status, class background, or LGBTQ+ identities, to name a few. And different generations have had their sense of possibilities shaped by shifting cultural norms. Mary, a white woman just a few years older than me, said it also took her decades to really start to look at how gender influenced her confidence. Indeed, this happened for her after she had started examining her racial privilege. In her late 40s, as coordinator of diversity programs for a community organization, she invited a speaker to talk about gender and work. For the first time, she said, she really reflected on the limits on her mother's and grandmother's lives. By extension, she thought more about how gender had shaped her life.

Mary realized how, even in her faith community, where she served as a church board member, "it was all men, and I was always feeling less than. Like there was something wrong with me because I was so different." It didn't help, she said, that growing up as a Baby Boomer, "I only saw doctors that were white men. And people in the world were white men on TV, and the women were Ginger and Maryanne [of *Gilligan's Island*], Mrs. Brady, or Julie London, the nurse. I mean, those are all my role models and all those things that I was seeing and not realizing what could be."

Mai, a Hmong woman in her late 30s, made a similar point about the absence of positive, mass cultural representations of women, especially women of color. Mai admired her mother who supported Mai at every stage of her education and career. But she noted, "Even on TV, movies that we would watch, I didn't have anybody [I could see to say] 'Wow, I want to be like that,' I didn't connect. That had a lot of effect on me. Because I do not have a lot of confidence in myself and didn't really think anything was possible for me. And so, I think that had a lot to do with me not initially going to school and taking any type of leadership role to better myself."

For Mai, confidence increased when she made an important decision about her career. She said she had "an awakening" while working in banking, after hitting glass ceilings with two internal job applications while she was pregnant, and getting turned down. "I loved what I did at the bank," she said. "And I don't mean to disrespect the bankers or the supervisor, or anyone involved in that matter." But one year, when it came time for a raise, Mai says, hers was "just pennies. And so, at that moment, I was just kind of like, 'You know what? I have to do better. I deserve so much better. I have to do something.'"

This was partly, she says, because of the messages she got from her husband, who always told her, "'Mai, you're smart, you can do it. You can do whatever you want. And I have faith in you.'... He always encouraged me." When her supervisor showed her the paltry raise, the combination of her husband's encouragement and her own accumulated disappointment led Mai to decide to go back to school, even while continuing to work and be a mother to four children. In college, she says "I felt empowered. Because I was learning. I wanted to learn. I couldn't wait for the next class or the next subject."

At the time of our interview, Mai was still finding her footing in a relatively new corporate job, but her supervisor was already offering her stretch assignments. "She's awesome," Mai said of the supervisor. "She's been extremely supportive through my educational process. She wants me to expand my wings and learn. She wants me to basically do everything I can. And everything that she does." Moreover, she said, there are two women at her company whom she's watching closely. "They're confident, intelligent ladies. So, I think just being in their presence and watching how they go about their work and their responsibilities, that has given me a lot of confidence as well. It's shown me that it's possible. We can do it. It's there and you can do it."

Confidence comes from stretching ourselves, and often, we don't make those stretches alone. We have our people (inside and outside of the workplace) pushing us along, reminding us of our values, believing in us. As some of the examples already discussed in this chapter suggest, confidence also allows us to clarify what we stand for, and how much we will stand for in a workplace. Sometimes this is about protecting our self-worth, as Mai did. And sometimes it's about protecting our integrity, as it was for Ronda. Often, these things are intertwined.

Sometimes when we're young, our voices are strong because our principles are clear. We refuse to re-traumatize a child because of a supervisor's callous decision; we slam a door. We quit a job, we join a union, we take the risk of showing anger.

From a larger angle, perhaps these moments could be written off as symbolic, or even as reminders that business goes on as usual after women make a principled stand. It's very possible that others were paid as poorly or even less than Mai and me after we left our jobs, that someone else in the D.A.'s office where Ronda worked was willing to order a rape kit long after it would be of any help. But we may be planting seeds and leaving some benefit behind us, even if we take off before we can see them grow.

In fact, I've seen it more than once in my consulting work: People voice their frustrations with inequities for a long time, or hold their critiques in, but then let them be heard when they're really ready to leave anyway. But the organization subsequently institutionalizes some of the very improvements the critics wanted, whether it's better education for employees on Diversity, Equity, and Inclusion (DEI), improved employee policies, or a commitment to using more inclusive language, even after the critics have moved on. For the next people working there, some of those fights don't have to be fought.

In addition to sometimes being a spark for changes we might not even know have happened in our wake, little by little, using our voices helps us too. This practice helps us grow into new and exciting roles, and potentially helps us become fierce advocates for others, too. Once we have our confidence and credibility better established, we can often negotiate and advocate more skillfully, and sometimes with more clear and lasting results. Early in our careers, when we take the long view, risks that feel so high stakes in the moment are often the very ones we need to take to grow our confidence, and to stake our authority in our values and integrity.

It's also important for women at every stage, including young women, to realize that at least parts of the process of establishing credibility sometimes need to be repeated over the course of our careers. As we grow in our professions, as we sometimes choose to leave (or even get pushed out of) spaces where we hoped we could belong, as we apply for leadership positions or even change careers, we can encounter new (though sometimes too familiar) sets of barriers and gatekeepers. In these situations, we may re-ignite struggles with confidence we thought we had left behind. Hopefully, though --and I have found this to be the case in my own journey-- we learn to value our strengths and keep encouraging people around us in ways that build over time and allow us to increasingly know our worth and help open the door for others.

REFLECTING ON YOUR
CONFIDENCE & VALUES JOURNEY

▶ What have been some of your own internal challenges in early career? E.g. Anxiety, burnout, distrust of the systems in which you work?

▶ How might discriminatory experiences have impacted your confidence, e.g. sexism, racism, homophobia, transphobia, ableism, religious discrimination, or other kinds of marginalization?

▶ What workplace barriers were significant for you as you sought (or are still seeking) to establish credibility and confidence? For example, gatekeeping, not being taken seriously, not being mentored or welcomed, facing a culture that revolved around people with more societal privilege than you had/have, lack of transparency about how to move ahead.

▶ Has the struggle to belong instilled in you the idea that you need to do a lot of smiling, people-pleasing and doing things "perfectly" to make a place for yourself and establish your credibility?

▶ When and how have you asked challenging and even potentially disruptive questions at work? What have been the results, including with respect to your confidence? What results might have happened that you could not see at the time?

▶ How did you make peace, if only temporarily, with the problematic systems in which you have spent time working, so that you could get some good work done, and make progress towards dismantling oppressive systems and developing your career goals?

▶ If you've experienced positive workplace cultures, mentoring, supervision, and growth early in your career, what was that like and what have you learned from those experiences to enhance your next chapter, and to help others?

▶ How do you/did you deal with anxiety and fear of failure?

▶ Has staying true to your values helped you find confidence?

▶ If you're at a later stage of your career, how can you mentor and help grow the confidence of young women in your sphere of influence?

▶ And how can you create space for young people's questions and challenges? How can you help them honor their integrity?

CHAPTER 4

FINDING MENTORS
AND BEING A MENTOR

IT'S NO SECRET that good mentoring is linked to women's career success, and that intentional mentoring can be part of important cultural change, leading to the development of diverse leaders who can transform our workplaces. The direct workplace mentoring received by Olivia, Tina, Lee, and others I already discussed in this section, remind us of the power of seeing the best in young people, protecting them when necessary, and helping them grow. Sustained and intentional mentoring by people in supervisory positions is life changing.

Recent research suggests that many women in business lacked mentoring themselves, and yet they are often committed to providing that valuable resource, despite what they had missed in this area at a younger stage of career. One study of over 300 women in business from 19 countries and 30 different industries surveyed a group of women who were themselves disproportionately in mid-senior leadership roles. (75% said this was their level at the time of the survey.) Of that group a striking 63% said they had never had a "formal" mentor. Just over half of the organizations for which they worked (56%) reported having a formal mentoring program. And yet, 75% of women who worked for a company with such a program said they "always" accept mentoring opportunities when they're available.[48]

When I look back on my 20s, I cannot call to mind any discussion of the idea of mentoring. I'm sure this was partly because I was the first person in my family to go to four-year college, and many aspects of organizational and higher education professionalism were new to me. But I also don't believe the idea was elevated in the late 1980s and 1990s the way it is today. I did not know what I might expect of a mentor, though I can also see that such people popped up for me at important moments, probably because of their own intentionality about how to mentor. There was, for example, the aforementioned undergraduate professor, Norm Rosenberg, who encouraged me to think more expansively about my career.

And then there was the Professor of Chinese History, Dr. Ann Waltner, in my graduate school years. I took Ann's courses for fun and interest; she was not my adviser. But she made me feel seen, in ways that my other professors often didn't. She saw my interest in the wider world, and she perceived confidence in me even when I could not see it. I remember confessing my insecurities to Ann about succeeding in academia, and she said, "I would not have known that, since we all see you as so confident." That's what mentors do: see possibilities in us, help us set our sights higher, and see our best selves even when we cannot.

Some stories collected for my research serve as reminders of frustrating missed opportunities for mentoring and the impact of that gap on the advancement and overall self-efficacy development of young women. For example, Morgan, who had worked at Planned Parenthood right out of college, had recently moved into a corporate career at the time of our interview. In her mid-20s and already experiencing some social justice burnout, she was seeking a better paycheck than she had found in reproductive rights and domestic violence work, and just as importantly, less emotional exhaustion.

In her new company, she found   excellent pay and benefits, and she "didn't cry so much after work." Morgan was also attracted to the mission of her health-related company. Unfortunately, she didn't feel connected to that mission in her day-to-day work. The transition to the corporate world, she said, had been "super challenging. I've felt really disconnected with myself and I felt very much like where am I? Where do I stand with my values? Am I using my values in this workplace and is this the right fit for me?"

The organization was actually investing in developing women's leadership in some important ways. Quarterly women's leadership events energized Morgan. "Those women's leadership meetings are super important to me," she said. "If those weren't there, I don't know if I would still be in the workplace, even though they are only quarterly. Just after them, I feel really empowered and I feel really re-energized, and I almost rely on them too much, I think, to feel energized."

In between the meetings, Morgan seems to have felt somewhat adrift, in spite of having a sister in the company who offered good mentoring regarding advancement. She felt isolated in her little corner of a large organization, and "when I have ideas, I just feel like, why even bring them up? Because they're not going to get anywhere."

Morgan's need for mentoring was not just about advancement. It was about figuring out how to align her values with her work and feel a sense of belonging in a workplace that was filled with male leaders, a workplace in which she had already "removed a bunch of my piercings to fit in," and in which she felt self-conscious about her tattoos. A male co-worker seemed to be seen as a cool, rugged individual with his tattoos, but she thought people looked at her as a "troubled woman" because of hers.

Morgan could see places she might go within the organization. "The organization is huge," she said. "There's so many avenues you can take, and I think I just need to explore these more because, I mean, I do like the business. I do enjoy the mission and the values and some of my co-workers are nice and relatable." But the health and wellness jobs that interested her "require so much experience. And how would I get that experience?" And yet, she said, "I do think there are other avenues that I could take to keep me here and to help me grow. There's a diversity and inclusion group. There's multiple women's leadership groups. There's an LGBTQ group, which—I identify as pansexual—so that's important to me. So, I think if

I also focus on making work not just work, but also connection with others, and trying to improve the workplace, then maybe if I incorporate that and those values, then I'll feel like I'm still being my authentic self and driving towards the social justice issue."

Despite usually feeling like her ideas were brushed off, there were a couple of exceptions. There was one "higher up person," a person of color, Morgan mentioned, "who has asked me directly for my ideas about how we could improve... He is absolutely great." And she said her former manager was "always very interested" in what was discussed in the women's leadership group meetings, and wanted her to review what she learned, "because he knows that I was a women's studies major, and he knows that I'm passionate about those things." He expressed that he could improve himself professionally because of what he had learned from her. "So that was always really empowering, and I really appreciated that." This person suggested she facilitate a meeting around these issues for her team of women. Unfortunately, she was assigned a new manager, and this project "never got off the ground."

Morgan's is a liminal story. She would love to know more about what mentors are supposed to do for her, how to find them, and how to decide, "is this the right fit? Where can I go from here?" At the time of our interview, Morgan was very young and hadn't found her place yet. This is of course not at all uncommon for women her age. Looking back, I suspect my confidence level was right about where hers was at that age. But clearly, she was trying to find a way to both belong and be herself, but at the time of our interview, she was falling through the cracks of her organization. I wondered if her organization would lose her, sending her on to a place where she could better bring her gifts, but losing her contributions to their work.

I believe it's always the work of organizational leaders to create a culture and structures around mentoring. Indeed, structures that attend to the way social inequality works, and the need to diversify leadership and voice. But it's also worth noting that impactful mentoring can happen in momentary encounters, or even just by looking up to people and being inspired by them. For women of color, among my interviewees, and among friends I've known and colleagues I've worked with, availing oneself of mentoring and inspiration from afar can feel especially necessary when they're in predominantly white environments. Rosalind, for example, said she has had "many mentors, and many people who did seek to help me navigate, even though they might not understand the exact walk I had to walk. Because they never could. We each have our journey." But "they saw something in me to help me continually grow in my personal and professional life."

That said, Rosalind pointed out that in her community, there are relatively few Black and brown people, "which makes an even smaller number of Black and brown leaders." Rosalind said that this has been part of the reason she "reached out nationally and internationally to other women leaders," such as those who had founded nonprofits, which Rosalind herself was doing when we spoke. "When you're seeking a mentor," she said, "you don't have to know them per se; you can read their books. You can say, what would Oprah do? Well, what would Maya Angelou do, or you know, what would Brené Brown do? And think of what their teachings are that they put into the world. You don't have to be best pals with them in any way."

Madeline said she was very appreciative of long-standing connections beyond her workplace and community that had sustained her career over decades. "One of the nuggets that I try and appreciate are those that cross my path. It could've been for a moment or two." Relatively early in her career, on a van ride from a hotel to the airport, Madeline had a conversation with the director of a nursing program in another state that opened up new worlds for her. She was already involved with the American Organization for Nursing Leadership and had an interest in leadership. But she learned from this woman "that there was a whole group of Native

American Indian nurses." The momentary mentor told Madeline, "'We're hosting this Native American Nursing Summit. I think you should come.'"

Madeline did go to that event and remained involved in the National Alaska Native American Indian Nurses Association (NANAINA) through her career. She was serving as president of that national organization at the time we spoke. "And so those connections sometimes are not long," she said. "They're like little pearls of messages that come, and it's a matter of being open to it or thoughtful about it in such a way that there is another path that might be opening up that you don't necessarily know what that is." These days, with the availability of online spaces and social media, we can find mentoring support well beyond our workplaces and our geographical confines even when we don't have chance in-person encounters like Madeline did. Surrounding ourselves with people who manifest positive potential can be especially important when we're struggling to see ourselves moving forward in our particular space and situation.

MENTORSHIP AS LEADERSHIP DEVELOPMENT: YOU DON'T HAVE TO WAIT TO BE A MENTOR

Clearly, it's helpful to learn from our elders when we're entering new fields, seeking a sense of belonging and connection to wider perspectives, and wisdom. It's also important to remember that even when we're young, we are potential mentors as well. Nina, for example, talked a lot about the power of being an ambassador to college and adult life for younger siblings, both for herself and for the students she worked with in her precollege program. Nina was only in her late 20s when I interviewed her, but her mentoring of college students through her Student Affairs position was framed in such an empowering way. She mentored in a way that leveled the playing field, lifting up young people by honoring their stories.

> Now, when I speak with students, [I say] literally tell me your story. I don't really take it as like, it's my job to tell you what you should do. If anything, I'm going to help you reiterate your story to yourself so that you understand what you're telling me. When those stories led to immediate challenges in the students' lives, Nina would say, "And now, what do you think we should do to fix this situation? Like what can we do? And the story isn't over. You know, like there's so much more that could be—that could happen."

In fact, no matter your age, you can mentor (in fact, you probably already have) and be mentored. It may be strange to hear this when you're not sure what you're doing, but we are all setting examples; we are all being watched by someone a little younger or a little less experienced in our field. And you already have a story. We might as well embrace this. It helps us be better human beings, while also helping us see that no matter how insecure we are, we all have something to give.

Mentorship is actually a set of skills, ultimately skills that are fundamental to practicing inclusive leadership. As the stories in Chapter 3 have helped illustrate, mentoring involves guidance, support, sharing experiences, offering and receiving constructive feedback, empowering people to navigate obstacles and build upon their genius ideas, and provide allyship and advocacy for that person. Mentoring to empower women committed to creating more inclusive, diverse, and equitable workplaces is especially nuanced. It means being careful about not trying to create a "mini me" or replicating the status quo in organizations. It's about two-way learning opportunities, listening, humility, advocacy, recognition of the leadership strengths of under-represented groups, empowerment. It's about promoting opportunities for emerging leaders who can bring original ideas and transform workplace cultures. It's a set of skills that you probably already have started developing. You can grow your awareness of them and practice them.

When I first started my tenure-track teaching job at the age of 32, I was thrown into teaching 195 students, in three different classes. The class was "World History up to 1500." I was trained as a historian of the twentieth century United States, and I was beyond underprepared to take on this challenge. I stayed up until somewhere between 11 pm and 1 am many nights writing lectures about Assyrians and Babylonians when I had just learned who they were, just trying to stay one step ahead of the students.

I was too caught up in my own professional insecurities (along with adjusting to a new community, while being the mother of a kindergartener and a two-year-old), to even think about the perspective of the students, except in the ways they might judge me wanting, not very Knowledgeable with a capital K. I just kept worrying about being found out for how ignorant I was about the subject matter and self-conscious about my fumbling attempts to convey it and make it interesting and true to the historical record. And it's true: some of my early course evaluations provide one unflattering window onto how many semesters it took for students to decide I was a decent teacher. While they were deciding, I was wondering whether I would make it in this profession, or whether the powers that be would kick me out.

So, imagine my surprise when a young woman came to my office hours during my first semester of teaching to talk about something related to class, perhaps the final exam essay, and out of her mouth spilled this surprising praise: "I really appreciate the way you teach. You're not like the other professors. You get us."

I have no idea what she meant, but it was a beautiful gift. Without my knowing it, I was already conveying something that at least one student thought was worth emulating, just as I had wanted to emulate my professors. What had inspired me was my professors' passion for justice and their eloquent ways of framing the world and its waves of change and continuity with the most exquisite descriptive vocabulary. I don't know what this student saw in me, but her kind words helped me understand that despite all the barriers between us, I was one of the people who was helping her think about her place in the world. Over the years, I leaned more and more into that mentor role, letting the "professor fills the bucket with information" model lessen, and orienting myself as much to relationship as to expertise.

To my mind, the sooner we can become aware of our potential to help young people (or people newer to a role at any age) see their potential, the better. It doesn't mean we have to be perfect. I clearly was no model of perfection. It does mean that we should strive to notice the chances we have to encourage, share our stories, and at the same time learn from people who see us as having something to offer that we might not even have known we have. A suggestion I've frequently seen shared on social media is simple but profound: "be the person you needed when you were younger." Honestly, it's never too early to start.

And as you're doing this, seek out mentors for yourself. In our early careers, we are learning how to struggle with our inadequacies, how to take feedback, how to understand ourselves in relationship to conflict, how to recognize our strengths, celebrate our successes, and how to articulate and nurture our wildest dreams for making a difference in the world. People who mentor us and teach us about leadership are critical at this formative stage of early professional life.

Overall, when grappling with the challenges and triumphs of early career, it's important to realize that you're never doing it alone. There's some continuum of support to obstruction around you. And in those varied environments, we don't just sink or swim; we often muddle through. We survive (not always without scars) obstacles, we challenge, we persist, and sometimes we thrive and shine.

I hope you'll join me in embracing the idea of yourself as a mentor and a person who has something to contribute to every structure in which you participate. As mentors of any age and stage, we want to develop strong future leaders, who can weather storms and prejudice if they're going to face that, own and leverage the privileges they may have on account of gender, race, class background, religion, ability, to name a few examples, and learn how to continually find and live in their own truths, while also staying in relationship with others.

As for those of us who are older in our careers and/or more experienced in our roles, we need to be attentive to the needs of younger generations. With an investment in those with less authority and privilege, we can be part of making the path easier for others while we're struggling, stumbling, or striding and sailing through the legs of our own work journeys. We can help create spaces, environments, relationships, conversations, and structures that empower young women and all people who have been under-represented in influence and leadership. This kind of investment points towards a future in which, someday, advice to leaders doesn't even need to be differentiated by gender, or any other systematic pattern of discrimination, a future in which we will have created workspaces rich, complicated, creative, and full of productivity built on diversity.

REFLECTING ON MENTORSHIP
IN YOUR JOURNEY

▶ Who helped clear the path for you? Who mentored you, protected you, or fought battles on your behalf or before your time, so that the way was easier?

▶ Who has opened up doors for you and shown you spaces of humanity, community, and exciting collaborations in education and/or the workplace?

▶ What were the positive impacts, and were there any negative aspects of your mentoring experiences?

▶ In what situations were you missing that help and protection, and what difference would it have made to have it?

▶ How did you (or did you) learn to mentor others and/or participate in their growth?

▶ Whom have you mentored, consciously, or even without realizing you were serving as a mentor?

▶ What structures and aspects of the workplace culture (if any) give women access to quality mentoring?

▶ What can you learn by watching your mentors? What questions can you ask them to open up their stories about how they learned to be good mentors?

REVIEW

MINIMIZING THE CHALLENGES AND MAXIMIZING THE OPPORTUNITIES OF EARLY CAREER

I HOPE YOU'LL SET YOURSELF UP at this stage of your career to minimize the obstacles and maximize the potential of this stage of life.

▶ Find support! Peers, mentors, even consider creating your own group.

▶ Develop mutual support around developing confidence.

▶ Have other people's backs when they ask challenging questions: keep clearing the path!

▶ Know your worth and become an advocate for yourself—and others.

▶ Watch for burnout and stress.

▶ Be a friend and ally.

▶ Leverage your generational power.

▶ Use the situation for what it can provide. Maximize what you have available.

▶ Do your work in the most authentic way you can.

▶ Start practicing boundaries and balance; watch your mentors and find out how they do it.

▶ Grow your confidence by flexing your values' muscles.

▶ Practice career-long skills like negotiating and working towards collaborative solutions.

▶ Figure out what help you need: find your allies and lean on the loved ones in your life.

A FINAL NOTE ON THIS CAREER PHASE

Throughout this stage of career and life, enter and find your place in the spaces where you're going to grow. Honor your questions and critiques, which may become the catalysts for making change and developing your authenticity and values. If you're fortunate, aware, and choosy about where you spend your energy, you may have all the ingredients in place to make such changes early in your career. That said, in most institutions, even supportive ones, you'll be in a limited role as a new professional. It's your questions and voice that will start to shift conversations and frameworks among those with more clout. Asking questions educates others, while offering the possibilities of new collaborations with those in more senior positions. Your questions can show the value of what's undervalued and shape the way institutions can change. Through this often-confusing chapter, find your friends and enjoy the journey.

PART II
MID CAREER

Balancing Acts and Barriers,
Resilience and Leadership

CHAPTER 5

SELF STRENGTHENING FOR MID-CAREER CHALLENGES AND OPPORTUNITIES

MID-CAREER IS POTENTIALLY a very long chapter, one that can include the triumphs of competencies and accomplishments, heartbreaking road-blocks, the complexities of caregiving that often shape women's lives, career pivots, and the opportunity to learn from and contribute through developing your leadership. My own mid-career involved all of the above. I learned how to be a good teacher and an accomplished researcher. I made some good noise on campus, especially speaking up and becoming part of coalitions on issues of gender and racial justice. I chaired a committee that implemented a part-time option for faculty with family obligations, which helped nurture and probably retain a number of talented women faculty on campus. All the while, I raised three children. Caregiving demands, and family joys mushroomed around me.

Yet, as my star rose, I ran right into bullying in my immediate department, and a related career crisis. Though I emerged from that experience somewhat scarred, I also continued to take on leadership roles and learned that I could grow into leadership by practicing, and that I could have some success mentoring and facilitating positive experiences for other people.

This section of the book couldn't possibly capture the complexities of those experiences that cluster in the middle decades of life, but the stories remind us of ongoing ways to combine self-advocacy with leaning into values and finding ways to thrive for some periods of the journey. We often also need to make changes, to get ourselves out of difficult situations; we need to learn to pivot.

Everyone's journey is different, but many of us arrive at this stage sometime in our early-to-mid-thirties and continue a mid-career type momentum through our early fifties. Even if we've changed careers, completed higher education at a non-traditional age, or pursued intense industry experience instead of formal education, we're likely to have accrued significant life experience, self-awareness, and social networks by this time in our lives.

It's not uncommon, somewhere in this time period, for professional life to take on a steady rhythm, because we've hit our stride. We might figure out where we might want to be in a context we now understand better (obstacles included) and begin pursuing new goals, potentially including accessing formal leadership roles. We might have more awareness of our worth, and the insistence that others acknowledge it. We might seek out broader platforms to do the work that animates us, raising our voices from different and sometimes more empowered perches within our organizations and fields. Or, we might be able to bloom in surprising ways, right where we're planted.

Another feature of the mid-career stage is that our careers overall can become important dimensions of our identities, and sometimes areas of significant self-efficacy and the satisfaction of making an impact. DEI work in particular can also be an essential way for values-driven women to be themselves at work, and to live by their values as they create expanded spaces of belonging for others as well as for themselves.

"Getting ahead" in these eventful mid-career years can mean different things to different people. It may just mean getting to a place that looks like empowerment to you in terms of balance for a period of time while you're focusing on your family. It may mean the opportunity to work on projects that satisfy you and in which you can have a positive impact, whether or not that involves a formal leadership role. Not everyone wants formal leadership roles, and we can exercise leadership in any position, as long as we're thriving: contributing, learning, connecting, working from and advancing our values, working with integrity. That said, the power of women's leadership, from any position, but especially with the platform of formal leadership positions, holds great potential in the mid-career years.

As we'll see, obstacles and barriers continue and shift in these years. To keep from being derailed and to keep adapting and thriving, mid-career women must learn to reflect, to advocate for others, to be a voice for structural change where possible, and to make deliberate plans in both the short and long term. We must develop resilience and keep restoring our self-esteem when negative situations threaten to drain us, so that we can continue to appreciate the value we bring and how we can share it with others. That includes mentoring younger people, and being mentored ourselves, because we can't do all this alone.

We need to figure out how to stay attuned to our shifting contexts, get help from our people, to stay on track with our sense of effectiveness and satisfaction, and forward movement, whatever that means to us. And we need to find strategies for resilience when we face setbacks, continuing to take the long view of our career and investing in ourselves. My interviewees exemplified this wisdom.

I met Connie in 2020; at a class I taught about women in the workplace through the continuing education program of my university. I was impressed by her passion for learning, her questioning mind, her ability to start critical conversations, her all-in engagement in her career, as well as her buoyant warmth and obvious, multi-faceted leadership competencies. Connie is a single mother who identifies as Native American but says she hasn't thought much about race in her career because gender has loomed larger. She has had to deal with challenges ranging from career stagnation to policing of her tone of voice and appearance, even to outright bullying; and she is well aware that other women are regularly treated this way in the workplace.

In one company, Connie says, "I kept getting passed over for management. And, you know, I had been the longest term one in the department. And it was always good reviews, I was told I was a go-getter, wonderful to have you." But at Connie's company (like many others) responsibility and praise for women did not translate into coveted leadership positions. As Connie put it, "you're in a company and you're that go-getter, employee of the month, you get all these wonderful rewards, but they don't look at you like management material, and you really don't know that."

During a long mid-career stint of working hard without advancing, Connie says she came to understand how sexism worked in her male-dominated company. She was told she was "brash" and that she laughed too loudly. "And then you go into a meeting with men, because... men dominate at the management [level]. I'm like hearing them argue and everything else and I'm thinking, I'm brash? I couldn't believe it; I'm like, okay, this is management, but when I do it, it's wrong. It was a constant, 'What you're doing wrong' or 'You are brash. You are too loud.'" She was told that her facial expressions made it too easy for people to "tell when you're mad." And yet, she could clearly tell when men were mad, and it seemed perfectly acceptable for them to express this emotionally.

Connie eventually left this organization, pursued additional education, and achieved a management position elsewhere. But her first management position was a glass cliff situation. There, she was immediately deployed to do the dirty work of a supervisor who "didn't like conflict." Her work" involved what Connie called "cleaning house." She said, "It was like getting rid of people, firing people. It was making sure they were productive. If they weren't productive, then we went through a process... with HR. And that was me. I was the person."

Connie tried to keep from falling off that glass cliff by being a team player, learning how to be a manager, "cleaning house," and "making sure people are productive," even though, she added, "nobody likes that person." But, she says, once she had done her supervisor's dirty work, he came to her with negative feedback: "He'll come in the office and say, 'Hey, people perceive you're this.' I said, 'Okay.' And then he would say, 'Well, I just have to tell you.'" The supervisor's comments focused on things that Connie found very odd and unrelated to performance, such as her loud laughter. Still, she told him, "'Okay, I'll work on that perception.'" And yet, she got the message: "you're too much of this, , stay in this little box." Connie found this experience profoundly discouraging. "Yeah, and you just experience all this stuff and you're like, how do you grow as a woman? You know what I mean? How do you grow as a leader?" The whole encounter made her feel like she was "going nowhere."

Like other women I interviewed who faced all-too-common mid-career roadblocks, Connie was not going to accept "nowhere" as a destination. She found a way to move through this experience with resilience. "I would be like okay, you need to just hold your head high, keep moving on, no matter what the roadblocks are."

When the manager who had made her "clean house" retired, Connie found a new position within the organization for which she applied. "I was reading some women's guides or [doing] Google research, listened to a podcast, and I thought, 'let's try for this position.' So, I did. I was nervous, but I did it. I didn't get the position, but what happened out of it was the CEO actually recommended me for some coaching, and it was with a woman that understood how I felt about women in leadership." Connie wished she had had these resources earlier, so that instead of undergoing "personal attacks," someone would have said to her: "'Let's look at what we can do with you.' You know what I mean? 'Let's look at your career.'" Now, the coach did that for her: "She was saying, here's your tools. Now, use them to be who you want to be, so people can see you."

Age 59 at the time of our interview, Connie had boundless energy and enthusiasm and was still pursuing every professional learning opportunity she could fit into her schedule, and looking for new ways to contribute. She grew through embracing change, learning, and filling needs that fit her competencies and passions, including mentoring younger people and creating more inclusive spaces. She was proud of what she had accomplished, and of how she was now being seen as a resource for others.

A younger woman in her workplace had recently asked to be mentored by Connie. The younger woman had told Connie that when she saw her "walking down the hallway, 'I thought, I'm going to stop her and say something, because I want to get to know her. She's got her shit together.'" At the time of our interview, Connie had recently proposed a formal mentoring program for young people, women of every age, and LGBTQ+ people. Her supervisor, she said, was enthused and "ready to roll out a pilot." Connie was triumphant, and excited to be a key player in that endeavor, which had the potential to impact the entire company. Connie channeled her leadership desires into project creation rather than high-level management, and this was working very well for her at the time of our interview.

Connie's path wasn't easy. She faced mid-career obstacles that are all too common. But she learned, adapted, built her portfolio and connections, extracted herself from toxic situations, and kept finding ways to grow and contribute.

ASSESSING YOUR STRENGTHS AND ENVISIONING THE ROAD AHEAD

One of the most thoughtful and intentional leaders I have encountered is Rosalind, who offered many lessons for navigating the shifting sands of mid-career. Her attention to context, to self, others, and the long view set her up for coping with any challenges that came up. Her advice is helpful for framing the mid-career stage, this time when we might change jobs or industries, adapt to new contexts and power structures, and hopefully grow in our ability to make our work our own, to choose our projects in ways that point us toward the possibilities of thriving and living out our values.

Rosalind's career has had exciting and ever-changing chapters, and she has also faced challenges and setbacks at times. Through it all, she consistently tapped into her own wisdom by marshaling what she calls an "intentional workplace presence." I wrote about Rosalind's journey in previous sections, from bartending to working for eight years in corporate settings where she had many positive experiences and a good sense of belonging. Listening to Rosalind during our interview, it struck me that she had an extraordinary sense of self-efficacy, based in large part on regular reflection about how to stay aligned with her purpose and her integrity, as well as nuanced attention to how to show up in different contexts relationally and intentionally.

Rosalind sees each career stage as just that, a chapter in time. Part of her regular reflection includes asking herself, "What does the end of my career look like?" Rosalind's effectiveness at work is based not only on self-reflection of course, but on multi-faceted competencies that have made her successful in many domains, including founding not one but TWO of her own nonprofits and pursuing her doctorate degree. As part of Rosalind's "whys" in the world, these nonprofits focused on empowering women, and empowering children through innovative education. At the time of our interview, shortly after the murder of George Floyd, Rosalind was also consulting nationally with corporate leaders on the topic of racial equity. She lived her values both within and beyond the confines of organizations where she worked, but her skills and dispositions across these arenas complemented one another.

Like the other women in this book, Rosalind knew how to draw on the strengths she had built over the course of her life story. In her case, her traumatic childhood gave her some important strengths to take forward in the workplace. Because of that background, she says, "I can get from point A to point B in an efficient way, and I can see things differently. I can kind of connect the dots on things, create something out of nothing, and through that, created a career." She used her big-picture, strategic, resourceful thinking every day in the consulting work she was doing at the time of our interview, saying she was able to be "a business strategist, in that I help people in organizations come together in order to build something profitable and sustainable."

Part of Rosalind's toolbox includes cultivating an understanding of herself as a "corporate entrepreneur." Her definition of this term is "being an entrepreneur in your fulfillment, in your 'whys,' to why you go to work every day and work for someone in that corporation, but you're navigating throughout the system as an entrepreneur for yourself. A corporate entrepreneur is someone who has an entrepreneurial spirit while working within an organization. So, you can curate and create your career within an organization. You don't have to actually be someone who's out on your own per se."

For Rosalind, this meant thinking creatively about positions as they had originally been defined by someone else, and using them to live out her "whys," and to grow and contribute to an organization's mission. "Over the years," she says, "I created my positions, in that, yes, I'm hired for the job title. However, when you see a need, you fill a need; and when you can really kind of understand your role along with what else you might be able to give and serve, it helps remove that glass ceiling feeling." She explains that if you can be "an entrepreneur in your career and in your personal life, that glass ceiling becomes so much more liquid. Because if you're showing up a hundred percent according to your values, according to what brings you in the door every day, you're not as closely tied to, well, I can't get that job, or I can never do that."

Rosalind wisely observes that shifting your perspective toward understanding your "why" doesn't just change your own outlook. "It changes perspective for those who might seek to hire you and help you grow into a new position, or mentor you because your perspective, and your presence, and how you show up becomes more, oh, I want to help that person because they're not just here for the paycheck."

In her late thirties, Rosalind began managing a major program within a large healthcare system, a pivot from the corporate world where she had been sharing her talents. Part of her pivot involved training herself to ask new questions and reach out in new ways. "I went straight to the VPs," she said, "and I asked for just five minutes of their time to really understand, why do they do what they do, and how did they get where they are?" They all ended up giving her at least 15 minutes of their time. "What was really empowering," she said, "is that one, they're not as scary as you might think. Two, they're happy to share their 'why' and how they got to where they are. Because quite honestly, if you think about it, as we're continually growing and going up in our journey, we're happy to throw down the rope to the next person or give out a hand." This initiative, she says "removed the illusion and perception that the C-suite is untouchable... you know everyone came from somewhere."

Talking with these senior leaders helped Rosalind feel more confident in her work: "I'm not stumbling over my words when I'm in a meeting, I'm not hiding in the corner, thinking, oh, my voice isn't important, because I had a conversation and I've humanized those upper echelons." And, she adds, "I'm on the radar." Now, people at the higher leadership levels understood her as an "interesting person" who "wasn't afraid to just say, hey, help me understand how you got here, and that was bold." Rosalind's skills in authentically connecting with people, working to understand workplaces, and taking the time to learn across hierarchy and generation meant that she was soon invited to be a part of other conversations at work where new opportunities would arise.

Rosalind provides many kinds of modeling of how women might navigate the middle of their careers. I wanted to highlight the tools and strategies that Rosalind articulated with such exceptional clarity, and which I saw echoed in other women's stories, because there are so many reasons, we're likely to need every tool in the toolbox in these complex years of career.

While the opportunities to contribute, accomplish, and lead are potentially greater in mid-career compared to our earlier years, the obstacles can feel very high stakes, and there is often more to juggle. We might be struggling to bloom, to get to our next goal; we might be encountering landmines of everyday sexism, racism, or transphobia; we might experience being denied raises or promotions, being bullied or harassed.

In addition, we may be caught in the middle of younger workers with new demands, and older ones who may still be occupying (and potentially dominating) the highest echelons of leadership.[49] We may come up against the limitations of an organization, industry, or ways of working. Or we may wonder what our own limits are, as we experience greater integration as well as a sense of fragmentation from incoming communication or service requests from all directions.

Whatever advancement means to you, there are lots of reasons why mid-career women get stymied in their efforts to advance, or even to do their jobs in peace without harassment. Discrimination and marginalization in mid-career happen through a variety of external obstacles. Self-doubt--socially constructed self-doubt also plays a role. As my interviewees attested, it's not uncommon to ask ourselves, did that happen to me because I'm a woman? Because I'm gay, because I'm Latina? Was it some combination of those things? Or is it something about an individual situation or individual differences that explains differential opportunities and treatment? Or something else altogether? The second-guessing of encounters, the wondering if you're just imagining something—all of this takes up headspace and contributes to self-doubt.

To make sense of both the challenges and the opportunities, it's worth understanding how sexism and other systems shift in mid-career.

WHAT WE'RE POTENTIALLY UP AGAINST IN MID-CAREER: AN OVERVIEW

DISCRIMINATION AND THE CHALLENGE OF FINDING BELONGING AND AUTHENTICITY

As we discussed in Part I, most large workplaces are shaped by rules and norms that reflect a history of male privileges (like assuming people won't need time off for children), whiteness, and heteronormativity. Even for mid-career women who have established significant credibility, these patterns can sometimes make it difficult to just feel comfortable at work and can hinder a sense of possibility about advancement.

What Dnika J. Travis and her colleagues have called the "emotional tax" of making others comfortable is especially relevant for women of color. This tax is the price paid for day-to-day vigilance, protecting oneself against racist, sexist or other microaggressions, verbal or body language slights that make people feel "othered" (such as being mistaken for a server at a corporate event, having your hair touched or commented upon, or being told you're pretty good at this job, for a woman).[50] Women of color also face challenges to their authority and credibility in many professional spaces.[51] Self-protection and guardedness can be a natural response, something that can also come into play for LGBTQ+ women, who may be cautious about revealing too much about their personal lives in heteronormative environments. The Human Rights Campaign Foundation found, as late as 2018, that nearly half of LGBTQ+ workers were still closeted in their workplaces.[52]

Code-switching, linguistic accommodations of workplace norms, can also make trying to "fit in" feel exhausting for people who are underrepresented on the basis of race, gender, or sexual orientation.[53] These day-to-day experiences often fall short of actual harassment and bullying, but nevertheless require significant emotional energy to navigate.

One especially gendered way where complex questions of "fitting in" shows up is the question of dress in the workplace. This topic sparked one of the most memorable conversations in that class I taught in 2020 in my continuing education class for working women. For example, one woman in the corporate world shared that management had repeatedly conveyed to her that she needed to dress in skirts and wear makeup, which felt micromanaging to her. Another woman argued that professional dress that was deliberately desexualized was an appropriate neutral norm that employers should expect of women, and that women should expect of themselves, in order to be taken seriously.

And yet, as Deborah Tannen, the prolific linguistics scholar has pointed out, "There is no unmarked woman," which is to say there is no neutral. Women, as Tannen pointed out in her 1993 article, have to make decisions "about hair, clothing, makeup and accessories, and each decision carried meaning... The men in our group had made decisions, too, but the range from which they chose was incomparably narrower." With women, no hairstyle, shoe choice, or decision about how tight or loose their clothing is can pass as "neutral."[54]

Corporate dress standards can be especially frustrating for women of color. As Ruchika T. Molhatra pointed out in *Harvard Business Review*, "Being able to dress comfortably at work sounds like a wonderful perk to have – but for women of color, who often have to repeatedly prove that they belong in corporate workplaces, dressing casually could further reinforce the stereotype that women of color aren't leaders. Close to 50% of Black and Latina scientists were mistaken for janitorial or administrative staff, found another survey."[55]

What's more, there is widespread pressure for Black women to conform their appearance to white standards, with hair being one big area of discrimination. In one recent survey, "More than half of the Black women surveyed felt like they had to wear their hair straight in a job interview to be successful" and "Two-thirds reported that they had changed their hair for a job interview." Making matters worse, "one-fifth of the Black women surveyed between the ages of 25 and 34 had been sent home from work because of their hair."[56] Advocates have responded by putting forth the CROWN Act to prohibit racial discrimination on the basis of hairstyle.

For trans and nonbinary workers, the complexity of dress codes adds additional layers of decisions as well, since dress codes often reinforce the gender binary, and genderqueer presentation challenges norms. The Human Rights Campaign Foundation 2018 report found that one in five LGBTQ+ workers report "having been told or had coworkers imply that they should dress in a more feminine or masculine manner."[57] This is likely related to other kinds of "othering" behaviors toward LGBTQ+ employees. McKinsey found, for example, that, "LGBTQ+ women and women with disabilities are subjected to more demeaning and 'othering' microaggressions, such as having colleagues comment on their appearance or tell them that they 'look mad' or 'should smile more.'"[58] And in the 2018 report, 53% of LGBTQ+ workers reported "hearing jokes about lesbian or gay people at least once in a while."[59]

CAREGIVING DEMANDS

At this career stage, many women are also juggling mothering or other caregiving responsibilities along with heavy responsibilities at work. About three-quarters of mothers of children under age 18 are in the labor force, with the labor force participation rate of single, divorced, or widowed mothers slightly higher.[60] The demands of caregiving connect to issues of emotional labor and gender in such profound ways that I've devoted a whole chapter to this topic. But since these issues are also connected to other barriers for mid-career women, I'll sketch out the basics here.

Caregiving work (for young children, for loved ones with special needs, for aging parents) is meaningful and rewarding. But it also tends to come with the so-called "caregiver penalty." As *The New York Times* neatly summarized in 2021, when gender gaps were exacerbating to crisis proportions:

> Substantial research has shown that most professional gender gaps are in fact motherhood gaps: women without children are much closer to parity with men when it comes to salaries and promotions, but mothers pay a large career penalty. Women tend to take on more of the burdens of caring for children and the family. To go to work, they need someone to help with that care. But fathers have been slow to change their behavior. And without subsidies, private childcare can be prohibitively expensive. Workplaces already tend to penalize women who choose to work fewer hours or need more flexibility, and that, too, is proving to be exacerbated in the pandemic.[61]

The caregiver penalty, the price paid for taking time away from work, scaling back hours, or asking for flexibility, hits women harder than men on average. It often shows up in limited opportunities for advancement, stagnating pay, lack of access to networks, and in the absence of paid leave programs, later gaps in women's access to accrued sick leave (if they took sick leave for maternity leave) and even later, reduced Social Security benefits for time away from work. As many studies have shown, assumptions about women's diminished commitment to work create discrimination in hiring and promotion. Women often wait longer than men to get promoted, even if they are not mothers, but motherhood adds a special penalty.[62]

Both the identity issues and the caregiving concerns speak to the difficulty of women, BIPOC people, and LGBTQ+ people in following the old norms of compartmentalized professionalism that were forged in systems created without inclusion in mind. Indeed, in many cases for the older institutions, with exclusion in mind. Jenny Vazquez-Newsum wisely observes in *Untapped Leadership*, her excellent book on how the leadership expertise of BIPOC leaders is developed and can be leveraged:

> We have a long history of disassociating our work lives from our personal lives, having been taught to check things at the door. The more we can compartmentalize from everything else, the more effectively and appropriately we can navigate our careers. If you didn't have to worry about how you would be greeted based on the color of your skin or if you were not saddled with caregiving duties and outsized household expectations, then the luggage you checked at the professional door (if it even existed) was much lighter. It is through this unrealistic lens that "professionalism" was defined, and only very recently have we begun to shed the surface layers of that facade.

Put more simply by Vazquez-Newsum, "leading is simplified when one's social identity does not add layers of complexity to navigate."[63]

ACCESS TO CAREER-ENHANCING ADVANCEMENT OPPORTUNITIES

This brings us to formal leadership roles and advancement. Overall in this career stage, when women aren't just trying to get in the door, but may be competing for leadership roles, the challenges of sexism and other discriminatory systems can shift. One recent study by Colleen Ammerman and Boris Groysberg, reported in *Harvard Business Review*, surveyed 100 senior executive women in different parts of the world. The women were asked at what stage in their careers they had "faced the most gender bias or discrimination. Half told us mid-career, that is, roughly their mid-thirties to late forties." Indeed, the women were often surprised by the level of bias or discrimination they faced; after all they had some career accomplishments behind them at this stage and had developed some clout and credibility.[64]

Interestingly, the study authors note that performance measures might become more subjective in mid-career. "Objective measures of performance that predominate in early career stages are a boon for women, as they make it harder for bias to creep into how they are assessed and rewarded. That changes in mid-career."

Many of the women in this study reported experiencing hyper-scrutiny as they sought advancement opportunities and having to "clear a higher bar." Some experienced the pervasive "assumption that women are less suited for leadership than men. One told us that when she was at the mid-career stage, about a decade ago, the prevailing view at her company was that only white men were able to successfully perform 'high-pressure jobs."

Moreover, the women in this particular study illuminated an interesting dimension of this career stage: exclusion from key networks needed to advance. "The women in our pool also told us that networks become highly gendered at mid-career, with men having superior access to senior leaders and often prioritizing relationships with male over female colleagues. By mid-career, one executive explained, 'men have established their 'cliques.'" She went on to highlight how these exclusionary networks limit women's opportunities. "If you are not in the club by then," she said, "chances of you getting picked for the next team dramatically decrease."[65]

A related issue is that the "niceness" challenge, discussed earlier, follows women into mid-career. For advancement, research shows that women need to spend a lot of time being "nice" as well as competent, while men can more easily advance in the workplace based on competence, and regardless of "niceness."[66]

Women are less likely than men to have allies with significant clout in their organizations, known as "sponsors," people who can showcase their work, open doors at higher levels, and brag about them in the right spaces. "Overall, women in corporate America are 24% less likely than men to get advice from senior leaders, according to a Lean in and SurveyMonkey study. And 62% of women of color say they believe a lack of mentorship holds them back in their career." To compound matters, in the post-#Me-Too U.S., 60% of male managers' report being "uncomfortable participating in workplace activities with women such as mentoring, one-on-one meetings or social outings." Indeed, men in corporate America were three times more likely to say they were uncomfortable mentoring women in the first two years of media coverage around #MeToo.[67]

The question of whether mid-career women "want" formal leadership positions in this chapter of a career is extremely complicated. It's mitigated in part by what they see leaders looking like, how they see them behaving, whether they think these leaders "have a life," or have a job that looks attractive, and whether or not their own sense of confidence can allow them to see themselves in formal leadership roles. The research is extensive on why there's a "leaky pipeline" to leadership, or even "broken rungs" on the ladders to more senior positions. From benign neglect of talented women who stagnate (who are not developed and encouraged), to glass ceilings, to pushing women out of their organizations through harassment or just unfriendly environments, risks of getting blocked from advancement abound. Potentially intersecting with external barriers are socially constructed interior barriers, like perfectionism, difficulty setting boundaries, or getting caught in the trap of overwork on projects that may not lead to advancement.[68]

One reason women may look skeptically at advancement opportunities in their organization is that they see the stress of fellow women leaders. And one reason for that stress could be women's placement in what gender and race scholars have called "glass cliff" leadership positions, like the one Connie experienced Gender scholars Michelle Ryan and Alex Haslam first identified this pattern in which women and people of color are disproportionately assigned to management roles in dysfunctional areas or struggling companies. In these situations, they become the face of unpleasant change, and are set up to potentially damage relationships in the process.[69]

As Ryan told *Business Insider* in 2005: "If women are appointed in times of crisis, it's not that women are unable to lead, but leading in a time of crisis is more difficult and more precarious than leading when everything is great." She added, "We might find that these women don't last as long in these positions or that they may be highly criticized because there's a lot going on. And that potentially reinforces the stereotype that women [and people of color] aren't good at leadership."[70] Given that women leaders are more likely than men to be judged harshly for any mistakes they make, these situations are especially risky, and yet often represent a rare opportunity to break into management.[71]

COPING WITH BULLYING AND HARASSMENT

As noted in the previous section, women of all backgrounds, and at any career stage, are vulnerable to harassment at work. Bullying and general harassment can be a hazard of mid-career in part because women seeking advancement, and sometimes outshining men around them, can create backlash that can show up in these kinds of toxic behaviors. While younger women are somewhat more likely to experience sexual harassment, it can still happen at mid-career.[72] Women of color are more likely to experience harassment in general (often intersectional harassment, based on both race and sex) than white women.[73] Indeed, women of color have been at the forefront of bringing the issue to light for decades. As legal scholar María Ontiveros noted nearly three decades ago, in response to the Anita Hill-Clarence Thomas sexual harassment scandal, "For women of color, sexual harassment is rarely, if ever, about sex or sexism alone; it is also about race. For us, racial epithets are spoken in sexist terms, and sexual or sexist comments involve our race and our culture."[74]

Moreover, with various kinds of harassment and bullying, women of all races are likely to decide that their best option is not redress within an organization but leaving. One 2017 poll found 41% of women who had been sexually harassed at work saying the harassment had led them to leave their jobs.[75] Women leave in part because reporting often doesn't work, and they often still see their harasser retaining his original position and status at work. Those who do report too often face retaliation. As *Harvard Business Review* noted, "One survey of federal workers found that two-thirds of women who had reported their harassers were subsequently assaulted, taunted, demoted, or fired by their harassers or friends of their harassers." To add to the burden, "Women who file harassment complaints end up, on average, in worse jobs and poorer physical and mental health than do women who keep quiet."[76]

Recent research found 38% of women who experienced harassment reported that they quit their jobs, and 37% reported that the harassment impacted their career advancement. Leaving costs them, while their assaulter, usually a man, remains in his original role. Such interruptions of individual women's careers can decrease their wages and lifetime earnings, and in the aggregate, add to gender wage gaps and a sex-segregated labor market.[77]

Harassing behavior doesn't just come from supervisors. And occupying leadership roles offers women only so much protection. Madeline recounted that once when she had to fire a white man, he referred to her race in conjunction with calling her a bitch during that "letting you go" conversation in her office. "And all I can think of," she said, "is, here I am in an office with him and he's in-between the door and me. And all I did was I just went through my calm sense of, so I think it's time for him to go. 'I think it's time for you to go,' I said. And he was swearing and he did leave. And I quickly got the administrator to help me both decompress from the situation, but also to navigate a lock on the building. I thought this guy could come back." Thankfully, he did not.

Other women of color have told me of having aggrieved men, all with less institutional power than they had, make not-so-veiled threats of violence against them in one-on-one settings. Women professors I know, especially women of color, have felt genuine fear from young white men with whom they have had disturbing encounters as they lash out, especially in   expressing their resistance to the classroom content on race and gender as presented by a woman of color.

BURNOUT

As work and home responsibilities tend to accumulate at this life stage, burnout is a real risk, and a higher one for women than for men. A 2022 report found 42% of women and 35% of men in corporate America reporting having experienced feelings of burnout in the previous few months (compared to 32% and 28% of the previous year).[78]

Back in 2016, when burnout hadn't yet become a household word in discussions of the workplace, Monique Valcour, writing in *Harvard Business Review*, identified three key components of this phenomenon. Burnout, she noted, often resulted from overwork, feelings of not being able to have a voice and make meaningful change in a situation: Exhaustion: "profound physical, cognitive, and emotional fatigue that undermines people's ability to work effectively and feel positive about what they're doing"; Cynicism, essentially "an erosion of engagement... Instead of feeling invested in your assignments, projects, colleagues, customers, and other collaborators, you feel detached, negative, even callous"; and Inefficacy: "feelings of incompetence and a lack of achievement and productivity. People with this symptom of burnout feel their skills slipping and worry that they won't be able to succeed in certain situations or accomplish certain tasks. It often develops in tandem with exhaustion and cynicism because people can't perform at their peak when they're out of fuel and have lost their connection to work".[79]

Women's increased risk of burnout is related to many factors, some of which are noted above. There are the challenges women face at work, whether from workplace discrimination or bias, from draining emotional labor and overwork, internalized perfectionism based on having to do things "better" to succeed, AND the greater likelihood that they're doing a lot of care for others at home while performing at work. Relatedly, according to recent research from LeanIn.org, women are about twice as likely as men to invest in DEI work, and yet 40% of women doing this work reported that such work was not acknowledged in their performance reviews. Not being acknowledged for the value we bring creates high risk for burnout.[80]

Indeed, women managers are often the key players in helping OTHER people manage burnout, and they're also not that likely to get credit for this critical work. As reported in *Harvard Business Review* in 2022, "Despite their own increasing levels of burnout, our research also indicates that women are much more likely than men to take action to fight it, for example by managing workloads of their teams, supporting diversity equity and inclusion efforts, and simply checking in on how employees are doing. This makes a difference: We found, for example, that when managers actively managed the workload of their team, their staff were 32% less likely to be burned out and 33% less likely to leave." Unfortunately, "companies are not recognizing or incentivizing this work," including work of strategic people management and project management. This means "they risk losing the very leaders they need right now."[81]

Women who are leading efforts to make their workplaces positive spaces of belonging, inclusion, sustainability, and community, are serving as leaders, whether they're recognized for those efforts or not. Fortunately, this work can be named, recognized, and seen as the leadership work that it is. The stories of women I interviewed speak to the intertwining experiences of confronting obstacles, innovating, thriving, and wherever possible, making workplaces more inclusive, rewarding, and positive for themselves and people around them.

STORIES OF FACING OBSTACLES
AND FINDING RESILIENCE

My interviewees often experienced at least one of the patterns I mentioned above. But they coped, pivoted, and learned to grow and thrive, claiming authenticity and leading through their values. A few examples below remind us that many of the women we work with, whose stories we may not know, have had scarring experiences just trying to move through their careers and make the contributions they value.

As reflected in the larger research studies above, Connie's experience of being stymied "on the way up" was not uncommon among my interviewees. Some women who worked for years in their fields either gradually or suddenly realized that the leadership positions they wanted were out of reach. There was Mai, whose paltry raise at the bank early in her career motivated her to go back to school, and who experienced sexual harassment in one of her jobs. And Claire, a mid-level manager in her mid-forties, who identifies as queer. Claire recounted that she had recently been passed over for a leadership role. She was well-qualified for it and indeed occupied a space one level below it. But top leaders within her organization directly told her not to apply. She then watched a procession of white men get interviewed for that job. Only one finalist, she says, was even qualified.

Claire was relieved that he got the job, but discouraged, nonetheless. "Had they offered that job to any of those other three candidates," she said, she would have quit: "I was mad as hell." She had professional connections across the nation, and people in her extensive network questioned why she stayed put. "I'm like, well, my family's here, right?" At the same time, she felt she was experiencing a form of "gaslighting" because "I have chops and people try to tell me I don't have chops." They do it "to keep me in place, to keep me doing the work I'm doing, to underpay me."

Again and again, my larger professional experience (and my personal history) has illustrated the phenomenon of women being harshly reminded of "their place." This may happen in particular experiences that called attention to their gender, race, or other "difference," in uncomfortable or demeaning ways. It can happen through subtle messaging about not really fitting or being right for leadership or advancement. One woman I encountered in my consulting work recounted being on a community board, with years of financial expertise under her belt, and having a male board member make a demeaning comment about women and their checkbooks, suggesting she was likely not capable of even doing that much financial calculating. Her frustration heightened her sensitivity to similar moments when her expertise was devalued, more subtly, in her workplace.

Women I interviewed for this book also described being talked over, being the victim of all kinds of microaggressions and subtle barriers and being outright harassed. Laura, for example, remembers being corralled with another woman of color (both of them fairly new in their roles, with little institutional power) by the top leader in her organization. This leader was feeling pressure on his professional reputation around social justice issues like addressing racism and bad press within the organization. After a larger meeting about racial issues, he was hoping these women could help rehabilitate his reputation:

> And so, it was just him and [my co-worker] and me in this meeting and we were standing, and I remember that because he is so tall... And he was basically saying, Yeah, I know I know that people are unhappy with me right now. And if the two of you who I respect so much could tell people that, basically, I didn't mean this and I'm not a bad person and I was acting in the best interests and like this kind of thing, I would really appreciate it. And then he just kept emphasizing how much he appreciated us and valued our work and respected us... and all of these things. And I just remember feeling so small and so brown in that moment.... I just felt very singled out and very uncomfortable.

Laura became used to feeling "my gender and my race," as when another tall white man with whom she worked routinely talked over her. Indeed, she said, "Professionally, I think a lot of white men have made me feel my race and my gender, but also my size in the ways they dominate space and dominate conversations."

As I mentioned, I experienced bullying that was less about getting to a particular formal leadership role but did feel a lot like "putting me in my place." It happened at a time when I was stepping outside some of the boxes that some of my coworkers seemed to want to define for me. When I was in my late thirties, supervising large federal grants and having recently published a book as well as ample research in my field, a mentor outside my department encouraged me to apply for promotion from associate to full professor. At the time, I was in the History department, and my supervisor there discouraged me, wondering aloud if I was really "ready," since I had only recently been promoted to associate professor. Over the course of about a year, his doubt shifted to outright bullying, as he and other colleagues contributed to marginalizing me to the point that I was almost completely isolated in my department.

Ostensibly, this was about how my workload was shifting due to administering the federal grant. Because of these administrative duties, I transitioned to teaching fewer introductory classes. When I sought to defend my opportunity to teach the specialty classes that defined my unique curricular contributions, while directing grants, I was shut out of meetings. Ultimately, over the course of that academic year, I sat on the sidelines without department allies, while the department literally changed its bylaws to prevent ambitious people like me from having the opportunity to teach upper-division courses while running grants or taking on other administrative duties. I would later learn that it would have been wise to not take all this personally. But at the time it felt profoundly hurtful and corrosive to my sense of trust in my colleagues, and even in myself.

I went forward with my promotion request anyway, preparing a portfolio to present to the larger university committee for promotion. In spite of a department promotion committee letter that seemed to damn me with faint praise, the larger university committee awarded me promotion anyway; by their estimation, I had earned it. But ultimately, I transferred to another department. I was able to do such an unprecedented thing because I had campus allies, people who helped behind the scenes and who supported me through the misery of that academic year. While I gained a great deal collegially in my new department, the truth is that I lost some of my sense of identity and belonging in the field of history for which I had trained for many years. It was a reminder that even with good self-advocacy skills, we only have so much control.

I would go on to redefine my career in a series of additional chapters, and like others whose stories appear here, I learned to see the experience as part of my story. I also sought to use my experience as a way to build understanding and compassion for others, and to be a better advocate for others in these situations. During that ordeal, I employed some of the basic tactics often recommended: documenting situations and encounters, attempting to use the reporting mechanisms of my institution, and though those were not very helpful, advocating, in the end successfully, for a departmental switch. I leaned on the networks I had been cultivating on campus.

I learned some coping skills at the time, but I learned many more from the kinds of conversations I've had with other women professionals over the years, including my wise interviewees. As we'll see, there is no one prescribed way to deal with these situations. But good strategies include: finding support, cultivating a long-term mindset, depersonalizing, documenting, assessing the risks and benefits of reporting, setting boundaries, and re-investing in your own self-worth. Some of my interviews went further, divesting from challenging spaces and creating new ones to build a thriving community and help others in these situations.

CHAPTER 6

STRATEGIES FOR MID-CAREERING ON YOUR TERMS

THANKFULLY, NOT EVERYONE will experience harassment and bullying. Often needs for mid-career shifts are due to more subtle situations at work, to our particular career goals, or to life circumstances. But it's worth beginning a discussion of strategies with some attention to how women can cope with the extra toxic challenging situations outlined above.

GENERAL ADVICE FOR COPING WITH BULLYING AND HARASSMENT

▶ **TRUST YOURSELF:** We are taught to downplay what is happening, and sometimes we're being gaslit as well.

▶ **DON'T JUST DOCUMENT: AUDIT** Unpack the problem and start figuring out your assets in terms of all kinds of support. (See the Resource Audit for Acute Situations textbox)

▶ **SEEK COMMUNITY, NOT JUST FORMAL HELP** Unfortunately, formal channels don't always work and can even be retraumatizing. This is not to say they never work. Find your people: colleagues, mentors, the people who love and support you outside of work. Lean on them!

▶ **UNDERSTAND HARASSMENT AS A SYSTEMS PROBLEM** Harassment can really undermine our self-esteem and we can subtly start blaming ourselves. But harassment is often part of a structural situation at work, including lack of accountability around bullying, or power structures, often not named, that your ambition and goals might have bumped up against. Again, your support system can remind you of this.

▶ **KNOW YOUR POWER** It will be up to you what that looks like. It could be redirecting your energy, tightly protecting your boundaries, exploring other work options, or, as we'll see below, building new community around these challenges in ways that can empower others.

▶ **TEND TO YOUR WELL-BEING AND SELF-CARE** This could look like accessing your EAP program at work, getting therapy or coaching, or attending a support group. And again, lean on your people and see the Resource Audit for Acute Situations textbox for additional ways to think about internal and external resources.

▶ **LEARN FROM OTHERS WHO'VE NAVIGATED IT** You're doing that here, and there are many more stories and resources. Step out of your situation and connect to the journeys and wisdom of others.

▶ **NORMALIZE CHANGING COURSE** Sometimes we have to withdraw energy from our work situations, perhaps riding out a particular storm, finding some shift in our work assignment and the people with whom we must interact. And sometimes we must walk away in order to honor our values and self-worth.

▶ **GRIEVE, AND THEN RE-NARRATIVIZE** Loss of trust at work can be traumatic, and grief and self-care are required. Part of working through that grief can be re-telling your story, discovering what you have learned, honoring your strength and wisdom, and letting go so you can move forward.

My interviewees and I incorporated these learnings into our own stories, and here is how:

STEP BACK AND DEPERSONALIZE

The women's stories I collected for this project reminded me of what I wish I'd known at the time I was experiencing a chapter of bullying and marginalization: stepping back and seeing the structures involved, including the incentive structures and cultural norms in the academic world as a whole.

And then there's the reality that people are often acting out their issues on us. Madeline, for example, remembers how she processed the threatening man whom she needed to let go. "I thought, Ok. I've never been called that before. I don't want to again." Madeline wisely refused to take this man's outburst personally, stepping back. "And so, I think as yucky as that situation was, I really looked at [and thought], Okay. You never know where somebody's at and their emotion and their level of, I don't know, whatever is an issue for them."

VALIDATE, DOCUMENT, AND CARE FOR YOURSELF

Having experienced outright bullying in one particular role she took on at work, Laura had sound advice for others: She advised documenting problematic situations, for example. This is wise because even if you don't end up reporting, your documentation can help you see the patterns. And if you decide to report later, you'll have the material you need. Laura also advised leaning on your people and being resourceful about your options. Laura leaned into the facets of her work she most enjoyed, set boundaries, and found ways to thrive as things shifted around her. She also described what she called "spiritual self-care," including media breaks and strategic discussions with her partner and other trusted people about where to invest her emotional energy.

SET BOUNDARIES & GET SUPPORT

As Laura suggests, it's important to find people you trust with whom to share and troubleshoot issues as best you can while you make a plan to resolve the situation. No matter how overworked you are in your role, try to avoid becoming isolated; this makes you vulnerable. Keep your networks fresh and wide. You'll have allies when you need them, and you'll foster resilience through community. I worried and thought myself into many corners when I was being bullied, but it was only through my allies on campus and my personal support system that I managed to get out of that difficult situation.

TAKE THE LONG VIEW

Whether you're facing harassment or just powerful roadblocks, always try to take the long view, whether it's about getting shut down personally or having your visionary ideas for change stymied.

Ronda experienced many moments of frustration when she was working to change systems in a large matrix of county departments interfacing in complex ways with the community. She recalls slipping out of a meeting to cry out the frustration, only to find she'd been observed by two older women whom she still considers mentors. They told her, "'You know if you're going to be able to accomplish what you've got to accomplish, you've got to stop that.' They said it nicer. That was my takeaway... very wise advice." This didn't end the frustration, and "it doesn't mean that I haven't argued with people. But what became my mantra over time was, you know what? I'm going to be here longer than these people. And I am going to be able to make change one way or the other over time because it may not happen today or tomorrow, or next week or next month or next year. And sometimes it was the next decade."

RESOURCE AUDIT FOR ACUTE SITUATIONS

Conduct a resource audit to see what you have available and how you could best access the support you need. Consider your internal resources, social resources, and organizational resources. It's always helpful to start within yourself and within your circle of trusted people, to remind you of the centering facets of your life.

INTERNAL RESOURCES

▶ Resilience, humor, general personal strengths

▶ Self-care strategies and practices

▶ Internal boundaries

▶ Spiritual resources

▶ Your story as resource: How have you handled adversity before? What coping skills, strengths, and ability to find optimism and make meaning have served you?

SOCIAL RESOURCES

▶ Who gives you love and support outside of work?

▶ Who has your back?

▶ Who makes you laugh?

▶ Who makes you feel seen?

▶ Who gives good advice and helps you strategize?

▶ Who helps you forget about it all and enjoy life outside of work?

ORGANIZATIONAL/WORKPLACE RESOURCES

▶ Where are the problem areas/problem behaviors and who is involved?

▶ Can you step back and see some of the ways the situation may not be personal, just to help you keep from being overwhelmed?

▶ Where might you seek help and/or direct your advocacy?

▶ What is the reporting structure for problem behavior?

▶ If your immediate supervisor isn't the problem, how might you approach him/her/them for assistance?

▶ Who are your allies?

▶ Are there structured resources besides HR? E.g. affinity groups, unions, professional networks and internal or external (to the organization) mentors?

▶ If possible (or maybe when the situation is less acute), could you create spaces to talk about problem behavior and how to respond?

WHEN REPORTING WORKS

The truth is, most of the time, women who face these situations end up leaving their units or their employers, which is why reporting for real satisfaction and a sense of justice is not a default strategy. But reporting can work, and employers can take proactive steps to develop trusted systems of reporting and to train managers to spot problems before they escalate.

Only you can assess your particular situation, but here's what the research shows about the conditions that tend to be in place to make reporting on bullying and harassment an experience that can bring some recourse, satisfaction, increased safety, or at least closure.

- ▸ Reporting systems are trusted and there is some independence to the reporting systems, making employees feel safer.

- ▸ Strong anti-retaliation policies are in place for those who do report

- ▸ People can see follow-through happening, and that ripple effect builds trust.

- ▸ Victims have external support (manager support, unions, legal support, peer support, social support in general.)

- ▸ Managers are trained, in trauma-informed ways, to recognize problems and prevent their escalation.[82]

CREATING NEW SPACES

In addition to coping and pivoting, sometimes we recreate and help ourselves and others, not just to cope, but even to thrive. We learn from our difficult experiences and bring that learning and compassion to others. We can name and get support for our experiences by knowing a little bit more about what we're dealing with and knowing that we're not alone. We can tap into our support systems, research and consider our options, find workarounds, and create new support systems for ourselves and others.

Laura's response to the chilly climate and microaggressions she faced was to create a dedicated organizational space for women of color to come together and support one another. She became a resource for others and contributed to the sense of belonging for other women of color in her organization. Laura was being that person she needed when she experienced workplace hardship. Similarly, Connie's response to hitting a glass ceiling was to create better opportunities for diverse young people while also providing a new opportunity to grow in her career by embracing mentorship.

Organizationally, you can be part of creating a culture that prevents harassment and bullying, for example by establishing strong ally networks, by pushing for systems of reporting and accountability, and by advocating for a culture of equity that recognizes how inherent bias can hold back potential leaders who are women, people of color, LGBTQ+ people, disabled people, immigrants, and other under-represented groups. You can even be part of a workplace culture that promotes healing, which is important even if your workplace is a positive place already, since people bring previous employment scars with them sometimes when they change jobs. For example, you can advocate for the availability of EAP programs and the promotion of information about processing experiences of workplace discrimination in these or other spaces.

Claire, the mid-level manager who was frustrated about not getting a higher leadership role for which she'd recently applied, says she let go of the idea of "belonging" inside an institutional structure some time ago. "I have never fit in the world," she said, "because the structures are not set up for me. I've always been a misfit. You know, my sexuality is weird. My body's weird. My brain is weird. My disabilities are weird. Everything is weird about me. And so, I've never expected to belong in any particular way, shape, or form." But she has accepted herself and her differences, and she knows how to find her people, or as she says, "to create a group, and then that becomes my group too, right? So, I create my own belonging in a lot of ways."

Claire is clear that in a workplace it's people, "not the structures," who help her belong: "I'm an aggressive woman, right? And that is very confusing to most people because I'm blunt, and I am I'm just a lot, I think for people to handle. And so, I got a lot happier when I quit expecting the structures to embrace me." Her clarity about how to accept herself and find people who do the same have also led her to open up space for others: "I think my goal is less to have me belong and more to create a sense of belonging for others so that they don't feel so outside of the spectrum as I feel." Claire did this through leadership of a mentoring program, and through significant, customized mentoring to create spaces of belonging, especially for high-potential women.

Remember, too, that acute situations like bullying and harassment require us to tap into and strengthen our inner resources and boundaries. We need every bit of humor, self-compassion, patience, and self-care routines that we can find We may access our spiritual well of resources, whatever that looks like for us. We can also tap into our own stories, remembering that we have faced hardships before, and reminding ourselves of how we coped and grew through those challenges. While the chapters that follow flesh out further strategies, we can learn some of the basics from the handful of experiences above.

The following forms of inquiry may be helpful in seeking resources, or, if you're in a position to help someone else, empowering others to tap into their resources.

ASSESSING AND CONFRONTING OBSTACLES

▶ What obstacles, if any, have you faced in pursuing your own professional aspirations?

▶ Do you think any of these obstacles may have been connected to your rising competencies and presence and the possibility that some people found your advancement threatening?

▶ Have you been bullied, harassed, or policed? If so, were you able to name these experiences at the time, or only in hindsight?

▶ Who supported you when you faced any of these obstacles? And whose support, which you may not have received, would have been especially helpful?

▶ What have been some of the impacts and outcomes of any of these experiences?

▶ How might some of the intersecting identities you hold have impacted the way these situations unfolded, and they impacted you?

▶ Knowing that even previous employment experiences can leave women on guard and tentative in their workplace, how can you create space for supporting women and people of all identities who may have been harassed, bullied, or held back?

▶ What mechanisms within your workplace are there to report and address harassment and bullying?

▶ In what ways does your organization explicitly and proactively work to promote opportunities for women and other under-represented groups to advance and become leaders?

▶ If you're unable to advance your core values and visionary ideas at work, where are the pain points? And where might you look for broader networks to start planting the seeds of new collaborations, potentially in new spaces?

THE MULTIPLE MEANINGS AND STRATEGIES OF MOVING FORWARD

As the stories above have highlighted, so many unexpected things, including barriers, can propel us into making changes and finding new ways to thrive and do the work we value. But regardless of whether we're pushed into change, we need to change to grow, whether that's taking on stretch assignments or moving into formal leadership positions. We can often take ownership of that change, using the habits of context awareness and self-reflection to take ownership of our career journeys.

Rosalind, for example, talked about a pivotal point when she needed a change in her career. She said she employed a coach who helped her think through the whole arc of her career. This process, she said, also helped her "release some of the self-limiting beliefs." For example, she had been telling herself that she needed even more education than the Ph.D. she was already pursuing. But through reflection, she realized, "No, I just need to really sharpen the tools I have. What happens a lot of times is we tend to look at where we're deficient, where our weaknesses are, compared to where our strengths are." Being strategic is also important. "If you've identified a career move," Rosalind says, "you need to be able to watch and learn and see what they're doing. How are they dressed? Where do they show up? Are they listening or are they talking? Are they taking a pause?" Rosalind rightly points to the need for exploration as part of a career pivot, and an attitude of growth and enrichment for yourself. Just as we have to have a diverse toolkit for moving away from challenging situations, we need to also equip ourselves for advancement, as much as possible on our own terms.

Mid-career women look to change jobs or even career paths, or to move into formal leadership roles, for many reasons besides obstacles. Desire for a career change could be as much about yearning for new growth and opportunities, or just about changing life needs, as it is about obstacles. Still, it's worth knowing that women leaders change jobs more than men do, and sometimes it's a push out of our comfort zone that leads us to listen to the call of whatever might be pulling at our aspirations.

For all the reasons discussed so far in this book, women have reason to look for greener grass. McKinsey reported in 2022 that "Women leaders are significantly more likely than men leaders to leave their jobs because they want more flexibility or because they want to work for a company that is more committed to employee well-being and diversity, equity, and inclusion." Their 2021 report also noted women's desire for advancement as a common reason for looking to make a change. Women at the director level have been leaving their jobs at significantly higher rates than in previous years, which leaves fewer women in any given company in the pipeline to the highest echelons of leadership. Add in the fact that, leaders or not, women are more likely than men to make job and career shifts around family needs and labor force breaks, and you have to picture a lot of women on the move.[83]

It's not uncommon to decide to pivot because of a disappointment around not gaining access to particular positions that interest us, especially if we're trying to move into positional leadership roles. But we can learn to depersonalize these situations too. As Rosalind pointed out, "as you climb, the ladder gets narrower," meaning there are fewer places "at the top." As she rightly observes, an organization might have one leadership position open, and hundreds of applicants for the job. "So, then that's where you need to decide, alright, well, if it's a numbers game and there are 800 people that have the exact same qualifications as me, or maybe even more, and there's one position, do I want to be in the game."

Rosalind ascended to a certain level and asked herself "Do I want to be in this room, competing for this particular job or career track, or do I want to make my own?" After all, she says, "applying for a job that's really competitive takes a lot of emotional energy." Rosalind eventually went out on her own as an author, consultant, executive coach, and nonprofit founder. She created these more independent paths for herself not because of negative workplace experiences, but more because she followed her primary career wisdom: "The number one" thing, she says, "is to be open. On my professional journey, it's to assume nothing, and just be open."

For many of us, not getting "the job," or even finding that our supervisor is not using their power to provide us a helping hand to that next place we can contribute, leads us to look elsewhere, including perhaps to pursuing further education. This is what Mai and Ronda did when they hit obstacles. For Olivia, it was a shift out of her organization that led to her next move. In general, Olivia felt valued at her public health position, saying that she had a sense of belonging and "felt supported, and that my contributions are valued and my coworkers genuinely care about me as a person."

But when her supervisor left, she got a new supervisor and applied for an internal position. The interview, conducted by her new supervisor, felt strange, and showed Olivia that the territory of support had shifted. She ruminated and second-guessed herself after this interview, feeling unsettled and somewhat devalued during the process. Ultimately, she didn't get the job. Within a short time, an organization that had felt like the right fit at a certain time didn't feel as much like a place she could grow. Within a year, Olivia had used this new information to orchestrate a move to a new organization where she could thrive—and she did! She basically stepped back and maneuvered around the obstacle.

For Mary, life circumstances weighed more heavily than career at a crucial turning point. Mary found herself in the midst of a career and life shift after her husband died when she was only 33. Pursuing her master's degree and having all the bills to pay while newly widowed, she was also dealing with fresh and excruciating grief. "It was all of a sudden like, I don't know what I want to do. I was rudderless because I had spent ten years of my life preparing for one career that didn't exist... I was so hurting." She says she "ended up" getting a job with a major company, which transferred her to the place she lives now.

Mary would go on to do wonderful things in her career, leading conversations around racial justice in her human resources and community roles, and championing disability justice. She would rebuild her life, but along the way, she clearly did not always feel that she was in the driver's seat as she adapted to change. It's important to be real about the fact that we're not always as in charge of our lives as we might like to be, that our pivots often happen because they must. But with anchoring in our values and continuous learning, we can bring our leadership skills along with us when life throws us curve balls.

We can also desire a career change because of burnout in a management role. On average, today's managers are facing heightened workloads and tighter budgets, stresses related to rapid change management, staff turnover, and the mental health needs of their teams.[84] Nina, who was much younger than me at the time of our interview, really loved her job leading a pre-college program on a college campus. But she also mentioned burnout as a challenge in her manager role, as well as inadequate pay, and having her credibility challenged by men who reported to her.

The above-mentioned institutional challenges certainly contributed to my decision to leave my university job before retirement age, as I was experiencing every one of these factors. Getting into the management role was itself part of a series of pivots for me. A number of years after I changed departments because of bullying, I found myself stagnating and somewhat depressed, in spite of a much better departmental environment.

In 2015, I was up for "post-tenure review," a bureaucratic formality to justify the tenure system. It was as unimportant as it sounded, and yet even the words "post-tenure" spoke to a sort of dead-endedness, the emptiness of the road ahead. In academia, once you climbed the long tenure and promotion ladder (to full professor in my case), there's often nowhere to go next, except into lots of service to help spare younger people the burdens of committee work while they get tenure. On top of that, pivoting from one department to another in 2006 had required that I develop a number of new courses in my teaching repertoire

I had just completed a book project on the history of motherhood that had taken me six years, while balancing a chapter of parenting that included some rough patches. I was coming into a particular place in my career where people knew I brought a lot of competencies but seemed to keep asking me to do everything without any more pay or recognition.

My tenure was renewed, but so was the mid-life crisis I'd been battling for a few years. Being at my university felt like that box of which I had already explored all corners and tested its flexibility in every way I could imagine: I had changed departments, taught new classes, run grants, published in my field, tried out some administrative work, served on committees to try to change the institution, even tried out part-time work. I had accomplished many things of which I was proud. I loved my students, and they often lifted me up when I felt discouraged. Still, no one "above me" was mentoring me towards any additional growth or considering me for one of the few higher-level administrative leadership roles I wasn't quite sure I wanted anyway.

Having learned a great deal about developmental editing from the editor who worked on my book manuscript, I set myself up to pursue that work independently, getting some mentoring, developing a website and an editing resume. I let people know I was interested in serious, writer-coach type editing opportunities, and I got a few enjoyable jobs. I was totally in the flow in that editing work, never doubting myself, knowing how I could help authors put their best foot forward, while encouraging them along the way. It was the start of work that I continue to enjoy.

I also applied for, and was offered, a part-time position as an executive director of our regional diversity council. When the position came up, I had already negotiated a part-time appointment at the university for the coming academic year because of some family health issues. So somehow, I was able to take on this role and continue a slightly reduced (via one fewer class to teach) workload at the university.

In that new role as nonprofit executive director, I found I was bursting with ideas and enthusiasm. I was out of the box! After three years of intense internal questioning about what was next for me, I was ready to invest in this opportunity. I set up a new basement office space in our house, where I could throw Post-its all over the wall and start dreaming of ways I could contribute outside of the bureaucracy of higher education. Granted, I still had a 75% appointment at work, and I was diagnosed with Stage 0 breast cancer within a month of starting the new job. I had my work cut out for me, but I was determined to do it well, and having a new canvas to paint on somehow seemed worth it even with all the stresses.

During my time at the council, I increased funding, created new community initiatives, helped create a more diverse board of directors, consulted with leading employers, created programming, and got out of my little university bubble. I worked with leaders across the city and the region, and I was constantly learning. I had not fully changed careers, but I had the freedom of having a new space in which to work, which actually made me a better contributor back at my university. I felt new energy there, which worked out well, since the diversity council work eventually ran its course for me. This was partly because, two years into nonprofit leadership I found myself thrust into the role of academic department chair, after the long-serving chair stepped down.

I found I had a few more years to give at my university, and I threw myself back in, but with more intentionality. I pared down my course offerings to make teaching easier, invested heavily in mentoring students because that fed my soul, and found ways to grow and contribute through my department leadership. Meanwhile, I kept the new community connections and skills alive for the next opportunity.

Even for self-chosen career pivots, it's important to recognize that change takes planning, vision, and a lot of work and energy. Rosalind, for example, remembers really learning how to find her strengths and autonomy in her career at a point when everything became a little too much, but she wasn't sure what was next. "My son was very sick, and I was traveling a lot, and I was trying to figure out what that next evolution for my career was, but then also, what's my next evolution for me as a person."

Rosalind started doing some reading that prompted her to take time for herself every day, time "in which to get silent, affirm, have visualization, move your body, exercise, read, and then also journal." Rosalind's story is a reminder that it's not so much which role we might transition into, but rather, what kind of process we undergo to empower ourselves through change that begins from within us, and connects with the external circumstances through our presence and our opportunities to make new things happen.

GENERAL GUIDELINES FOR TRANSITIONS

▸ **SIDE-STEP TROUBLE:** Even consider making lateral moves if it's your only way out of a toxic situation.

▸ **CONSIDER ADDITIONAL HIGHER EDUCATION** as a highly structured way to start a new path, as a disproportionate number of my interviewees did, never with any regrets (Caveat: older women had it easier in doing this; cost-benefit analysis is more challenging for younger women)

▸ **GET HELP:** Lean on coaching, therapy, mentoring, the people in your personal life whom you lean on, those who have a flexible enough mindset to not be too attached to their own version of you and what you should be doing. Listen to stories of other people who have pivoted.

▸ **TRY NOT TO OVERTHINK:** Doing the "next right thing" (credit to Glennon Doyle here) to get unstuck is more important than having a whole vision mapped out. After all, curve balls come along and throw off big plans anyway. It can feel empowering to practice doing a "next right thing," while also cultivating a practice of dreaming and planning, including writing down those big picture life plan ideas.

▸ **INVEST IN YOURSELF:** Especially during my middle-years career crisis, of bullying and burnout, I invested heavily in myself. I sought out expensive career coaching when I was being bullied. I took a class on web design when I was getting burned out, so that I could start advertising my editing skills; I later invested further, in coaching, in professional development learning, and in time spent with people who could help show me and inspire me towards a new direction. Others in my group of interviewees did similar things.

▶ **KEEP LEARNING:** Continued learning is the key to vitality, including among all the women over 40 who were part of my group of interviewees.

▶ **DIVERSIFY YOUR ASSETS:** If you see yourself even possibly wanting to get out of where you are in the next few years, invest in making sure you have transferable skills and a diverse network of colleagues outside your organization or perhaps industry. Consider your "stretch assignments" with these ideas in mind.

▶ **HAVE PATIENCE:** Career transitions are often quite slow, and as many books on the subject point out, we often move step by step away from our original industry, bridging into something similar to the original industry for the first or second move, and slowly making our way towards something that better feeds our passions and purposes.

STRETCHING AND THRIVING

Stretching and thriving go hand in hand. Looking back on my career, I tried to lean into times of thriving, times when I felt that people were listening to me, my voice was making a difference, my ideas were actionable, I had enough balance in my life, and my work and my values aligned. Things were never perfect, but taking stock of what was good always helped, and my friends helped me with that.

Once, in my early 50s, while running with my friend Sanna and kvetching mildly about work, she said, "You're at the peak of your career." Yeah, such as it is, I joked. But she really made me think. I WAS at a certain peak of professional reputation, expanded networks, and ability to use my privileges to help others. It helped for her to reflect that back to me. And who could say how long that peak would last? This perspective helped me use what clout and energy I had at that moment.

If we keep learning and growing, we are going to have beautiful stretches of thriving in our careers. Indeed, we can appreciate those times more from having known toxic environments. Sue, for example, whose experience in the male-dominated spaces of medical school were harrowing, says, that "actually having that experience, Jodi, was probably one of the great experiences of my life because it really allowed me to see... some of the worst environments I would not want to be part of."

At the time of our interview, Sue was very happy at work: "I feel supported... I feel encouraged. I feel empowered. And if you don't know what it's like not to [feel those things], how can you appreciate what you have when you do have it?" Sue had recently begun an exciting leadership opportunity after negotiating an exception to a corporate policy that would have required her to stay in an initial role for a year. She had practiced self-advocacy and found a role that she enjoyed. Sue articulated the empowerment and opportunity to thrive that she was currently feeling in her role:

> When I'm empowered... when I fit in well... with the values of an organization or the culture... My definition of empowerment is my ability or the autonomy to be able to do the best thing I can. To improve a process, bringing forward a best practice... when I am able to improve something or make something for the better, or bring together a certain amount of people or achieve a common goal. That's when I feel most empowered.

The ideal situation is rarely handed to us. For most women, it's necessary to co-create our environment, our workloads, and our opportunities to pursue our passions. We have to assess and negotiate and work from the space of our values and passions. For Mary, for example, her big wins were about lending her advocacy and service values to projects that empowered the people her organization served, as well as the employees who worked there. She pointed, for example, to working on a plan to improve the use and awareness of the organization's Interpreting Services division to serve people for whom English was not their first language. "I didn't do the work," Mary says, but "I helped the person move it forward." Another rewarding project was helping create employment opportunities for youth with disabilities:

> We're providing internships for students with developmental and intellectual disabilities... That's a huge win. I really felt like we really moved it forward. And to have someone in a department say, "being a mentor to one of these interns is the best thing I've ever done in my work here." And she was retiring the next year. And she said it was the best experience she ever had. Just to see the interactions that people had and the connections that were made. So, I think in those ways, I've really been very encouraged.

Mary also found great satisfaction in knowing she had established a reputation as a knowledgeable resource around leveraging the possibilities for empowerment, not just compliance, related to the Americans with Disabilities Act. "And to have people call me and say, 'So what do I do about this situation?' as far ADA, felt really good."

Madeline recalls her decade-long chapter as Director of Hospital Operations as an especially enjoyable time of thriving. "It was fun," she says "because it was uncharted territory. There hadn't been anybody in the role before." The position involved building significant partnerships across teams, and innovating responses to a rapidly changing environment, including the emergence of electronic medical records. "So that was a very dynamic time," Madeline said. "And what I found exciting was that I'm a pretty good problem solver. And I also enjoy working with people and helping to figure things out." She also loved that "everybody was working together" in ways that made hierarchy feel less important in the day to day.

So often in the stories of these values-driven women, "thriving" was about more than career advancement or fiscal remuneration. Connie, for example, thrived by learning new technologies in her 50s and by throwing herself into the mentoring group she had created for younger employees. Laura noted that in order to thrive, you can work to cultivate gratitude for the opportunities in your situation. For example, as a professor, she enjoys being able to follow her curiosity, to work in a field that's "expansive and has ambiguous boundaries," and to publish accessible work that advances social justice. Laura also helps students of color, especially women, navigate systems and structures in academia in ways that help them empower themselves. Despite hardships and obstacles in her career, Laura is grateful to have found such a happy fit in being a teacher. From the time she was a graduate student teaching assistant, Laura found a "comfort, and just joy" in being with students in her classroom. It came "right away," and that foundational, consistent piece of her work has helped her thrive.

For Madeline, already well established in her career as a hospital administrator at age 60 when I interviewed her, thriving in her vp role at the time felt like continuous learning. She knew a lot about race and the issues women faced in their career, but she wanted to educate herself about "the LGBT community, and how I can be an advocate within the work I'm doing." Madeline finds it important not to just "stay in my own world." She says she thrives on the "richness of really learning and leaning out into other ways that people are looking at the world."

Rosalind found that the places where she could thrive were inclusive and created a sense of belonging, such as the healthcare organization where she worked for five years. There, she was "truly able to own my own work and navigate owning that work, while having colleagues that were extremely supportive, like a family situation." These experiences, she says "really molded my expectations and standards for a workplace that I could thrive in and where I wanted to grow." She says this organization was also smart about investing in their employees "because as you feed your staff with the opportunity of that belongingness, employees want to grow the business." Organizations who provide these opportunities can grow employees' expectations for what workplace culture can look like.

Often, thriving connects to a sense of being an empowered and effective advocate for your values. Mai, for example, worked with a supervisor by whom she felt very supported to institute an inclusive pronoun policy in her workplace. Mai recounted that one co-worker who had seen Mai put her own pronouns in a signature started a conversation with her about how she should respectfully address pronouns with a transgender member of the team. Mai was very pleased to be seen as a resource in modeling gender identity inclusion in her workplace.

Olivia, who started out working in explicitly feminist public health organizations early in her career, later brought these feminist values to her work in more general public health spaces. As discussed previously, she blossomed for a significant career chapter in that space, in part because of great supervision. A highlight of this chapter was when a state legislator pushing for funding for mental health coalitions invited Olivia and some colleagues to testify at the state capitol. "That was really empowering," Olivia said. "It was me, maybe one or two other women," and (overwhelmingly male) law enforcement representatives. "And I was just advocating and speaking my truth," she said, proudly, explaining the work she and other mostly women public servants did to prevent and address mental health in their communities.

Olivia also advocates passionately for more inclusive workplaces and better-informed public health services, for example in pushing for trauma-informed care. At the time of our interview, she was working to be an educator to her fellow mostly white colleagues on how whiteness shows up in the workplace, and how LGBTQ people struggle with disparate health access and outcomes. She was also spearheading new conversations around equity and how "oppression manifests in health and health status," in part because of historical trauma, such as through the intergenerational impact of the decades-long boarding school movement that targeted indigenous families.

Like the other women I interviewed, Olivia found purpose and thriving by being an advocate and an educator on inclusion. This and other values-based advocacy can light our fires through our own mid-career journeys. In doing this work, we can join arms with like-minded people, innovate, take risks, and grow our skills.

That said, even those who are passionate and outspoken about social justice may need breaks from their level of involvement in this work. Women of color, in particular, are sometimes expected to do this work for minimal reward, often on top of multiple additional responsibilities. DEI can become "the job within the job." Madeline, for example, talked about "ebbs and flows" in her work priorities. "There are times," she said, "where I've done a lot of cultural sensitivity work." But "there are times when I just need to take a break" from that work. "Because there's so much energy that goes into something like that, and to have that really deep meaningful conversation, you've got to take a little step back and say, okay, it's time for somebody else to take the load for a while." In addition, younger women, especially if they face potential discrimination around other aspects of their identities, may not feel safe speaking up until they have a greater sense of security, for example as women of color in predominantly white spaces.

For any dimension of our work, thriving must involve some calculated moves towards self-care for the long haul. For me, ebb and flow were essential as well. I thrived for many years in teaching, for example—the core definition of my role at the university. But sometimes I needed to step back. Some of the best career decisions I ever made, decisions that allowed me to thrive, involved deliberately cutting back on my workload in my assigned roles at the university, even with parallel pay cuts or use of sick leave. I did that in the academic year before I finished my book on the history of motherhood, losing 25% of my salary to meet my goals as an author.

A few years later, I took a big chunk of sick leave to reduce my workload to 75% for the year, for family reasons, and ended up using the time to lean into my new nonprofit executive director role. And my last year in the academic world, I deliberately chose part-time work, (a 60% appointment), so that I could walk to the finish line of my 25-year career at my university, instead of running. Letting go of teaching, I focused on doing everything in my power to use my department chair role set my department up for success after I was gone, to leave a legacy of deep mentoring, transparent ways to operate, and as many resources as I could advocate for in my remaining time.

Periods of thriving are periods when the trade-offs are basically working for us. We continue to thrive by regularly reassessing our commitments and our energy level and not depleting the singular resource we have in ourselves. Career investment is a decades-long project, so pacing ourselves is important.

CHAPTER 7

CAREGIVING AND EMOTIONAL LABOR

Lifting Up the Work That Sustains Workplaces,
Families, and Communities

IF YOU ARE NOT A PARENT and currently do not have significant care-giving responsibilities for an elder or someone else in your life, please don't skip this chapter. For one thing, being an advocate for caregivers is an important piece of inclusive leadership and indeed justice-making at work, and this chapter will help explain why. For another thing, you may be a caregiver of sorts at work more than you already know, and it could be draining you. And finally, life changes. As Rosalind Carter famously said, "There are only four kinds of people in the world: those who have been caregivers, those who are currently caregivers, those who will be caregivers, and those who will need caregivers."

Fortunately, more workplaces are becoming attuned to the needs of caregivers. McKinsey's 2024 report on women at work found that "Half of companies now offer support for caregivers of sick and elderly adults," and one-third offer compassionate leave.[85] Yet Sarah Wells' research with mothers transitioning back to work found that 50% of the mothers with whom she spoke had not had any communication at all with their employers about support for working mothers.[86] So much work remains.

CAREGIVING AND TRANSITIONAL WORKPLACE IDENTITIES

As anyone who has cared for young children, an elder, or someone with special needs knows, caregivers could write entire books on work-life balance—if only they had the time. Caregiving is an important piece of the puzzle of seeking (I won't say finding) balance and setting boundaries. Of course, these are valuable goals for everyone to strive for, regardless of their caregiving responsibilities. But the reality is that gendered expectations around caregiving shape women's experiences at work, whether we're engaged in caregiving or not. Expectations about women's level of commitment to work have been shaped by notions of women as mothers for centuries, and women's caregiving of their co-workers can be a tacit expectation in the workplace, on top of expectations at home.[87]

In your personal life, becoming a mother or a caregiver of any kind can shift your career (and life) perspective, and can create unique challenges along with many relational joys. It is also a space from which to learn and share with others the value of care work. We need to not only acknowledge people's personal lives, but to transform our organizations towards supporting people as full human beings and towards valuing the work of caring for and being in relationship with other humans.

Women who have transitioned to motherhood have often felt their place in the workplace subtly become less comfortable. Working while pregnant can itself be a daunting experience that brings up sexism you might not have known was there. Erin experienced intrusive scrutiny when her pregnancy became evident at work. She says pregnancy brought a "hypervisibility in a way that felt really uncomfortable." She faced "unwanted comments about my body," and felt that people were "seeing my pregnant stomach and not my full self, and that felt kind of gross."

Erin says she felt her gender most in the workplace when she was pregnant. The comments about her body made her feel diminished in her professionalism. Indeed, pregnancy discrimination makes women especially vulnerable to losing their jobs. One study noted that "complaints of workplace pregnancy discrimination to the United States' Equal Employment Opportunity Commission (EEOC) rose 46% between 1997 and 2011" and that being terminated from a job was an especially common experience. Law professor and founder of the Center for Work Life Law, Joan C. Williams, coined the term "maternal wall." The term encompasses not just pregnancy, but ensuing motherhood, as a dimension of sexist discrimination at work. Williams has shown how high performing women's careers can go south from the moment their pregnancy is revealed. *The New York Times* quoted Williams in 2018: "Some women hit the maternal wall long before the glass ceiling... There are 20 years of lab studies that show the bias exists and that, once triggered, it's very strong."[88]

Mai recalled that when she was about eight months pregnant, she interviewed for an internal job, which she didn't get. She learned that someone outside the company had been hired, who had no previous experience in the area of banking where she had developed expertise. "I didn't really think anything until I came back from maternity leave and then they had another opening." The company slotted Mai into that new job opening without her even needing to interview for it. Mai thought this was strange but considered that maybe she had been the number two choice for the first job before her leave. However, she talked to a female co-worker a year or two later, who "mentioned that I probably didn't get the job the first time around because I was pregnant." Mai was shocked. "You know, I didn't think of it; I didn't even see it. It was another man interviewing me and that never even crossed my mind. So, I was a little bit upset. But it is what it is."

Some of the most overtly sexist experiences of my own career were connected to pregnancy. There was the time, in my very low-paying teaching gig just after earning my Ph.D., that I walked into the History Department office in the small liberal arts college where I taught, and an older male colleague exclaimed, "Wow! Do you have two babies in there?" And there was the time, when I was pregnant with my third child, that a young male colleague thought it would be funny to joke, publicly at a department gathering, that the baby I was carrying might just be the offspring of the department chair. Yes—super funny! Or the time when a female colleague reportedly complained, six years after the birth of my last child, that I had received special treatment through my maternity leave.

Those are only the surface comments, revealing the underlying contours of the family-unfriendliness of my profession. Indeed, I often felt that I should not discuss my children at work. At least in the academic world, the mere fact that they existed seemed to make many people uncomfortable, as though mothers cannot also be serious scholars and teachers. I especially felt like an alien in my 30s in a History Department where there was only one other woman with children. She was halfway out of the department, too, with one foot in an administrative role. The only man in the department who had children was married to a woman who was a full-time parent.

On the other hand, especially in female-dominated professions, women who don't have children can be made to feel uncomfortable, as Olivia noted. She and her partner decided against having children, and she said she doesn't think her co-workers "know that that's intentional. Like I don't plan to. That's something that I wouldn't necessarily share with many people... I'm also a little afraid of how people might perceive me." Indeed, with the "motherhood mandate" of patriarchal cultures, most women who do not become mothers feel societally judged for it.[89] The mother/not-mother dichotomy (for which there is not a father/not-father parallel) can also lead to the kind of "horizontal hostility"—women disliking or sabotaging other women—that probably shaped my female colleague's reactions to me and my maternity leave.

"MOMMY PENALTIES"
AND OTHER CHALLENGES OF CAREGIVERS

In addition to pregnancy discrimination (which is illegal but can still happen) women who do become mothers might face what many have called the "mommy tax" or the "mommy penalty"—career stagnation in terms of pay or advancement. If you become a mother, you may be "mommy tracked" into less upwardly mobile positions. Or you may not. Especially if the balancing act is difficult because of a relentless workload and/or an inflexible workplace where formal leaders seem stressed or overwhelmed, you may find that shifting priorities make you feel like "leaning out" could be a better option for a while, even if someone else doesn't deny you a promotion. A recent Pew Research Center study found about 23% of working mothers, compared to 15% of working fathers, saying they had turned down a promotion because of parenting responsibilities.[90]

Navigating potential promotion opportunities while mothering can connect to childcare challenges. The Center for American Progress found that about half of U.S. families say they have a hard time finding childcare. Their 2018 survey showed that "mothers were 40 percent more likely than fathers to report that they had personally felt the negative impact of childcare issues on their careers. Too often, mothers must make job decisions based on childcare considerations rather than in the interest of their financial situation or career goals."[91] The financial challenges alone can interrupt career progress. Not only are quality childcare slots hard to find, but childcare costs are steep—as are the costs of giving birth or adopting a child. Many women go without income to do caregiving in the early stages of their children's lives.

Well beyond children's early years, caregiving shapes the workplace decisions and experiences of mothers in profound ways. Historically, women have always worked while rearing children, either working alongside their children in pre-industrial times or in agriculture or leaving their children with family members (including fairly young older siblings) or neighbors when they needed to work outside the home. The industrial revolution drove the separation of home and work spaces for many, resulting in the daily lives we have today: daycare drop-offs, after-school care if we can get it, and the sense of separation of "work" and "life," though indeed home life involves lots of work and family life often intrudes on our thoughts and our time while at work. With the advent of email and our ubiquitous phones, the lines have become even more blurred. Contexts and access to resources vary. But today, outside of the wealthiest women who can out-source most care work, there's a near-universal experience of holding the chaos at bay while trying to enjoy both work and whatever brings you happiness and meaning outside of the context of work.

Of course, coronavirus pandemic experiences, most prominently the closing of schools, put the chaos I and other mothers my age experienced in perspective. Our version of maternal juggling acts really can't be compared to what younger families have faced, and from which they are still trying to recover, financially, emotionally, and in terms of career and sometimes family health. In March and April 2020 alone, about 3.5 million mothers residing with school-age children left their jobs.[92] In the fall of 2020, one quarter of women dropped out of the workforce to care for children, and in March 2021, McKinsey found that "One in four women are considering leaving the workforce or downshifting their careers versus one in five men."

Moreover, McKinsey noted that all women had been impacted, but three groups "experienced some of the largest challenges: working mothers, women in senior management positions, and Black women." The disparities were especially evident when children in the family were under age ten. Additionally, "women in heterosexual dual-career couples who have children reported larger increase in their time spent on household responsibilities since the pandemic began." Indeed, one survey in 2020 showed that "70 percent of women said they do all or most of the housework during the pandemic. Another 66 percent said they were responsible for most or all of the childcare."[93]

By spring of 2022, mothers were starting to recover in terms of actual employment status, in part because of the flexibility of many white-collar jobs with the advent of remote work. But the pandemic did nothing to alleviate the gender pay gap, and mothers of young children had not recovered their labor force participation rates. 90% of fathers of young children were working in mid-2022, compared to 69% of mothers.[94]

The pandemic merely foregrounded what was already an entrenched pattern in a culture that still assigns so much invisible caregiving and logistical work to women. Yes, there are many involved fathers. But so many logistics and emotional labor still fall to women. Decades of research bear out these conclusions, summarized neatly in *The New York Times*, based on recent research: "In the U.S. women spend about four hours a day on unpaid work, compared with about 2.5 hours for men according to data from the Organization for Economic Cooperation and Development." The gap has not narrowed nearly as much as most people think, even with women's heavy labor force participation.[95] Indeed, *Harvard Business Review* recently implored men to do their share at home—and employers to step up with paid leave for men to incentivize their involvement—as part of creating gender equity at work.[96]

As in childcare, there is a significant gender gap in who is caring for our elders, with women taking on more of this labor than men. 61% of caregivers were women, compared to 39% men, in AARP's regularly published research on "Caregiving in America" in 2020.[97] Indeed, the idea that women are the primary caregivers is taken for granted by many people, even progressive ones. When I talked about the issue of elder care with a male colleague once, I remember him half-jokingly observing that his sisters would be handling that when his parents needed it. Of course, not all men feel or behave that way, but the casual nature of the comment reminded me that people don't always think critically about the gendered burden of care. In addition, considering the growing mental health problems of teenagers today, parents of teens and young adults face special challenges. They may need modifications in healthcare benefits or paid leave to deal with family crises that are less happy than the arrival of a baby.[98]

MAKING IT WORK AT WORK AND AT HOME

I wanted three children. It felt like the right size family. I managed to time pregnancies for births around the academic calendar (two August daughters in 1992 and 1996, and one early February son in 2000), and negotiated an awkward informal maternity leave arrangement for my third child (the one I had while in my assistant professor role). Everything was confusing because my university had no protocols. Like most American women in a society that provides so little support, throughout my years as a mother of young children, I generally just hurtled through the chaos to keep body and soul together and to savor the moments with my kids.

There is no magic formula for work-life balance (or, aspirationally, life-work balance) while raising kids. But the fight to prioritize them—to prioritize my family life—became central to who I was. My first year in my tenure-track job, with just two kids, ages two and six, I carved out one day a week to stay home with my younger daughter, and I managed to volunteer occasionally in my older daughter's kindergarten classroom. I almost never worked weekends, and, even when my children grew up, I kept to that pattern. Having children helped me set boundaries at work. I became a model of efficiency, though I would learn by my 50s how much that hypervigilance was working its way into my nervous system and the stress I held in my body. Still, it served its purpose. One of my old friends once said, you can tell which women are mothers because they run meetings so efficiently.

Health risks are only one part of living life around efficiencies. Hypervigilance and anxiety are the lot of working mothers in a capitalist economy largely without paid leave and other significant supports for caregiving. I often wondered how much more I might have enjoyed my children's early years had I lived in a country that acknowledged the work of caregiving through public policy like paid leave. That said, without family around for much of our child-rearing, my spouse and I leaned in as best we could to equitable work at home; he was actually a stay-at-home parent for a big chunk of our kids' childhood and worked part-time jobs while I had my full-time one. In addition to my supportive spouse, I found "my people" outside my department, including a warm and kind network of mothers with whom I could acknowledge more of the fullness of myself as a professor and a mother.

For my spouse and me, the key to our survival as working parents included not only his many stints in a part-time or even at-home role, but also, as people living far from our families of origin, the relationships we intentionally built with friends who became like family. Beyond carpooling and the occasional shared babysitting opportunity, friends can be critical in the work-life balancing act when the chips are down. For example, when one of our children was struggling with a health issue in middle school, my nearest and dearest shared in the driving to and from appointments and also provided critical emotional support for our family.

As the mothers among the women I interviewed attest, becoming a mother just becomes part of who you are, and you work with it. You can't afford to think of it as holding you back, even if it does sometimes. It's also true that it doesn't always hold women back. Erin found that becoming a mother did not have a negative impact on her upward mobility at all in her organization. She was offered an advancement opportunity as soon as she got back from parental leave. You can never entirely predict work (not to mention shifting family situations), so you have to live the life you want to live and make a career work around it.

Interestingly, Connie believed that having children as a single mother helped her with her career. When her kids were young, she worked three jobs, including waitressing and retail, only dropping one of these jobs when she went back to school. Of the school decision, she says, "I wanted to do something for my family, for me," she says. "I had to do all of it, but it helped me. I just think, keep striving over those roadblocks... Just keep moving forward."

As my kids got a little older, I discovered that integration could be as good a strategy as balance. I published an article on the Berenstain Bears children's books' portrayal of Mama Bear as part of my emerging scholarship on the history of motherhood. The article padded my publication record for tenure. Since we read these books to our kids, the research was right at my fingertips, and the article practically wrote itself. As time passed and my children became teenagers, I brought them to university events, showing them what it's like to be proud of meaningful work.

We can't always predict when we decide to take the plunge into parenthood—although with protections of reproductive rights unraveling or, in some states, disappearing altogether in the wake of the Dobbs decision, we may not always get to decide. But we often get some help along the way. As noted above, partners can be key. Laura, for example, reflected that "I think I sort of knew at my core that I wanted to be a mother and a very present mother, so to be able to do that, I have to have a supportive partner." And she does. "I'm really lucky... with regard to the family and caregiving demands," she says, because her partner supports every undertaking she feels called to take on. "He always is like, oh, okay, you should do that."

Laura and her partner, like my spouse and I, prioritized part-time childcare for as long as they could. "We just had to fit our work in the gaps around them when they were little." But, she says, "that clear commitment was helpful." It represents the empowerment of making your own decisions, decisions that others may make differently (or may not have the option to make). There's no judgment there for Laura, who noted, "I think that there are so many ways to raise kids who are healthy and kind and wonderful... I think we get into trouble when we think that we might be doing things wrong. We can just do our best. You know, that's not really advice, but I think to just figure out what your best is and then move with that, with conviction and know that it can change at any time. And that's okay too."

Help can come from surprising places. Once, during my first semester teaching, I dropped my daughter off at kindergarten, came back to the car to take my two-year-old to childcare, and found that my car wouldn't start. I was going to be late to class, and my anxiety went through the roof. A teacher at the elementary school, whom I had never met, understood my situation without my even approaching her. She walked up to me and said she could tell I was going to be late to work, so I should take her car. I was stunned, but I took the offer. I still see her in the community, and I still want to keep saying thank you to her, for being the best Samaritan ever.

Connie had a similar experience. She had just gotten divorced, had three small children, and her car battery died. "I was walking with my children to work," she recalls, when a top leader in her organization—someone she really didn't know—saw her. "She said, 'Do you not have a car?' I said, 'Yes, it broke down.' She goes, 'Just take it to the shop, they'll bill me, you can pay me back.'" Connie was blown away by this woman's generosity. "Back then I was young, and she impressed me; boy, I remember her."

Madeline pursued a master's degree while her kids were in high school and she was working full-time as a hospital administrator. She almost abandoned the educational endeavor. "I just couldn't keep doing my schoolwork and being a mom of teenagers, so I dropped off for a period of time, and I thought, 'Oh, I'm never going back. How do I go back?'" But one of her sisters "was just persistent: 'You can do it. You have to go back.' And then I went and met with the faculty, and that took courage for me because I thought I'm just not going to be able to do it. And they were like no, you can do this... in fact you have more credits than you need to graduate." Madeline just needed to finish her thesis, which she managed to do, constraints and all.

At the time of our interview, Mai had four children and was finishing her undergraduate degree while working full time. It was a struggle, "not being able to mommy 100%" even when she was home, but she was making it work. "Luckily, you know my husband is 1000% moral support... He picked up everything that I wasn't able to do. He did the laundry, did the dishes, he cooked dinner, he helped the kids with homework, he did everything that we would have shared together. So, I missed out on a lot. I was not able to go to some of the concerts. I wasn't able to read to them every night." She wondered, "Is this right? Is this okay? Are they going to be okay? Do they miss me? Do they need more mom time?" The encouragement she received at home helped Mai feel reassured about these questions.

Looking back, all of these questions came up for me and for just about every working mother I know. But somehow, we adapted as needed, our kids got through childhood and moved forward, and we made family lives even as we made working lives. Most women today are not in a position to even consider choosing work versus motherhood or vice versa. Indeed, such a choice is not something most women have ever had, and doing both becomes part of our identities. Work is part of who we are too. Of her work as a hospital administrator, "It's my life's work. I can't not do it." I feel the same about my own professional work. Whether out of necessity, calling, or both, women find a way to work and to care, and to build lives alongside careers.

IMPROVING OUR WORKPLACES FOR CAREGIVERS, FAMILIES, AND COMMUNITIES

In addition to our families and friends, our workplaces can do so much to help us along. Gina, for example, knows that she is "among the very, very few fortunate people that work for an organization that is just incredibly supportive of new families." It's true. The U.S. is the only industrialized country in the world where paid leave for new parents is not required, and only about 20% of American workers enjoy employer-paid leave. But Gina's mission-oriented organization is among those who offer it. They did so even before the pandemic, and more organizations stepped up this benefit as the pandemic unfolded.

But by 2022, things were shifting backward for many working parents. A Society for Human Resource Management employee benefit survey found, in October 2022, that "Organizations offering paid maternity leave dropped to 35 percent (from 53 percent in 2020) and the number offering paid paternity leave dropped to 27 percent (from 44 percent)."[99] Many workers cannot even access unpaid leave. The 1993 Family Medical Leave Act provided for 12 unpaid weeks of leave for events like childbirth, adoption, and illness. But according to the U.S. Department of Labor, in 2020 only 44% of workers meet the eligibility requirements, which include time of employment, level of employment, and company size. Only organizations with 50 or more employees are required to offer this benefit, and workers need to have logged about 24 hours a week for one year before qualifying and need to have "a physical work location ('worksite') where at least 50 employees work within 75 miles" of the site.[100]

But at Gina's workplace, the parental leave program encouraged leave for any gender. And family support went beyond the leave policy, including, for example, rooms for nursing mothers. In this context, as a manager, Gina felt empowered to live out her values of supporting parents. Gina says those values came from a sense of being able to see people in their full humanity—something she credits to her Hispanic culture, her background growing up in foster care and struggling with that stigma, and the resilience and learning she'd cultivated throughout her life.

Of course, her own experiences as a mother added to the mix. "Obviously, I have some really strong feelings about parenthood and caring for children," she said. "I think that comes from me growing up and my relationship with my own children. It's by far the most sacred piece of my life. And so, I am so supportive of any kind of parenting issues that come up in the workplace." Gina reflected on her luck in working "for a company that backs that piece. I think that I would still be very supportive of it in another environment at another corporation. But again, you can only go so far with that."

The family friendliness of Gina's workplace was also facilitated, she said, by a culture of trust in employees at different levels. The organization gives "a lot of authority in managing people to the people directly managing." Having worked in a top-heavy organization that did not operate that way, I can attest to the struggles of trying to facilitate work-life balance for people who reported to me. My authority to do so was quite limited by people above my level, and sometimes by policies made by a central campus authority beyond our own campus. In contrast, structurally, Gina had more authority to live out her family-friendly values as a leader.

This is not to say boundaries are easy, even for Gina and those like her who have supportive workplaces. Overwork is held up as an ideal in the U.S., and some jobs do require significant availability in after-work hours. Gina reflected that she had "not always been the best" at setting boundaries: she described being texted or called at all hours of the day or night, needing to respond to lots of work-related emergencies. But she thrived on the adrenaline of solving problems, and her relationship with her son grounded her: "Somebody close to me is very good at telling me when I'm spending too much time at work. And that's my 11-year-old son... He's phenomenal at saying, 'Mom I think you're working too much this week. We haven't played one game.' He says it not in a guilt way, just sort of like 'Come on back. Let me help you balance this out, Mom.'"

To add to the happy mix in this particular moment of Gina's career trajectory, she loved her team, felt incredibly supported by her own supervisor, and felt empowered in empowering others, including telling her direct reports to go home on days when there was downtime. "I tell everybody that has ever worked for me or that ever will in the future... family comes first." She added, "there's nothing that is worth missing significant pieces of the lives of the people that you love. So, whether it's a birthday or a first haircut or whatever, whatever is important to you... I mean that's why we all come to work, right? I really like my job... But also, we come to work to earn a living, to be able to provide for the people that we love. So, let's not shortchange them with the most valuable thing we have, and that's our time and attention."

In her management style, Gina said, she leans on the idea of "always assume good intent," which she links back to that positive college experience, when supportive professors "just always went the extra mile to help me out because, it could have been very easy for them to be like, 'No, you didn't turn this in, it was due this day, I don't care about your excuses, done'." I don't operate that way at all." With people that report to her, she says:

> I'd much rather sit down, talk with somebody about their struggles and you never know when somebody got a flat tire on the way into work or they found out that morning their grandma was really sick, or their dog died the night before. You don't know that, and those things significantly impact people's lives. And they would for me too. And so, you have the opportunity in that struggle to strengthen a bond and have somebody come out of that experience with more respect for you, which is good. I mean, on a personal level, but also from a business perspective, right?

Other managers I interviewed understood the obligations of work and life in similar terms. Madeline, who was in a high-level leadership role in healthcare during the height of the pandemic at the time of our 2020 interview, saw the struggles of mothers and remembered her own earlier years as a working parent. She encouraged stressed mothers on her staff to "let it go and go home and be a mom" some days, saying "Let's just take another run at this tomorrow." And Olivia, who did not have children herself, appreciated being part of a flexible organization, recognizing that for parents in less supportive workplaces, "it's a lot to shoulder."

Erin decided to funnel her appreciation for the paid family leave she received from her company, and her commitment to gender equality, into action. She worked to shore up her organization's paid leave program, persuading senior leadership to hire a consultant to evaluate its efficacy and impact. The external evaluation provided concrete evidence of the strong value of this program in easing the challenges of working parenthood, fostering strong employee loyalty to the organization in a generation of young workers, and just contributing to the greater good of the lives of employees.

Because fathers were just as encouraged to take leave (and did so at roughly equal numbers) as mothers, the program also contributed to gender equity. Other research shows that paid leave programs like this not only help foster more equitable gender dynamics at home among heterosexual couples but also help level the playing field at work. They also contribute positively to maternal health, infant health, and familial financial well-being.[101]

Individuals helping one another can be critical, but intentionally supportive workplaces make an even bigger difference, creating norms that can keep people from needing to scramble for so much help in the first place. Research shows that people can create caregiver-friendly and work-life friendly environments that contribute to recruiting and retaining diverse employees, and also have a documented impact of increasing women's access to senior management roles.[102] That said, we can't expect companies to voluntarily create such structures on their own: We need family-friendly and worker-friendly public policies that make them mandatory. We also need to be rebuilding communities so that kids have more safe spaces and fully-staffed "surround care" options, and promoting active involvement in childcare from men—who are often deeply rewarded by this work too.

At the level of the workplace, a work-life friendly work environment must support ALL caregivers—but must also attend to the gender dynamics: women tend to pay more of a price for prioritizing family care than men do. The need to care for school-age children at home during the pandemic underscored gender inequality in caregiving, as well as the reality that caregiving is not just infants and preschoolers. In a labor market where workers are greatly needed, and where parents are now struggling to help their children catch up from lost learning and helping their teenagers and young adults with the mental health fallout of the pandemic, the need for family-friendly workplaces has never been more urgent.

At the same time, inclusive workplace cultures create space for people without children. Indeed, work-life issues are not just about caregiving for others—though it is women's caregiving for children that forced the issue of any policy change on the issue, and opened the doors to further potential change. Particularly since the pandemic, fostering life-work balance and employee satisfaction also means addressing the need for remote work options for people with chronic illnesses and immune-compromised health status, for example. Since the enactment of FMLA in 1993, increasing numbers of workers have used leave for their own health crises, or those of intimate family members. Flexibility in our changing workplaces might also mean re-creating absence policies for women who need to travel to another state for reproductive healthcare.

The data is clear that flexibility is good for retaining women and investing in their productivity. McKinsey's 2023 report on women in the workplace found one in five women reporting that "flexibility has helped them stay in their job or avoid reducing their hours." Moreover, "a large number of women who work hybrid or remotely point to feeling less fatigued and burned out as a primary benefit. And a majority of women report having more focused time to get their work done when they work remotely."[103]

All of this relates back to creating a workplace culture in which people's family and personal lives are acknowledged as important, and where people can be as openly as possible "themselves" in the workplace. For example, research shows that LGBTQ+ people often attribute their ability to be out in a workplace to a strong network of allies.[104] In turn, their family and personal needs, including medical and caregiving ones, can more appropriately be addressed if their workplace is LGBTQ-friendly.

Can we actually find work-life balance, even in people-friendly/family-friendly workplaces? Rosalind said she preferred to think about "work-life alignment" rather than work-life balance, because balance can be elusive. But workplaces that proactively help with fostering alignment can really make a difference, reducing stress, facilitating diverse contributions, and making it easier to attend to all that matters in life outside of the workplace.

Savvy mothers and others are evaluating workplaces as they consider where to work. As Rosalind described it to me: "When I'm looking for a career move, as a woman and as a mother, I'm not looking per se for the income as much as the flexibility." Could she take her child to the doctor as needed? Would she be "working until eight o'clock at night?" And what was the benefits package? Rosalind said that although income could be a factor between one job or another, things like benefits, insurance coverage "are the top things because I'm a mom." She also wants to know about the workplace culture: "Do they encourage family, or are they encouraging work first? If family is first, excellent!" And what about the individual manager to whom she would report? "Because it could be very different within different departments."

Rosalind is absolutely right. Wise leaders of large organizations look for those shining light departments or units, and find ways to lift them up, supporting what they are modeling for other areas of the organization. Wise leaders also recognize emotional labor and caregiving work WITHIN the workplace, whether as part of the job description, such as for social workers, healthcare providers, or K-12 teachers, or as an often-invisible add-on involving skillsets such as diplomacy, conflict mediation, relationship building and maintenance. To be really expansive about supporting caregivers, we also need to recognize the caregivers who nurture others and provide social coherence for a team within the workplace. This work is often ignored as part of workplace skillsets and is disproportionately expected of and done by women. There is also emotional labor involved in managing your own emotions in the face of microaggressions, trying to make others comfortable. Being thoughtful and maintaining relationships can bring joy and satisfaction, and using your emotional intelligence to do your job well can bring joy and satisfaction.

But the work of making other people feel comfortable, even when they have slighted you, is a burdensome part of the equation. It's part of paying the "emotional tax" discussed earlier, a tax disproportionately borne by women of color in predominantly white workplaces. The scholar Arlie Hochschild first pointed this out back in the early 1980s, when she observed that some people (especially women) needed to manage and regulate their emotions as part of the fulfillment of certain jobs, for example in customer service.[105] Rose Hackman, who recently authored the book *Emotional Labor: The Invisible Work Shaping Our Lives and How to Claim Our Power*, observes that everyone has to be prosocial in the workplace, but people with less power are more expected to be attuned to, and deferential to others, doing things like "finessing tone, being careful of the status and egos of others," putting others' emotional needs above their own, creating space for others' emotions at work while stuffing down our own.[106]

Power is connected to expectations of emotional labor, Hackman rightly observes, which often breaks down in ways that reinforce social hierarchies. "Who is expected to do emotional labor the most is not about ability but who has the least perceived power. In a work context, that means more emotional labor for junior people, but it also means people with marginalized identities – women, people of color, LGBTQ+ people – will be expected to do even more of it, regardless of rank."[107]

Leaders can make a difference here too, expanding the vocabulary of emotional labor, breaking down the skillsets involved, and making sure those skillsets are recognized with pay, promotions, and in strategic planning decisions for the organization. The work of creating more inclusive organizations involves addressing unconscious bias and microaggressions, and acknowledging the emotional tax paid by those most affected by these patterns. Naming emotional labor remains a critical feminist and anti-racist project, and this work has its place in our thinking about the work of caring so long gendered and delegated to the less powerful in our society.

Again, this work has myriad satisfactions, when not exploited or misused to maintain power structures. And it makes critical contributions. It can feel great to be part of the hospitality team of your organization, to organize celebrations for the births of people's children or their work milestones, or to send a caring note to acknowledge their struggles or loss. Care workers, unpaid or paid, knit our society together, invite us to celebrate life's joys, provide comfort and support to those who need it, and bring emotional intelligence to bear on every critical ethical issue in our society. It's vital that our workplaces play a role in lifting these caregivers up and supporting their contributions.

As the above discussion highlights, the value of a flexible, inclusive workplace that supports caregivers is crucial to the advancement of women and to creating more humane workplaces all around. Consider how you can be part of this, regardless of your caregiving status.

EXAMPLES OF WHAT WORKS

▶ Policies on leaves and workplace flexibility are clear, available to all employees (not just salaried), and as generous as possible. .

▶ Attention is paid to cultural diversity and anti-racism in creating work-life policies, for example attending to community care, elder care needs, and diverse religious and cultural holidays and rituals.

▶ People can move from part-time back to full-time work: there are on-ramps and off-ramps to reconfigurations of working hours.

▶ Paid leave is generous, inclusive, and available regardless of gender or employment category (e.g. available to waged as well as salaried workers).

▶ Remote work and flexible scheduling are available, and those who participate in this work have their work accomplishments celebrated and highlighted; and structures are provided to keep them integrated into the workplace community.

▶ Disability accommodations are up to date, generous, and supported by a human-centered workplace culture that celebrates the contributions of people with differing abilities..

▶ The organization is up-to-date and mindful of LGBTQ+ policies, in areas such as healthcare, pronoun usage, and more. The Human Rights Campaign's Corporate Equality Index provides a helpful index for employer competencies and friendliness.

▶ The organization takes an interest in, or even supports childcare options available to working parents, and elder care options in the area, perhaps even providing on-site childcare.

▶ The organization communicates and operationalizes its commitment to caregivers and people with commitments outside of work, while also making space for people who want to be "all in" for at least part of their careers.

▶ A significant portion of formal leaders demonstrate their own commitments to life-work balance.

▶ The company monitors indices of gender equity and the potential for "caregiver penalties" for those who take time out for caregiving, ensuring that such workers continue to have access to promotions and pay increases.

▶ Employees can show their community spirit by donating sick time to others. According to the Society for Human Resource Managers, this is a practice which "allow employees to donate accrued paid time off (PTO), vacation or sick leave to a general pool to be used by fellow employees who experience medical emergencies or who are affected by major disasters and have exhausted all paid leave available to them."[108]

▶ Companies resist a culture of overwork, the clearest drain on personal and family well-being. All the policies in the world can't compensate for the expectation of a 60+ hour work week.

▶ Extra points for innovation: companies offer paid time off for community involvement and service, which could include employee's children's school or nursing home. Ben and Jerry's offers 40 hours a year annually of paid time for such service work.[109]

▶ Other companies offer sabbaticals, touted by policy experts as especially relevant for mid-career parents juggling too many responsibilities.[110]

▶ In the workplace, organization is conversant in the language of emotional labor, and recognizes the work of relationship maintenance, community service, and servant leadership often done by women and people of color within the workplace. These vital ongoing contributions are recognized in how work is evaluated and celebrated and considered part of advancement criteria.

OUR WORK TOGETHER

We need to encourage public policy and/or corporate community invest-ments to promote paid leave and other social supports, like after-school care, safe neighborhoods, meaningful support for communities of color and LGBTQ communities, reproductive rights, pay equity, subsidized childcare, universal pre-K.[111]

We should support unions and their life-work advocacy. Although unions can be difficult to access in some professional workplaces, they can definitely be helpful in the family-friendly fight. Union workers are not only more likely than non-union ones to have employer-sponsored health insurance; they're also more likely to have paid sick days, and more opportunities to shape work schedules. Unions can and do bring people together to advocate for public policy change.[112]

REFLECTION QUESTIONS ON CAREGIVING AND EMOTIONAL LABOR

▶ To what extent, and how, are caregivers supported in your workplace?

▶ How can caregiving work be elevated in its importance to society through the vehicle of your workplace? This can include not only the care work done in people's off-work time, but also the care work done to sustain people within the workplace.

▶ What could your workplace do to better support mothers, with attention to diversity?

▶ How much and in what ways do you perform emotional labor in the workplace?

▶ How can you use your voice at any level of the organization on these issues?

▶ Which parts of that labor do you find rewarding versus draining?

▶ Are you doing the amount of emotional labor that feels appropriate to your position and to your own well-being and goals?

▶ Are those who perform emotional labor being acknowledged for this work?

▶ If you are a caregiver at home, are you getting the support you need? And are you investing in your long-term career and life trajectory while practicing self-advocacy and self-compassion?

▶ Who can help you in your continuing quest for alignment and/or balance? And how can you work with others to facilitate these possibilities for everyone in your workplace?

CHAPTER 8

LEVERAGING MID-CAREER CLOUT

Becoming an Inclusive Leader and Change Maker the Many Faces of Leadership

IT TAKES VISIONARY and hardworking leaders to create cultures of trust and employee empowerment where women and people of all backgrounds and identities are most likely to thrive. If you've been using your voice and choosing your projects based on pro-social values of equity, diversity, and inclusion, you've already been leading. You don't need a title to be a leader. You can think of leadership as simply expanding your platform and voice, regardless of whether a new position is involved. You may be a manager at any level, someone who sits slightly outside the hierarchy by being, say, a community engagement coordinator, or simply a thought leader and powerful voice. Or you may be a vocal leader on a project or issue.

Wherever they may be, effective leaders use the tools of their platform and stay attentive to their growing power, which they use both to disrupt problematic systems and to make exciting new contributions. Leaders wanting to bring social justice to work often have a keen eye for opportunities to work past the boundaries between arbitrary categories, such as between the workplace and the community, between work selves and full, embedded-in-families-and-relationships selves. They also tend to shake up hierarchies when those hierarchies don't serve the people and work of the organization, often resulting in better organizational effectiveness through increased communication and unleashed talents.

Even if you're ambivalent about the formal leadership roles that you can see in your current organization or industry, consider how influential those leaders can be. These are the people with significant decision-making authority, access to budgets, and access to the ears of higher-level decision-makers. They're the people who can do a great deal to create team cultures that help people thrive and advance workplace culture change.

Your potential movement into leadership roles can have an enormous ripple effect. Direct supervisors and departmental cultures are key to women's satisfaction at work. For example, research shows that women of color are less likely to leave a company if they have a good relationship with their supervisor. Unfortunately, a 2022 McKinsey report found that "Only about half of women say their manager regularly encourages respectful behavior on their team, and less than half say their manager shows interest in their career and helps them manage their workload."

But, as previously discussed, women managers are most likely to show this kind of interest. A pattern of women's leadership tends to make a difference in the aggregate, according to a great deal of research. Women leaders are more likely to invest their time in efforts to improve diversity, equity, and inclusion—twice as likely according to a recent report by McKinsey.[113] Another study found that "having more female managers appears to reduce the likelihood of pregnancy discrimination in the workplace."[114] And still another found that "firms with a higher proportion of women on the board of directors and firms with a female CEO experience less sexual harassment. An increase of one female director is associated with an 18.2% decrease in the sexual harassment rate. The mechanism for reduced sexual harassment is linked to overall improved social policy."[115]

Even though leadership can happen from anywhere, we need more women to open themselves up to formal leadership roles. If you have such an opportunity and are considering it, it's helpful to recognize the leadership skills and dispositions you have, no matter your position. You can begin demystifying formal leadership as a concept and practice. It's something you can probably grow into, even if it can look daunting from the outside.

I mentioned earlier that I "found myself thrust into" the role of academic department chair. I was not seeking this role. The reality was that, in our small department, I was the obvious person to take on this position based on my faculty rank, and the department needed a chair. At that moment, I was stretching out into the community with the Diversity Council position, and I was leery of having my energy drained by university bureaucracy. Though I appreciated my predecessor's leadership in the department, I didn't think I wanted my days shaped by endless email, meetings, and bureaucratic tasks, which is what the role sometimes looked like from the outside.

But then the department chair job surprised me—in a good way. I grew enormously from doing this work. Indeed, it reminded me of the growth I had experienced as a leader of large federal grants, facilitating learning for teachers across two states and many grade levels. The department chair role expanded my platform and voice in the larger university. It also allowed me the opportunity to support every person on our team, to build community within and beyond our department, to serve students in a broader way, and to work with others to dream up new ways to put our department mission and social justice expertise into action. Ultimately, this leadership role gave me a chance to lead in a new institutionally focused way, and an opportunity to cultivate and model an ethic of support, kindness, community care, and advocacy. And I embraced those opportunities for my last six years at the university.

Roles that may appear scary or unappealing because you might only be able to see one part of them at first can be incredible teachers. As Laura said of an administrative role she took on, it helped her to learn "a new skill set and seeing how the university works and kind of testing the waters of admin." Even when she let go of that position, she says she had new wisdom for her work elsewhere in the organization and more empathy, understanding, and effectiveness because she understood the work it took to be a supportive leader.

TRANSFORMATIONAL LEADERSHIP THROUGH VISION AND VALUES

Although many leaders of any gender work their way into high-level formal leadership roles by replicating the same dynamics of leaders before them, this pitfall can often be avoided through the grounded, strategic, values-based approach that keeps coming up in the stories of the women I interviewed. Madeline, for example, now a vp in the healthcare world who describes herself as a "quiet leader," says she has always been "a bit fearless when it comes to asking questions." Madeline's sensitivity to context is borne of years of experiences, and likely also from being an Indigenous woman in healthcare. She notes that in decision-making spaces, "the egos sometimes that are in the room or around the table... can be a barrier. Or it can be challenging for individuals to have a dialogue or a discussion with someone if that title is bigger than theirs."

Madeline says she has tended "to be more of a quiet observer. And within our Native culture that is considered respectful." She says she has cultivated the "ability to step in then and ask questions or to understand how to partner" across those barriers of hierarchy. When she's run into leaders who "might have been perceived as barriers themselves," she has approached them with a spirit of partnership, in order to "shape that relationship in such a way to help teach others, why and how they're doing what they're doing, to build that trust and understanding and then partner with them so that further change could happen going forward."

Madeline helps these leaders be more transparent with others, too. What she calls her own journey of diversity learning helped her understand how different people approach different situations. Her leadership quietly subverts the barriers created by hierarchy in favor of belonging. When I asked her about her experiences and ideas about belonging at work, she said, "It's kind of like having a circle, so that's not necessarily being known or having that kind of visibility. It's about the circle of people around me and having them understand who I am. So that builds the trust of 'we're in this together.'"

Like many of the BIPOC leaders Jenny Vazquez-Newsum interviewed for her book *Untapped Leadership: Harnessing the Power of Under-represented Leaders*, Madeline employed a leadership style that could be described as "leading from the back," spending a lot of time (and emotional labor) building trust and learning from different people's perspectives. This kind of "quiet" leadership is foundational for organizations because functionality is built on trust. It is transformational, moving workplace cultures away from top-heavy, gatekeeping, exclusionary decision-making processes. Research shows that leaders make better decisions when multiple perspectives are gathered and incorporated into the thought process.[116]

Transparency, too, is a commonly practiced value of transformational women leaders. So often this is driven by a deep awareness of social identity, an ability to leverage the lessons of having been marginalized, and a capacity to listen and to be intentional. Claire, for example, attributed her intentionality around transparency to her queer identity. Because she was partnered with someone whom she said "presents as male" at the time of our interview, she said she often had to remind people in her life of that queer identity.

> It's this constant making transparent. My queerness still shapes who I am and that I still inhabit that identity. And it shapes the way my brain works. And it still shapes the way I see the world.

> And so, I think... that constant making transparent actually allows me to make transparent other things as well... I've gotten very good at saying things to people like, I said to somebody the other day. "Do you understand that I'm honest with you because I respect you?"

This was a hard conversation, she says, but "I've gotten good at that because I've had to do a lot of meta work in my life all the time. And I think that comes from queerness... having to articulate what I know in my body to people consistently... Because normal is not a thing I'll ever be, even if that would make people comfortable."

For values-driven, intentional women at or near the top level of organizations, the transformational power of intentional and values-driven leadership can be remarkable. The only woman among my interviewees who was situated at the very top of her organizational chart, Tina, has executed her leadership role in a way that deserves a deep dive here.

As previously noted, Tina's early career experiences in a pharmaceutical company provided her with excellent mentoring, and she took those lessons with her. She went on to a variety of roles in government and the nonprofit world after her corporate experience, growing her leadership capacity along the way and sharpening her understanding of how inequality had affected her journey. At one point she realized, for example, that she appeared to have been "given an opportunity because I was white, over a Black colleague" at the pharmaceutical company. While working as a lobbyist for animal rights, she noticed that flirtation was expected of women who worked with politicians, but not of men in the same positions: women's ideas weren't just advanced on the basis of merit. She also understood that "because I don't have children and I don't care for parents or a disabled sibling, and I have a partner who knows that I am very career oriented. I am very privileged in that way," and this probably helped her advancement.

Another key lesson for Tina was about hierarchy in organizations. She learned what a "flatter," less "top-heavy" organization could do to bring out people's talents when she worked at the Humane Society. This was the kind of organization that was "trying to empower people and get the best out of them." It was a pivotal experience in her growth as a leader.

In her 40s, Tina took over as executive director of a large anti-poverty nonprofit that served thousands of needy people in the area. Until this point, one director had been in place for some thirty years, overseeing the same, fairly rigid workplace culture. Building on her past experiences and her keen attention to discrimination and the flaws of hierarchical culture, Tina was ready to operationalize a sweeping vision of "flipping the hierarchy on its head" when she assumed leadership. She wanted to transform the organization so that employees would be empowered to lead strategic thinking and so that communication would flow more smoothly throughout the organization, across arbitrary boundaries of position and rank. Having wanted to be an activist since she was a kid, Tina said that she knew at this stage of her career that "the hierarchy never served me. So, when I come into an organization, I blow it up."

Of course, Tina couldn't do this in a scorched-earth way. Nor did she want to. She wanted the organization to thrive. She wanted to preserve the expertise of the people who worked there and partner with them to transition the organization into a new chapter. Culture change and policy change required a massive investment in interpersonal relationships and deep listening. "In the first two months I was there," she says, "I met one on one with every single employee involved here." This involved meeting 50 employees and an even larger number of volunteers, just asking them about themselves and getting to know them a little bit, making a personal connection.

Tina oversaw seven division directors at that time. She told them, "Heads up. I am going to be reaching out to every employee on your team and I'm going to ask them for a one-on-one, so I get to know them individually. And let them know that I'm not scary, I am here, they can always talk to me." Initially, she says, "the directors were so uncomfortable. 'What are you going to talk about? What if they say something bad about me? Are you going to report back to me what they say?'... They were just really uncomfortable with it because that opened doors." Tina addressed this discomfort directly, by working with people and bringing everyone along, not by letting anyone in the leadership circle go, as some new leaders do.

Rather than implementing a vision from the top down, Tina began with people across the organization, reassuring these nervous directors while getting to know all employees. She also opened doors to board meetings, inviting any employee to attend. She began shifting decision-making patterns, empowering teams with more control of their budgets and more access to her as the executive director, without having every decision go through a huge chain of approvals. "Employees collectively choose a health insurance plan, for example. All staff are invited to participate in key decisions. We got a big grant through the CARES Act to use for anti-poverty efforts and emergency services. We did not make a decision on how to spend that money until we did a survey. All employees have the opportunity to tell us how we could use the money."

In addition, Tina made sure that employees can come to management meetings, which are now open to anyone. "You can stop by anybody's door and just talk. There is no fear anymore. It is so reassuring to see that happen." As a "servant leader," Tina speaks about her role in the organization as, in some ways, the least important. If she took a vacation, she says, the real work of the organization, helping lift people out of poverty, would go on. "Employee empowerment is the highest priority for me. I always tell my team that I am the executive director and that means I work for them. My job is to remove barriers so that they can do their work. My job is to get them the resources that they need to do their work. My job is to work for them so they can do great things. I don't impact anybody, except my employees."

From her past experiences, Tina understood the way family-work conflicts for caregivers could add stress, leach productivity, and create unnecessary burdens to talented people, especially women, whom she wanted to see grow and blossom at work. So, she instituted a slew of policies to support caregivers, including parents as well as those who provided elder care. For example, new policies allowed people to bring their babies to work for the first year, instituting flexible work hours for everyone, and reshaping leave policies so employees didn't have to use their vacation days when they were sick. Even more proactively, she explains:

> We expanded the definition for the parameters of sick time. So, it's not just if you or one of your immediate family members are sick, like physically ill, we allow you to use it if you need to focus on other parts of your health and wellbeing. If you have a meeting with a financial advisor, that is your financial health. You can use your sick time. Or if you have a class at the gym you want to take... [or] if you need to use it for any mental health. We have expanded it to pretty much any aspect of health and well-being in your life. Financial, physical, mental, you can use your paid sick leave. And that is really intended for that need to navigate life along with work.

A few years after our original email, Tina's organization implemented paid family leave, a rarity in nonprofits in small urban areas like the one where she and her employees work.

Every year, employees evaluate Tina's performance in an anonymous survey that goes directly to the board of directors, so she can keep communication flowing and provide feedback mechanisms. She intentionally practices trusting people to do their jobs:

> You have to pick people and put them into jobs where they can really use their strengths. And then just let them go. There is not one way to do it. Everybody has a different way. We can learn from

> each other. If you give them the freedom and the training-- I say, "You're free to lead." I say that to everybody. People come to me, and they need a decision, and I say, "You're free to lead." If you give them their freedom to make decisions-- they're going to make good decisions on behalf of the organization.

That decision-making capacity is fostered by the Project Future team that Tina co-created with her team. Anyone can join this group, which meets with Tina once a month to talk about strategic planning, workplace culture, ideas for programs and services for employees, or anything else on their minds. She also works to create situations where people can communicate across hierarchy, for example, where staff and board members can connect and get to know one another. Employees are encouraged to grow because Tina pushes people to get experience in a variety of areas in the organization, which also presents an opportunity to understand other people's roles and develop a more connected workplace culture. Cross-training, Tina says, promotes "organizational resiliency."

In addition, Tina has worked to decouple performance reviews from wage increases, based on her awareness that performance-based pay increases tend to reproduce gender and racial hierarchy because of unconscious bias. Instead, raises are across the board, and performance is seen as a reflection of team effort. Meanwhile, individual performance is a matter of ongoing check-ins and coaching. Peer coaches are part of the culture, and people are compensated and recognized for that emotional labor. Teams create collaborative goals as part of strategic thinking and teamwork. "If there's a performance issue" with someone, Tina says, "that's where coaching and training come in." Of course, she says, "not every job fits every person," and leaders sometimes have to make hard decisions about letting people go.

Tina is clear that transparency, flexibility, and trust are key to how people are treated and how the organization thrives. But this doesn't mean that the organization is run in a loose way. Fiscal policies are tightly managed towards responsibilities to funders and communities. But all of what functions well in her organization, including making the organization more diverse and reflective of the communities it serves, Tina attributes to the people who work there. "Protect the culture," she says, "and the rest will happen."

Any leader can talk about their leadership philosophy, but if, as a leader, you don't have feedback mechanisms to check your reality against that of other people, you're likely to be less effective. You may be blindsided by negative feedback because there was a dam that finally broke of people making complaints without your knowledge and ability to engage with and learn from people on your team or in your organization. Without feedback loops, you may also wonder if things are really working and perhaps live in your monkey mind of perfectionism.

Tina made sure that didn't happen by instituting employee engagement surveys, which, in 2023, had an 88% response rate. Employees were asked questions about whether they felt trusted, felt the organization was transparent, trusted the leadership, felt proud to work at the organization, felt cared for, felt their work and ideas were valued, felt they could bring their best selves to work, and would recommend the organization to others as a place to work. The combined average of "yes" responses to these multifaceted questions was 90% in 2023.

WORKING WITH "CREATIVE TENSION"

Of course, when you're a high-level leader, not all feedback you receive will be so positive. And there will be some feedback you'll never hear. People in leadership roles are experienced differently by different people. Adding to that, as Vazquez-Newsum points out, we tend to both associate leadership only with "the top" and to make heroes out of our top leaders, expecting no mistakes from them.

When you do receive feedback, it's important to listen to it. If you can make changes and then get better feedback, you know you're becoming more effective. When you get negative feedback, you have to work with your most trusted people to help you process in a way that mitigates the natural shame response. You can then go back and ask more questions and find out what you can learn from someone's negative feedback. Not all feedback is going to make sense, be actionable, or even feel relevant, and that's part of the messiness of leadership and of humans working together. Check in with your values to see when and if particular kinds of feedback can be useful for your goals, the health of your organization, and your integrity.

On a related note, leaders in large institutions must always balance formal processes and procedures with attending to the complexity of human beings. This pertains not only to an organization's employees but also to the people served by that organization. As a hospital administrator, Madeline reflected on the "creative tension" in the cancer center, the imperative to understand "where there needs to be that structure. For instance, you can't have ten different ways of deciding what imaging needs to happen for a particular cancer, right? So, unless you have some structure around that, you're going to have variation in both probably clinical outcomes or impact, but also in cost."

At the same time, she says, "each patient is different," and the question becomes "how much structure do you have to give you the best chance in cost and the quality. And then it's the freedom to navigate that, the nuances of how that happens for the individual patient, their condition, that physical, mental, emotional... how the impact of someone's mental health and emotions make a difference in their healing in their recovery." There's always a need, Madeline explains, "to delve into that human perception of what's been going on for them."

As these examples illustrate, effective leaders, even in high echelons of an organization, find ways to stay very connected to the fundamental human focus of the work of their organizations. Of course, this is also true of women who lead from the middle rungs of an organization, where there tend to be more positions and thus more opportunities to practice leadership and to enact change. As always, a culture of support helps. Rita Sever, author of *Leading for Justice*, talks about how important it is for middle managers to be supported, for example, by creating regular meeting space for them to talk about issues at their level.[117] A culture like the one Tina has co-created with the people who work with her promotes this kind of multi-level mutuality.

Gina, a director in what has long been a male-dominated field—the dairy industry—knows what it means to be supported at the middle levels of an organization and to have that support come from above. Her department is full of women, including her supervisor, one of the few women vice presidents in the company. Reflecting on their relationship, Gina says, "There's a personal connection there that I haven't had with previous supervisors... I told her about how I was doing this interview with you, and she was just so excited... She's such a champion of empowering women." Her supervisor is, she said, "a little powerhouse of a woman. It's funny, we talk together a lot. We hit it off immediately and I think a big piece of it is that we are so much like each other. Even though, historically, we share very little in common about where we come from and our upbringing. But we somehow have come to this very similar place and lives we're doing very similar work, very similar personalities and value very similar things." This supervisor has also built a specific team culture that nurtures Gina's own leadership style. She continues:

> We're all very strong. I wouldn't say they're all as outspoken as me, but we're all very much on the same page with just making sure that the things that are important to us in our department and our [organization] are represented across the board, regardless of the type of work that we do... We're kind of this force of women and it's awesome to be a part of it and to be able to lean on each other too. Because I know that we experience things in different ways.

While some of her team are mostly office-based, Gina toggles back and forth between their safe departmental environment, where she has a leadership position, and frontline regulatory work with male plant managers, some of whom she says have "ginormous egos." She has to calibrate her communication in a kind of gendered dance between male-typed old school agriculture—" guys that have been in dairy a really, really long time before any of this regulation and oversight even existed"—and being the female face of government regulation. "Sometimes you just have to be forceful, matter of fact, this is how it is. You know, sometimes you can be a little more delicate in the approach so that you don't raise anybody's hackles and still be effective. It's just really interesting how you have to navigate that landscape." Gina enjoys the challenge and says she's "well suited" to the work.

Gina is very intentional about translating the good leadership from which she benefits into her own work as a manager, and she appreciates how all of this flows from feeling valued: "I don't feel like I need to be quiet, or I'll be hushed or whatever because I am loud, so that helps I suppose. But then the other piece of that is—outside of wanting to be valued and respected—the other piece of that is I just always want to be a good human in life and where I work. And I think that has been, I don't want to say hard, but it's been a focal point of my life, especially since I had direct reports." As discussed previously, this translates into very intentional support for her employees' balancing acts with work and life.

"MANAGING UP":
Education Across Hierarchies for
Workplace Transformation

No matter where you are in a workplace hierarchy, you may be able to create opportunities to "manage up." As your networks, institutional knowledge, and competencies expand, if your organization has room for new ideas, you can find a space for your voice to be heard, to be a thought leader, a mentor, or an ally. All of these are facets of transformational, values-based leadership.

Mary, for example, spent a good deal of her career in Human Resources, never at a director level, vice president, or executive level. But she didn't need a title at that level to be a leader in her organization in making organizational change. Mary's approach to change was always grounded in learning and listening to people's experiences. Interested in cultural diversity from the time she was young (she served with a mission group in the red-light district in Amsterdam), Mary was very intentional about learning from people who were willing to share their cultural experiences. A white woman, Mary, jumped at the chance to attend the White Privilege Conference in her community and eventually joined the board of a community diversity organization, where she developed her capacity to advocate for building inclusive communities at work and beyond.

Through seeking out a sort of re-education process for herself, she rethought how Western models of leadership are social constructions and can be challenged, thanks to what a Dakota Sioux person shared about leadership. Through ongoing learning, Mary also continually reconsidered what it meant to help others, especially as she later transitioned into a more human services role in the community. In that role, she focused on "coming alongside" people, decolonizing her thinking about how to help in a humble and respectful way. "You can show people resources and provide information, but 'fixing' was not your job." Mary exemplifies the ways that lifelong learning and self-reflection can continually improve the way we can bring our values to work with a grounding in cultural humility.

While she was still in her HR role, Mary took on projects she could do at her level, including changing some of the imagery of her organization around race, ethnicity, and gender. Mary's work advancing disability access in her organization was impactful. It resulted in significant structural improvements to the buildings as well as greater awareness of diversity and interpreting services. But the impact went beyond policy change and into culture change. Within HR, Mary pushed away from the idea of compliance and from preoccupation with the question, "What do we need to do to not get sued?" Instead, she advocated for creating inclusive spaces and being attentive to diverse needs. These days, she said, "No one says, 'What do we need to do for compliance?'" They're thinking more about serving various groups, for example through translating key public-facing documents.

Anti-discrimination laws, Mary says, can sometimes give organizations an incentive. "Laws are helpful in our country in that we can now, if they're paying discriminatory wages, we can take them to court. But that is costly to the victim." Laws, she says, are just "the backbone" for when something goes wrong. Because of the law, organizations are told, "Here's your goals; don't discriminate. Don't harass, all of those things." But "how many places in the United States, how many businesses have all of those laws set up that say you can't sexually harass, and how much is it still happening?"

For Mary, "it's all about culture. And what's important is the training and educating of those leaders, and how you're letting voices be heard, and the culture you set up." Creating that "resilient system" includes making space for challenging voices as well as training people on interventions. When something is problematic, "Are you saying something? You have to have leaders understanding what they need to say and saying it." It means empowering people at all levels. "We can empower all our leaders," Mary says. But "when something happens, it's often other team members that have to support a team member," and so "you have to empower your team."

Organizational leaders at every level, Mary says, need to think about "how can we look beyond compliance and into really making it work and making people feel respected." In her vision for this kind of culture, Mary drew on her past experiences and role models, including a male mentor at work who had "a passion for treating people well. When I think of an equitable place, I think of him and how he led. So many women [who worked with him] would have told you that they felt respected, they felt heard, and they felt safe."

Mary was especially gratified by the impact of work she did in the creation of a mentoring program for young people interested in her industry. Like so many other rewarding and impactful projects that energize our careers, this one came out of seeing an important need and deciding that if she didn't figure out how to fill that need, perhaps no one would. "There came a point where I realized it wasn't going to happen unless I took it on," she says. "And so, I walked into my performance appraisal and was asked, what do you want to do next year? And I said I want to do this." Her director agreed, other people got excited, and the project quickly gained momentum. Because of advocacy leadership like Mary's, not only are people working in or served by the organization treated better; there is also a positive impact on other advocates: Mary noted that as a result of this program, "I've seen other things blossom and bloom and other folks come into their own."

Through her advocacy leadership, Mary became a known resource for others and became aware that she advanced values important to inclusion that others appreciated. She had shown people what was possible and was creating new thought leaders in the organization based on her work.

QUESTIONING ARBITRARY DIVISIONS

Women leaders at any level, and their allies, can think critically about who benefits from the divisions, categories, procedures, and titles created by institutions and traditions that were created long before they arrived. One arbitrary division is the one between our workplaces and our communities. Bridging this division allows the resources of employers to add more value to the communities where they do business. Some of the women I interviewed enhanced their overall profile and contributions as leaders by embracing the creative disruption of those boundaries in impactful ways.

In my three-year stint as executive director of the Greater La Crosse Area Diversity Council, thanks to some wonderful mentorship from others, I learned a great deal about how porous these boundaries are. I learned more about how much this mattered to people of color in a mostly white community and in mostly white workplaces. Professionals of color who work in the hospitals, schools, universities, and companies in a medium-size town like ours also often raise their families in these communities. If their children experience racism in the schools, this can impact how they feel about the whole package of living and working in a particular situation. If their relatives visit the community where they're making a home, and those relatives do not feel welcome, this too can have an impact. The professionals themselves need to shop, get healthcare, purchase homes, and live in neighborhoods, navigating spaces beyond the workplace. Similarly, LGBTQ+ colleagues can face spaces that can feel unwelcoming or even hostile in the community, impacting how they feel about working in a community.

As Mary said, "we have to work really hard at making sure that people belong [at work] ... and we have to do it even harder in the community." This is why Mary spanned the boundaries of workplace and career by serving as a workplace representative in community DEI work, by bringing in thought leaders on DEI topics through her work with a community professional association, and by joining community learning initiatives like the White Privilege conference. Making our community spaces welcoming, diverse, and inclusive impacts the ability of anchoring employers in medium-sized communities to retain their talent and to help that talent flourish and contribute.

My interviewees who had influence over hiring and promotion continuously looked for ways to make their organizations reflect more of the diversity that did exist in the community. Some of the most innovative thinkers saw and built these connections. As previously discussed, Madeline, in her vice president role, regularly engaged in work that helped her healthcare organization meet the needs of diverse communities, including newcomers from the global population shifts that are part of so many cities today. When I asked if it was hard to balance community work like this with her designated administrative duties, she said, "I do try and balance my time and my energy but no. I just look at it as: it's my work. It's my life's work."

Madeline was a tireless advocate and learner, on a journey at the time of our interview to learn more about the LGBTQ+ community. But even with her high position at work, she felt somewhat discouraged by her workplace's lack of acknowledgment of racial issues beyond the workplace itself: "I never talk about any type of a tribal or discriminatory situation, even with George Floyd. May he rest in peace." Madeline was involved in national organizations that were "wanting to come forward with different statements of support" in the wake of George Floyd's murder at the hands of Minneapolis police. "It was a no brainer." Yet, "The response of my organization was something internal; it wasn't external, and the internal message was certainly fine. But it was—what more could the organization I work for do?"

A few weeks later, a physician approached Madeline and said, "'I think we should be doing something.' He happened to be a white male. 'I don't disagree with you. Where do you think you need to go with that?' Indeed, he took it up. But nothing happened with it."

Though Madeline is active on racial justice issues within her organization, she says she stops short of commenting on issues like this beyond the immediate workplace, "Because I think it could be misconstrued being a person of color wanting to discuss it versus somebody who is non-Native or not Black talking about the situation. But I can tell you that as soon as I knew the Washington [team]　announced their name change, I texted my husband and son and said, 'Do you believe this?'"

Madeline's story is a reminder of how people with marginalized identities do not leave those identities at the door when they go to work. Indeed, Madeline noted that in the predominantly white community where she lived, white people often seemed to think that "everything is fine," while "for people of color there's a different experience." Even highly positioned leaders can face the challenges and burdens of self-policing speech and frustrations about arbitrary boundaries between workplace, community, and the world. My interview with Madeline took place well before the anti-DEI backlash of Donald Trump's second term.

In today's instant news environment, in which various communities can instantly learn of and try absorbing news of identity-based violence, chilling executive orders, or other disturbing events, compartmentalization is a myth. If we can learn from the leadership of people like Madeline and Mary, we can begin to incorporate that idea of mutable boundaries between workplace and communities, these false and problematic compartmentalization of "the world" and "the workplace" can be challenged in ways that promote better mental health for everyone. Together we can carry on with the work through these long-standing commitments, even in the face of a hostile backlash.

In another situation, Erin used her awareness of racial inequity and her white privilege to ask critical questions about how larger political events might be impacting employees. During the "Unite the Right" summer of 2017, Erin found the absolute silence at work "jarring," she says. Having previously worked professionally in higher education, she says that in that kind of space, people would have done the processing around "What does this mean for us as humans and also in our roles?"

Erin broke the silence in her company in 2017, connecting with a handful of people at work with whom she could have those conversations, and then going to her supervisor to ask about creating a space for processing around racial justice. The supervisor invited her to provide leadership on the issue from her learning and development coordinator position, an answer which she found less than satisfying. Still, Erin continued work from within her team and circles of influence to develop conversations, vocabulary, and ally and advocacy networks around racial justice in her workplace, in a way that acknowledged the porous boundaries between the workplace and the wider world. Leadership through challenging arbitrary boundaries and expanding organizations' missions into the civic realm is yet another kind of contribution that can be lifted up.

None of these women work in or create perfect systems. They are all complicated human beings and imperfect leaders. But they use their leadership, as advocates, as positional authorities/managers, as thought leaders, as educators, and as allies, with wisdom, acting from their values. The opportunity to carve out key areas of efficacy through our values can be the secret sauce to creating chapters in our career where enough pieces are in place, where we feel good about our work and our contributions. Hopefully, the people who work with us are positively impacted by the spaces we're helping create.

The above stories remind us of the necessity of making visible and fighting for the value of the work done by and on behalf of women and/or people of color/queer people and social justice. Consider the value of your own work as a values-driven person, and the work of social justice initiatives or units within your organization, and female-dominated areas of your workplace, like customer service or community outreach, whether you're part of them or not. Who is amplifying that value? With whom can you find community when these values are under siege? How could reconsidering resources and language make it possible for you and your work allies to better show the value of the work that embodies your values? No matter where you work in the organization, how can you be part of amplifying the value of that work?

A SAMPLE OF INITIATIVES TO PROMOTE AN EQUITABLE WORKPLACE

▸ Mentoring and sponsorship opportunities, including formal mentoring programs with training

▸ Returnship programs to help people transition back into the workforce, to support people through the ebb and flow of family and community needs

▸ Employee engagement surveys to assess and address issues of inclusion, belonging, and opportunities for advancement, to get more ideas for what all of these "investing in your people" initiatives could look like and how they could really serve people's needs

▸ Diversity, Equity, and Inclusion committees, or if necessary, committees with more subtle names, like Belonging and Community. If your organization doesn't have one, you might start one, and make sure it contains an empowered network of champions who represent every part of the organization, and who have the funding and other support they need to succeed.

▸ Structures that incentivize, lift up, and provide resources and voices at many critical tables for DEI thought leaders and activists

▸ Reading groups around anti-racism and other social justice issues

▸ Proactive policies and procedures around celebrating diverse holidays, community needs, ongoing health needs, and veterans' obligations

- Leadership development strategy that includes an in-depth assessment of what leadership contributions and competencies can look like, and what kinds of biases might be keeping leadership pipelines too homogenous

- Pay equity: study and implementation committees and action plans

- Work-life friendly policies, conceptualized broadly and inclusively

- Celebration of remote workers' accomplishments and help them stay integrated

- Community engagement initiatives, including considering how large employers' local giving can reflect a restorative relationship with marginalized communities and can empower leaders working on issues like LGBTQ+, racial, and gender justice

- Task forces on credentialing, hiring, and performance review criteria, including attention to the transparency of processes and the rates of advancement for women, people of color, and other marginalized groups

- Support for and engagement with union initiatives around equity

- Language equity task forces, including for employee handbook and all workplace policies

- Communication channels for regular feedback loops

As the many stories in this section show, when empowered and centered, social justice leaders at any "level" of an organization take the long view, the holistic view. They see how systems intertwine with one another. They are lifelong learners. They mentor better than they were mentored. They create belonging for themselves and others, as part of contributing to workplaces where more people can thrive and contribute.

As you move through the decades of mid-career, you can continue to anchor in your values to work with authenticity as a means to navigate shifting challenges and opportunities. You can and will be a leader if you do this. If you know your own contribution as a leader, regardless of position, you are in a good place to amplify the diverse leadership contributions of others.

PART III
THE THIRD CHAPTER

*Adapting, Leaving A Legacy,
and Building Bridges Across
Generations*

CHAPTER 9

THE THIRD CHAPTER

Reflecting on Your Career Moment

LIKE SO MANY OF US, by the time I reached my early 50s, I could look back with some pride, satisfaction, and a little bit of awe at how very hard I had worked over the years that had quickly become decades, and what I had accomplished in my career, even while balancing so many commitments. Sure, there were deep disappointments, missed opportunities, mistakes, and some wounds that had not fully healed. But on balance, I knew I'd been fortunate. I'd done many things I'd dreamed of doing in the decades of academic toil, contributions in teaching, grant administration, activism, research and publication, leadership, and community and nonprofit work.

But also, like so many of us, I was tired and confused about the emerging final chapter of my full-time career life. Looking back from that early 50s perch, I hardly recognized the younger version of myself. Who was that woman in her 30s who had driven a minivan from the country home and dropped off kids at three different schools every day while her spouse was in nursing school, only to begin a long day of teaching and/or working on a lengthy book manuscript, or strategizing about the next stages of the large grants I ran during the 2000s? I did all that while trying to strike the right balance of involvement with necessary department and university politics and duties, not to mention the needs of my kids.

I was also unsure of what my options were for the remaining years of my professional life. As I mentioned earlier, my friend had already primed the pump by making me think about being "at the peak" of my career. What could I do with that peak, I wondered? Or was the other side of that peak already here? After all, it was clear that many 40-somethings were now the rising stars on my campus, being tapped for institutionally centered leadership positions that had somehow eluded me, or I had avoided. Which was it? For years, I had "looked up" in my little campus environment and not seen many positionally placed leaders, especially women, who seemed empowered to both live their values and have some sense of peace versus constant overwhelm.

For the most part, the higher positional roles (Dean, Associate Dean, etc.) hadn't appealed to me, and I preferred leading grants with external funding, doing my own research and projects, taking on special projects, like faculty fellow for grant advancement, or even sidelining into nonprofit leadership, and eventually embracing the department chair role But my potential institutional leadership growth had also not been encouraged or cultivated. Although I'd created other opportunities for myself, I'd still done a LOT of teaching, and I was dead tired of grading papers and preparing so many lectures. I was having a hard time keeping up with the rapid-fire changes in how we talked and taught about social justice in the Trump era, and how we were supposed to help students with their mental health and social anguish in the changing world. The department chair leadership I was doing had many rewards, but it also sometimes drained me. By my early 50s, I was beginning to imagine fewer commitments, especially at a moment when I was leading a department and a nonprofit. After three years of service, I passed the leadership torch in the nonprofit role, and I was actually beginning to envision an end to my time as an academic. I wondered how many years I had left in this environment, and what my legacy would be when I was gone.

One thought kept coming through, loud and clear: At my age and stage, I wanted and felt that I deserved less heavy lifting and more consulting. After all, I had long since proven myself professionally. And personally, I was still reeling from having had (stage zero) breast cancer three years earlier, a diagnosis and treatment process that had overlapped with my first semester balancing leading the Diversity Council with my ongoing university work.

The path towards that ideal of less heavy lifting/more consulting was easier said than done. As it would happen, my heavy lifting years were definitely not over, not with all the crises going on in higher education, not with COVID-19, and not with a workplace context where I lacked mentors and role models (besides my peers, who were struggling with similar issues). Sometimes when we think we're done with something, it's not done with us, not least of the reasons being the need to keep a salary coming in from a position that has some security. In my case, I had three kids in college over these years.

Nevertheless, the intentionality I felt around where I wanted to go was a guiding light. It helped me set boundaries in the midst of intense periods of work, including a ramped-up final leadership project for me at the university: overseeing the merger of two academic departments. This intentionality helped me see that it was now appropriate for me to use that consulting/sharing emphasis to sow the seeds of what I wanted to leave behind, in academia in particular, but in my career overall. I wanted to be intentional with my remaining years of giving my talents to the world. I also wanted to lean into mentoring, driven not only by a need to be useful and relevant, but also by curiosity and love and concern for upcoming generations.

This intentionality also helped me say no sometimes (though not always). It helped me own my industry and institutional knowledge, and quite frankly, my wisdom. It also helped me take stock of what the rapidly fleeting decades of my early and mid-career had meant: what legacies I had left, what legacies I might still be in the process of creating, and how I might stay open to making a meaningful difference in the world as I kept moving into real elderhood.

How can we keep the energy flowing across generations as our roles and identities shift in later career? What does it mean to leave a legacy of whatever kind of leadership we have embraced in our careers? What are the possibilities of the final decades of paid work in our fields? And how can all of us, at any age, support and leverage the value of older women? After all, as Aviva Wittenberg-Cox noted in *Harvard Business Review*: "We are moving into a world where there are going to be proportionately many, many more older humans than we've ever, as a species, experienced before. What they want and need, how they live and behave, who and what they vote for, and what they actually do with all those extra years, will affect everyone."[118]

More and more older workers are in the workforce. And they often want (or just need) to stay there. Overall, people over 65 are the fastest growing segment of the workforce, and that age group is projected to continue to grow as a share of the working population.[119] The Great Recession set back people's retirements. The decline of defined pension plans and shifting Social Security benefits have also led to increased retirement ages for Americans. Pew Research reported in 2023 "the older workforce has nearly quadrupled in size since the mid-1980s."[120]

Women's career-long pattern of lower earnings can certainly contribute to that need to stay. And their earnings decline can begin earlier than men's. According to PayScale, "Women reach their peak earnings at the age of 44, earning on average $66,700. Men reach their peak earnings at the age of 55, earning on average $101,200."[121] The last chapter of a career has its own patterns of sexism.

Yet this older workforce is an important asset to employers. Compared to previous cohorts of older workers, today's employees are healthier, allowing for more longevity in the workforce, and highly educated, a trait that is correlated with staying in the workforce. Add to that, the global "demographic winter" of declining birthrates and an aging population, and we can see how important the skills of older workers can be, filling important gaps in the labor market.[122]

LEADERSHIP AND LEGACY FOR OLDER WOMEN WORKERS

By now, we have unpacked this concept of leadership, acknowledging that leadership happens at all levels and at all stages of career. As your career advances, you're likely leaving many leadership impacts, including signature projects, policies, and perhaps the creation of new programs and networks. Maybe you've created tangible things (publications, programs, new roles in an organization) that have significant staying power. Maybe some of what you created got lost in budget cuts, corporate mergers, or other changes. You may not be sure what your imprint has been, and truthfully, you'll never fully know.

A bright spot of living in today's age of professional discourse is the way people frequently quote Maya Angelou in talking about leadership: "I've learned that people will forget what you said, people will forget what you did, but people will never forget how you made them feel." As Angelou reminds us, you can leave a legacy at any stage of your career in the most unforgettable, and I would argue, most important way: "how you make people feel." Because if you make people feel that they belong, and if you make them feel that you are a collaborator or co-conspirator in advancing humane values in the workplace and beyond, you're planting seeds. If you make people in power feel uncomfortable at times, with your challenging ideas, that too is planting seeds and potentially providing necessary disruptive energy in the direction of transformation. Even if things don't change quickly, perhaps someone else who heard you ask that question does pay attention, and their thinking and actions are reshaped. If you've been a career-long courageous leader, you've made a difference in your workplace culture, and in the sense of possibilities of people coming up behind you.

The networks of older women are often wide and deep, though some can be diminished by the loss of peers and older colleagues who retire or move away. Older women can bring hard-earned and deeply informed presence to advanced leadership roles. Most have a greater interest in leaving a legacy at work, regardless of whether they keep moving up a ladder. They may long to protect the programs or initiatives where they have given years of their energy. Many are also interested in nurturing upcoming generations, helping them develop as leaders for the next chapter of the work.

It can be hard for many older women to recognize their accomplishments, in part because of ageism and the present-crisis thinking that tends to infuse workplace norms. Smart organizations, and smart colleagues in general, can help support older women, empowering them to grow and claim their legacies, while tapping into their hard-won wisdom to inform approaches to current challenges and growth opportunities.

Seasoned women professionals (generally 50 or older) must adapt to new challenges in the last stage of their career while seeking to name and claim their own legacies and opportunities. Meanwhile, some may be reckoning with realizing that their career advancement, in the formal sense, has gone as far as it will go. Some may be shifting sideways into consultant roles or moving into more community involvement. Some may be downshifting as grandparenting, other elder care responsibilities, health needs, or simply long-neglected passions and interests call for their attention.

Regardless of the decisions (or necessary shifts) about the configurations of their working lives, the older women I interviewed and so many others I have worked with tend to be practical and wise. They're adept at using all that they have learned and cultivated through their intentional workplace presence, projects, values, and hard work, to model worthwhile possibilities for others. They are often engaged in intergenerational bridge-building, even as they are reflecting on and taking pride in the value of their many years in the workforce.

Because my in-depth interviews for this project were a small cohort and were diverse in age, only a handful of the women I interviewed were in the later stages of their full-time careers. The words of wisdom of these seasoned women professionals are highlighted here as a way to explore leaving a legacy and thriving through what Dr. Sarah Lawrence-Lightfoot wisely calls the "third chapter" of life, and by extension, career.[123] I offer them not as an authoritative examination of how older, values-driven women navigate the "third chapter" of their careers, but rather as a coda on a larger story of intergenerational wisdom as it accrues over time. The insights and the practices of these women can be understood as resources for intergenerational awareness and bridge building in service to the values highlighted throughout this book.

MOVING THROUGH THE CHALLENGES OF THE THIRD CHAPTER

In a historical moment when generational change is rapid-fire, it can really be a gut punch for women who have been contributing and leading for so many years when they begin to feel overlooked or considered somewhat less relevant or nimble. Lee's experience, for example, prompted her to do some reflective writing on how these attitudes showed up at a particular stage of her journey in her 50s. She recalled:

> In my workplace, which I joined at age 55, I noticed a subtle yet undeniable "coolness" in how team members interacted with me. I believe this is largely because I joined one of the more innovative teams at the large hospital where I work: the team responsible for

the development of our mobile app. This naturally draws the younger, more innovative thinkers – mobile app developers, UX designers, and tech-savvy project managers. I am literally old enough to be the mother of some of them, and I'm sure they subconsciously placed me in that category the moment I walked into the room.

Imagined or not, my sense is that I was assumed to know less about the frontiers of digital products and to be less able to produce innovation. It took some time to prove my ability and experience, even though I came back to this organization after four years working with some of the health startup industry's most talented "code-slingers" and product developers, as the content and behavior design lead for this health management startup.

Lee's experience is not unique. Sexist-inflected ageism can sometimes prevent others from seeing the new kinds of value older women may be adding in these years. Ageism is real, and its intersection with sexism can be demoralizing. One study that queried 10,000 companies, asking whether age is "a competitive advantage or competitive disadvantage in your organization" showed that more than two-thirds of the companies regarded older age as a disadvantage.[124]

Women may be surprised by ageism because we may have been told throughout our careers that we're too young (to supervise, to lead, etc.) only to be given the subtle signal that now we're suddenly too old. As Amy Diehl, Leanne M. Dzubinski, and Amber L. Stephenson reported in *Harvard Business Review*, "Gendered ageism sits at the intersection of age and gender bias and is a double whammy where there is 'no right age' for professional women." The authors' study of 913 women in four different U.S. industries found that perceptions of age had negatively impacted women across the span of their careers. "In our research we found no age was the right age to be a woman leader. There was always an age-based excuse to not take women seriously, to discount their opinions, or to not hire or promote them. But for women over 60, there was a special inflection."[125]

As one of the physicians in this study observed, "While men become wells of wisdom as they age, older women are seen as outdated, harpy, strident." Older women in the study frequently reported feeling discounted, ignored, no longer invested in, and "discouraged, burnt out, and resigned to not advancing any further." One college leader noted that some hiring committees discriminated against women in their late 40s because of perceived family responsibilities, while also suggesting that "women in their fifties and sixties may not have 'aged well' and do not 'look vital.' Yet the jobs were given to similarly aged men."[126]

On the one hand, we live in an era when some aging women command the national stage in ways that would have been inconceivable to these same women when they were young. I think of Kamala Harris, Nancy Pelosi, Janet Yellen, Angela Merkel, Oprah Winfrey, or the many actresses, like Helen Mirren and Maggie Smith working into their elderhood. And we do have some legal protections for older workers, notably the Age Discrimination in Employment Act of 1967, which protects people over 40 from employment discrimination on the basis of age in hiring, promotion, discharge, compensation, or terms, conditions or privileges of employment. On the other hand, research shows that inflexibility and top-down leadership drive many women, and their talents and institutional wisdom, right out of the workplace. According to *Lean In*, "For every woman at the director level who gets promoted, two women directors are choosing to leave their company."[127]

It doesn't help that the overall needs of older women workers (and older workers in general) rarely receive attention. I mentioned my own lack of mentoring "from above" in my mid and late career, because I have found that it is a structural issue, all too common in academia as well as in other spaces. It's something I see with my peers and colleagues, and in my coaching practice today. People tend to lose mentors as they age, and that can add to the challenges of the last decade or so of intense, often full-time professional life.

Madeline, for example, in her late 50s at the time of our interview, observed: "I think now that I'm at the age I am, and professionally having worked as long as I have, I'm seeing less of my elders that I would reach out to as leaders. They're retiring, they're at their cabins...So professionally it's not a stark landscape, but definitely a landscape that changed, it's not as profuse with other leaders around that same sense of either wanting to dialogue or learn in that way."

Claire, though still in her forties, grieved the day-to-day presence of female mentors who had recently moved on or retired, while she herself was negotiating the complexities of a relatively new associate director-level role. These days, she said, "I often feel like the only woman [and] I'm often the only queer person in the room. That's why I'm really sad about [the person one-level-above-her leader] retiring, because her presence was really important to me." With another senior-level colleague (also queer-identified) having recently retired as well, Claire said "I've been left by all my female mentors now really." Without their presence, she sometimes doubted herself: She wondered, "Can I show up for [younger people] the ways that other people who showed up for me" while still executing all the duties of her job? "I'm still uncertain about that."

That said, Claire was fortunate that one of these leaders, a former supervisor who had been "very formative" for her, still lived in the area. When they had worked together, Claire said, this supervisor had invested time and deep attention in her. "She would come into my office and stick her little, short feet on my desk and take the time to talk to me. And that was important. And she's still doing that!" Claire was thrilled that this person "hasn't stopped mentoring me even though she's retired. She's still like, 'Hey, how are you doing?' I think that relational work is something that I'm trying to make sure that I hold onto as well."

This story is one illustration of why we need to think about what it means to tap into and amplify the wisdom of our women elders, to not let them (or us, if we're the elders) fade into obscurity in the final decade or two of their careers. There is so much that older women workers can bring to the table: their expansive networks and connections, to which they help link younger people, their opportunities to see systems and potential for innovations in new ways, the security some of them have that allows them to leverage their power to help younger people make change in the workplace, and their hard-earned perspectives on a myriad of issues.

STAYING, SHIFTING, GROWING, SHARING:
Opportunities of the Third Career Chapter

In spite of the exodus of many older women workers, others are finding ways to stay and thrive, leveraging the values and propensity for connection and learning that have driven their whole careers. It helps when they're supported by their team members. Connie, for example, worked hard at being an active learner as she aged, including staying up to date on new technology. She also continued to leverage her learning about effective management and about being a facilitator of constructive relationships in the workplace.

Embracing a role that more seasoned professionals often handle well, Connie learned how to step back and help mediate conflicts in the workplace. "I feel like I'm a better listener, and I learned that maybe a month ago." And after many years in some pretty rough and potentially damaging corporate environments, Connie was not moving in a direction of hardening herself or withdrawing. Instead, she insisted, "you need to show that you're vulnerable" at work, "to show you make mistakes, but then you recover." Connie lives out her philosophy that as we age, it's so important to "keep yourself open to learning." Indeed, being mentored by younger peo-

ple, not just being their mentor, can lead to rich and satisfying relationships.

What was gratifying about listening to Connie was that her energy
came from a place not of fear of being irrelevant or dismissed, but of genuine continuing passion for her work. She was able to take pride in her
ongoing learning. Because of her self-development, she said, she believed
she was a better manager during the COVID-19 crisis (which we were in
the thick of during our interview in 2020). "There's managers out there
that feel like they have to touch and feel people to know what they're working on...Well I was changing ours a little bit before [the pandemic] happened, using technology to communicate and things like that. And because I had to regroup myself, I felt like I had the time to focus on my
team," including biweekly check-ins remotely. "So, we have the tools in
place, and I absolutely love it now," she says. "I also understand people's
time," including a need for flexible hours. "If they have situations, it may
have bothered me years ago to be honest with you, but it doesn't now. If
they have a child and they have to do this and they're offline for two hours,
who cares?" Though Connie came through corporate America as a young
mother at a time when there was less flexibility for childcare, she made herself into the flexible leader she may well have benefited from when she was
younger.

Connie's team members fueled her fire. One woman who came to
Connie for coaching helped her feel good about what she can share: "I can
help other women...I can be there now and go, 'I get it, you are a woman,
you are strong. I get it.'" In fact, some members of Connie's team were
actively trying to retain her. "My team was really there for me." Seeing her
begin to "check out" a bit after a setback, "a couple of them came up and
said, you know we still need you."

Connie acknowledged that even now "I still have challenges being
heard, but I don't let them take me back from who I am." And she throws
herself into being a resource for others. "So maybe I'm not involved in this

area and maybe I really feel I could fix it." She tells herself, "Don't worry about it because if they need you, they'll come to you. Otherwise, there's plenty of other things that you know from your experience, what to do, how to help...I used to be involved in all the projects. I used to do all this stuff. I'm not anymore. That's his [her supervisor's] role. But the wonderful thing is now I have more time to coach my team, my staff." She takes pride in her experience and knowledge. She works closely with people in ways that she enjoys and takes on special projects to improve processes.

Lee's strategy, as she adapted to the youth-leaning and male-inflected world of technology in the healthcare communications realm, was to frame the situation in light of her own strengths and intentionality. "I am more interested in contributing to a greater whole from the position of my most important strengths," she says. In fact, from this mid-50s transition to mobile app work for her hospital, she went on to embrace a very energetic career revival in her early 60s at that same employer. Seizing the opportunity for a role that brought together many of her professional talents, Lee said she had "had a chance to build something new" late in her career. "I have just a huge opportunity," she said. "I am leading our multimedia efforts in the area of patient communication. And I get to help drive choice-making in how groups and individuals are represented. Pictures and visuals are just so critical. And it's so critical because [our organization] is perceived as a place that's 'not for' people that are from under-represented communities. So, we have a lot of ground to make up." Not surprisingly, this was the chance to bring Lee's years of expertise to the values of social equality, including the representation of race in healthcare imagery. The new work reinvigorated Lee and helped her ground in her own value in ways that leveraged her age and experience.

At age 62, Lee said that she was currently happy with how she and other older workers were valued as resources in her company. "We're the go-to people," she said. "We get things out of the way for people." The older workers smoothed the way in part because they had refined competencies beyond a particular work task. After all, as Lee said, "It takes a long time to learn how to communicate effectively."

As the above examples suggest, the women I interviewed confronted ageism with many of the same tools and mindsets they had used throughout their careers. They grounded in their values, cultivated curiosity and connections across differences, attended to shifting contexts and their place in them, and made themselves into continuing learners. They continued to embrace new conversations in a rapidly changing culture. They embraced humility, boundary-setting, self-awareness, and self-compassion, while not foreclosing new opportunities.

Women who flourish professionally in their 50s and 60s, and sometimes beyond, often have a deep sense of continuing an ethic of service while also continuing to set boundaries. They spend less energy trying to prove themselves because they recognize they have already done so. They spend more energy modeling and gently advising and mentoring and demonstrating respect for younger generations. They often need to learn to let go of being "leading edge" and having the most "relevant" or "up to date" answer for every problem, but they find ways to leverage what they do know.

And sometimes, they're fully coming into their power, and they know it. Age 54 at the time of our interview, Ronda was right to believe, as she long had, that she would be in her space of county government administration longer than many others. And she would keep working at the changes she hoped to make. "There have to be people who are willing to be in it for the long haul," she said. At this stage of the game, Ronda said she knew how to "use the people who are in power, including white men. Do I love that? No. I'm very pragmatic about it. Who can I get to do what I want?"

Ronda could look back and see how systems had slowly changed. One slow-moving hard-won win, for example, was community integration and support programming for women in the criminal justice system. At the time, this initiative had "caused a big community uproar. It was the only time in my entire career I thought there could be somebody who might actually do me physical harm." But looking back, she can say, "Wow! That was amazing! I did good stuff, right? But it's hard for me to see when I'm in the middle of it because it's never done. This work is never done. So...when I am working on something, it just feels imperfect all the time. But that's how change is and that's how systems change. There's the perfect way and then there's how it is and there's working to make it more perfect."

Ronda could now recognize what change-making took, including leveraging allies with power, building coalitions, bringing in experts, coordinating numerous departments, and continually finding ways to be responsive to and engaged with diverse communities. Not long after our interview, Ronda moved from being Associate County Administrator to the top position, County Administrator, after her long-time supervisor retired. She continued to expand her platform and leverage the long and deep connections she had made by staying the course over decades in government service work.

While some women are upshifting, some are stepping sideways into mentoring, and some are also reaching outward into projects that build bridges between workplace and community. Sometimes women over 50 or over 60 are feeling the freedom of diminished responsibilities, allowing them to grow professionally in new ways. This was Lee's situation when she took on leading-edge technology work in a large hospital at age 55, and Madeline's when she moved into a vp role in her hospital in her early 50s. Mary, meanwhile, completed a degree at age 59 in theology and worked her way into community ministry work. Mary said she stayed energized through her faith and through ongoing opportunities to "make a difference" through her work, even as the nature of that work would begin to shift. Within two years of our interview, she moved from her HR role to a small community ministry, where she practiced "coming alongside" people with significant challenges of poverty and encounters with the criminal justice system. Mary kept her faith-based continual learner social justice orientation, combined with decades of real-world wisdom, and leveraged her gifts in her new community role.

TAKING STOCK

▶ In what ways are you coming into your power? This may not mean institutional power. It could mean something else. What does it mean to you?

▶ How can you use that power, whatever it is, for good?

▶ How have you and how could you support younger women trying to use their voices and access institutional resources to transform workplaces, de-emphasize hierarchy, and create diverse, equitable, and inclusive workplaces?

▶ How have your priorities shifted in the past 5-10 years? Take stock of past projects and responsibilities and consider what has changed.

▶ List your current responsibilities and do a gut check about how each one makes you feel.

▶ List your current life commitments, sources of joy, responsibilities, and longings, and consider what is pulling you in directions beyond the workplace.

▶ Are you still trying to prove yourself at work? Still doing more than your share of heavy lifting?

▶ Could you delegate some tasks that would allow other, less senior people, some learning and growth, while tending to the projects and responsibilities that feel good, energizing, and growth oriented?

▶ What have been your proudest moments in your career?

▶ What situations have brought out your best with respect to nurturing others, helping them feel a sense of belonging, and helping them grow?

▶ In what ways have you "left a legacy" in the various chapters of your career and how does this legacy advance social change values?

▶ What have you learned from the times you have been thwarted, marginalized, and felt ineffective?

▶ How does reviewing these themes help you consider where you really want to go in the final decade or two of your career? Are you looking to expand your responsibilities, keep them about the same, shift the overall work landscape without increasing or decreasing responsibilities, or are you ready to consider downshifting to allow more space for other life needs?

▶ Are you interested in building something new in your career? Taking on a new role?

▶ Are you interested in expanding your positional leadership and leveraging the salary possibilities of your experience through more responsibility?

▶ Can you find ways to work across generations in ways that feel generative and connected?

▶ What next steps could you take to move in the direction you're longing to go at this stage of your life and career?

CHAPTER 10

BUILDING BRIDGES
ACROSS GENERATIONS

Creating Connections Across Generations

IN THIS CULTURAL MOMENT, we find a lot of humor that points to friction among generations in the workplace. Cultural memes sometimes do this in ways that rightly draw attention to the economic generational privileges that were more widespread in the Baby Boomer generation. But the thinly veiled resentment in some of the intergenerational humor sometimes suggests that we have nothing to learn from one another, only slightly amusing exasperation to pass along in our cultural currency.[128]

These tropes obscure important truths. Not only have my years as an educator shown me over and over again how much respect and appreciation younger women often have for older ones, and for women's history in general, but I also see a lot of evidence that the respect can go both ways. Researchers Ken Dychtwald, Robert Morison, and Katy Terveer point out: "AARP has found that a large majority (70%) of Americans like to work with colleagues of various ages, and in our research more than eight in 10 U.S. workers across all generations say they wish older and younger people took more time to learn from one another."

Older women I interviewed showed both curiosity and high regard for younger generations. Indeed, they were often building their professional identities around a kind of humble but confident elderhood. They were positioning themselves as resources AND as learners, using the habits, dispositions, and values orientation they had practiced over a lifetime to remain relevant and useful, in spite of the ageism of our culture and/or of individual workplaces.

Though they had plenty of wisdom and had earned the right to take pride in their own competencies and approaches, the older women I interviewed expressed awe about young people. Mary remembers listening to a woman about 10-15 years younger on a phone call, noticing her "standing up for herself," and thinking "Could I do that?" Another young woman in her orbit reminded her about the possibility of being very "clear" in communication. Mary was "taught to be nice and kind. And you don't think being clear is being kind. But it is." These encounters are a reminder that "we can learn from any generation."

Claire, too, admired younger women's directness and sense of entitlement to take up space, and to reach out across hierarchical divisions within an organization. Madeline noticed that "the younger generation are much more versatile" than women her age. "They come to work and try new things."

We've lived through times of change so rapid that those of us who are older are often bewildered, while young people, like their Baby Boom counterparts in the 1960s, feel the urgency of a "world on fire," and a frustration and sometimes despair about the cruelties of racism, colonialism, and other historic systems whose violence is exposed before our eyes. It is not for us to tell young people to wait, and hope things get better. Indeed, we should be fired up by their urgency as much as possible, while also understanding that we may have limitations in our capacities (emotional, physical, and otherwise) to participate in social change in the same ways that younger people do.

Younger people can also learn from history, including the history of their elders, that while some change is rapid, other kinds of changes are the result of years and years of advocacy and coalition building. Ronda, for example, reflected:

> I think when I was younger, I was very short-term oriented, like immediate. And I think that could be just part of being young. Now I am much more [interested in] what's the long-term effect? I am always future-focused. Where can we go? What can we be like? How can we be better? I don't dwell very much on mistakes except to try to learn from them...When I do look back and realize things that were accomplished, I realize it just takes years for something to really change. And if something does change really quickly, I think it's magical that it happens. It does happen once in a while but usually change happens over a very long period of time.

Recent rapid change in county government and community relationships had happened with the help of Ronda's leadership. She wished she and others had been better equipped earlier to confront racism in communities with the tools that they were using at the time of our interview in 2020, and certainly people of color in the community also wished that more of their concerns had been centered years earlier. Ronda tried to focus on the positive and look forward. In the years leading up to our interview, in part through her Associate County Administrator leadership role, government ties with community organizations had significantly increased, the county was responding to "disproportionate minority contact in the criminal justice system" in ways that she hoped would "have ripple effects into the adult system." At this point, she said, "I think that we have enough people who are interested that it's going to make a difference." And soon, "we are going to hit our stride." Ronda expected to be right there pushing things along, with no plans to step away from the work.

When asked what advice she'd give young people, Madeline spoke first about what she loved about them, how she marveled at "their fast pace, the conversation, and the technology." Sometimes, though, she felt that young people could "spend a little more time at that job or take a little more time, to anchor in a bit, more than kind of skipping on the pond so to speak."

But ultimately, Madeline's advice was about trusting themselves and honoring their own contributions and gifts: "I really believe that your journey is yours," she said. She encouraged young people to "not only look at what you're getting from that experience or that situation," but also recognize that "it's also what you're giving back. So how are you influencing and how are you sharing part of yourself? Because it's a two-way street. Sometimes you think you're there to learn from [the more experienced colleagues] and in fact, they are there to learn from you and sometimes it's the other way around."

Our workplaces can facilitate intergenerational connections (even while navigating the intensified intergenerational tensions of this historical moment) and offer generation-specific opportunities for older women to leverage their many gifts and talents.

Connie's advice for younger women was succinct: "Be true to yourself...There's nothing wrong with who you are. You just have to learn to channel it in this business world. That's all. That's it. It's really that simple. Everybody walks in and thinks they have to make all these changes and do all these things. There's a plethora of tools for you. Go out there and play in that big sandbox and figure it out."

Connie remembers her own learning from a previous generation, when she was in her 20s. Her employer's son-in-law was her supervisor. This man had reprimanded her for talking to a fellow employee "for 20 minutes," which he said was too long. Connie had countered that she was salaried, and she worked long hours. Though she stood up for herself, the encounter left her shaken. Connie says she "reached out to an older generation person there." Connie cried in this woman's office, "saying 'I can't do anything good enough...I can't even talk to anybody now.'" The older woman "calmed me down," and said "'You are a good worker, a hard worker. Don't let anybody make you feel that you're not. Always think of success. How can you turn this around to be successful?'" Connie says, "she got me thinking about that...and it sticks with me to this day," 30 years later.

EMPLOYER SUPPORT FOR WOMEN WORKERS IN THEIR 50s, 60s, AND BEYOND

With all the ageism and sexism (as well as other intersecting patterns of discrimination against women with marginalized identities), colleagues and leaders looking to support and benefit from women over 50 should remember one thing: we should not make assumptions about the needs, wants, and potential for contribution of older women. But we should pay attention, with the lens of age and life stage in mind.

It is heartening to hear about companies like Lee's and teams like Connie's, in which older women can grow and share their multifaceted value. Indeed, for some women, growth opportunities and intense full-time work well into the 60s provides for rich levels of career satisfaction. For some, intense family responsibilities can slow down, the energy drain of proving oneself can diminish, financial obligations may decline, and women can feel ready to take more risks and ramp up their ambition for long-deferred opportunities to contribute, innovate, and lead in their careers.

As we know, the socialization of women to spend their younger years caring for others tends to influence their career opportunities in powerful ways. Writing about working women, author Aviva Wittenberg-Cox notes, "It's the first half of their lives that is spent balancing professional growth with serving and caring for a variety of others: children, parents, communities. And the second half that affords them the possibility of prioritizing their own voices and ambitions."[129] At the same time, she notes elsewhere, "Most companies focus on thirty-somethings as high-potential talent to be developed and accelerated with job mobility and stretch assignments, acting as if careers are made (or not) before the age of 40. But this approach has never served women (or parents) particularly well."[130]

Wittenberg-Cox has written about four phases of career, from the ambition characterizing the 20s, to the "culture shock" of the 30s, focused on women who have children, to the "(re) acceleration" of the 40s "refocusing on career priorities in the foundations built," to, finally, the 50+ chapter, which she calls "self-actualization." Her focus is on women, mostly corporate, who have the resources, health, family stability, workplace reputation and successes, and financial resources, to make the 50+ period just that: one of growth and excitement, at a time when men's more typically single-focused lives may be shifting away from an interest in careers.[131]

Wittenberg-Cox argues that companies should re-think their talent management plan and avoid making assumptions about leadership or any other role readiness based on age or stage of career. They should use the lessons learned from flexibility programs designed for parents and remote workers to help workers of any gender and age to "craft the path that works best for them across decades." Taking stock of women's career cycles and how they may differ from men's should make companies reconsider "the up-or-out model still dominant in most talent management programs," in which if people aren't all in in their 30s and early 40s, they're already on their way out.

But there isn't just one set of needs for older women workers. With the heightened potential for energy-consuming health needs for self-and/or family members, or just accumulated burnout, some women want and/or need to slow down while still holding onto their jobs, for money, and also for meaning and identity. Research has shown how important meaningful work is for contributing to people's sense of purpose.[132] As parenting and other relationships shift, work can be an anchor. Add to that, older workers often need to keep their income going due to rising health and housing costs, and perhaps a need to catch-up retirement savings based on earlier life circumstances or lower earnings that prevented that saving.

Many women of the "seasoned" age are looking for ways to keep contributing and even growing, while still conserving their energy. The variations in how people age continue to be stunning to me, as I move into my late 50s. I am increasingly aware that as we get older, we may need to hold more of our energy for ourselves, recognizing the needs of aging bodies, changing family life cycles and needs, and social and spiritual needs that may have been neglected during the decades when being "all in" at work felt like a non-negotiable requirement. AARP's 2023 "Value of Experience" survey found that, even among the 40–49-year-old age group, over half were "caregivers of a parent, friend, partner or spouse, in-law, or another adult relative. Many of them acknowledged having to work remotely, change work hours, reduce hours, use accrued sick or vacation leave, take temporary leave, use paid caregiving leave, or quit their job altogether to provide care."[133]

Although none of the women I interviewed were actively seeking a downshift at the time of our interview, a wider lens suggests that this would likely be on the horizon for a number of them. It would be wise for their organizations to work with them to preserve their talents and leadership. Overall, when older workers maintain their engagement, our economies and our communities are stronger. Moreover, employers should recognize that addressing the needs of older workers can represent another opportunity to create an inclusive, humane workplace that channels resources into pro-social values for individuals and communities. Many older workers want to work part-time, phase out, let go of management responsibilities in favor of individual contributor roles, and be involved in mentoring. Their experience can be preserved, replenished, shared, and leveraged by wise employers.[134]

OPPORTUNITIES TO SUPPORT OLDER WOMEN WORKERS AND EVERYONE ELSE

▶ Promote intergenerational wisdom sharing, encouraging older women workers to share their stories with younger people, while also listening to the ways young people see the world and their futures differently.

▶ Leverage the strengths of older workers and make sure those strengths are visible to younger colleagues.

▶ Assume and promote an interest in lifelong learning for older workers.

▶ Tap into the wisdom and talents of older women (and all older workers), for special projects, for mentoring, for self-driven initiatives, as well as for formal leadership roles.

▶ Pay attention to gender and race pay equity as it relates to age.

▶ Pay attention to ageist language.

▶ Make part-time work available to preserve professional competencies and institutional memory for those who want to transition slowly into retirement.

▶ Create mentoring programs that encompass all career chapters.

▶ Create book discussions on topics that invite different generational points of view.

▶ Empower people from each generation to be teachers and learners.

If you're a younger worker reading this, consider what you can learn from women of all ages who work alongside you. Also consider what legacies you'll be leaving in each role and workplace context, as well as in your career overall. If you've been thinking about yourself as a mentor and a mentee all along, how does learning about the challenges and opportunities of older workers inspire you and challenge you to start new conversations? How does it help you consider the ways our workplaces can be spaces of dialogue, respect, and innovation by respecting the long arc of age, experience and wisdom found in women's stories?

STORY SHARING FOR INTERGENERATIONAL WISDOM AND VIBRANT CIVIC SPACE AT WORK

Americans have long been a youth-worshiping society. A corollary of that obsession is the tendency to dismiss our elders, although this varies among cultures within the U.S.[135] And in our current historical moment, language is changing constantly, along with social mores, while intergenerational resentments show up in a variety of ways, from humorous memes to social segregation by age.[136] People's age also correlates to what kinds of media they consume, and therefore the kinds of cultural and political conversations in which people engage.[137]

In the midst of all of these trends that pull generations apart, we have workplaces with four generations of adults spending their days trying to get along, collaborate, and hopefully respect one another. On the bottom end of the age scale are disproportionately anxious Gen Z workers, who have faced runaway inflation on housing, food, and healthcare costs, and may be struggling with student loan debt unimaginable to Baby Boomers. Many in younger generations grew up watching *The Office*, with its dim view of the meaning of work, and/or saw their parents experience devastating financial loss during the Great Recession. Some experienced profound shifts in their worldviews as a result of events like 9/11, the escalation of the impact of climate change, and the murder of George Floyd in 2020, and the overturning of *Roe v. Wade*, taking away bodily choice and dictating the terms of motherhood to younger generations, in 2022. All had their youth impacted by the global pandemic. Many have been exhausted, demoralized, and made to feel a sense of constant fear or unease by the overt racism, sexism, transphobia, and anti-immigrant sentiment coming from the most powerful political voices and so many emboldened hate mongers who follow them.

But these younger people work alongside generations of people who often suffered in silence and even lost their jobs or entire careers in situations where there seemed to be no recourse for discrimination. They could be fired for being gay, lose out on marriage benefits with same-sex partners. They, too, may have endured sexual harassment while watching the harassers get promoted in workplace cultures of silence, and/or deafening silence around institutional racism even as leadership echelons remained stubbornly white and "colorblind." If they suffered from mental health challenges, had their work and family lives impacted by trauma, they often had nowhere to turn to address their own or their families' mental health concerns. Few employees had access to Employee Assistance Programs at work before the mid-1970s.

Many Baby Boomers were shaped by the reality that before 1964 (Title VII of the Civil Rights Act), people could be overtly discriminated against in hiring and promotion on the basis of race or gender with no legal recourse. Before 1973 (*Roe v. Wade*), they may have had to figure out how to keep their paychecks coming in in an environment where abortion was criminalized in all but four states. Before 1978 (Pregnancy Discrimination Act), they could be fired for being pregnant. Before 1990 (Americans with Disabilities Act), there was rarely even a minimum expectation of accommodations for workers with disabilities. Before 1993 (Family Medical Leave Act), employers had the right to fire a person with a uterus for missing one day of work for having a baby.

It is our workplaces where people with such divergent experiences (not to mention political views in a nation divided by partisanship) must coexist. By fostering genuine connections, conversations, and responsive initiatives for age-friendly workplaces, we can do better work together but also do better as a society. Our workplaces are civic spaces, day-to-day environments where we can build and rebuild some of what has been torn apart by division. We can be part of the healing by doing good work together and being human alongside one another.

CONVERSATION STARTERS ACROSS GENERATIONS AT WORK

▶ What were your earliest aspirations for your career?

▶ What options were available to you for education and work when you were young?

▶ Who influenced your decisions about work and family?

▶ If you had children or didn't have children, how do you think that influenced your journey?

▶ Did you have other family or community responsibilities that shaped your approach to and experience of your career journey?

▶ Did you experience discrimination, pay inequity, harassment, or other problems at work? Who supported you through challenging experiences?

▶ What were the workplaces where you worked in your younger years like? Were there opportunities to grow for women of all backgrounds?

▶ What were the most exciting parts of your career journey, times when you felt energized and like you were making a difference?

▶ Did you have any mentors? And if so, what did they teach you?

▶ Do you see yourself as a mentor? If so, how do you try to approach the opportunities and challenges of mentoring younger people?

▶ How did you create space for yourself at work over the years?

▶ How did you work to create space for others, to make workplaces more inclusive, diverse, and equitable? What worked and what didn't with these endeavors?

▶ What were some of your proudest contributions to the work you did and/or to the culture of your workplace?

▶ What do you wish younger women understood about the workplace and work journeys?

▶ What do you want to better understand about young people?

▶ What do you think about leadership, and specifically about women's leadership? Do women offer different styles of leadership?

▶ How can women support one another, including across differences?

▶ How did you bring your values to work? How did that work out for you? Successes and challenges?

▶ What advice would you give to younger people?

▶ In what ways have younger people challenged and stretched you, maybe even mentored you, especially with their moral imagination and their ways of approaching making social change?

▶ Who do you most admire in younger generations, whether at work or in the larger culture?

CONCLUSION

CONCLUSION

AS I WRAP UP THE WRITING of this book, in the world-shaking mid-year days of 2025, I find myself in awe and not for the first time of the resilience and creativity of courageous women. Women at work, women at home, women in the community, women online, women gathering in new configurations around the world. Raising our voices, caring for others, and trying to nurture our own dreams.

I'm a historian at heart, living in a moment of the ever-explosive urgency of the present, and the constant divisiveness that obscures what history teaches. History teaches us about change, but also about continuity and throughlines. We can find this continuity in people's courage in the face of brutal and more subtly damaging kinds of authority, in organizing and resisting in many venues. One piece of continuity I have highlighted here is women leaders' persistence in crafting our own working lives deeply rooted in inclusive values, with ripple effects on the workplace and, by extension, the fabric of our civil society As this book reminds us, this is not a new effort, even if the contexts keep shifting.

I hope you have seen yourself or women close to you in the stories of this book. When you picked up this book, you may have needed a spark to reclaim both your own empowerment at work and your sense of efficacy and hope about living your values in the workplace. I hope you feel more confident in both ways. I hope that you've broadened your concept of what leadership looks like and deepened your appreciation for the long-term efforts of ordinary women working simultaneously for their own dignity and empowerment and for a more humane world in the workplace and beyond.

Building upon the stories of this book and the insights of the intrepid researchers who illuminate the workplace patterns, let me remind you of throughlines to cultivate in your own journey:

▸ **PEOPLE:** You need them, always. The close relationships that hold you, the work friendships and networks, the allies and confidants, the mentors, the mentees, the fellow builders and dreamers that collaborate with you on exciting projects. You can find new ways to build connections and to learn from others, across all kinds of differences.

▸ **CONTEXT:** Context awareness is key not only to survival in the workplace, but also to finding the levers for change to build more inclusive spaces.

▸ **BOUNDARIES:** Boundary building is life-sustaining, and women often need extra reminders on this one. Beware of over-identifying with any particular role or workplace situation. When you find it happening, strengthen your boundaries, and enlist your people to help you with those efforts.

▸ **AUTHENTICITY:** Working in integrity and through values provides the most solid foundation for surviving hard times, making critical and even everyday decisions, and dreaming up new possibilities, projects, and partnerships.

▸ **LEARNING AND HUMILITY:** Learning and humility are truly part of the resistance of our moment. They seem to be in short supply in our larger culture. But when we look at the arcs of the stories here, we see how fundamental these habits are, not only to women's career success, but to their joy and sense of connection to others.

▶ **SELF-COMPASSION:** I am grateful for the more critical stance younger women often take on perfectionism, for the naming of it and for the compassionate work they do with themselves and others to mitigate it. I am grateful that self-compassion is a vibrant discourse as we confront so much cultural toxicity and try to find a way forward. Practice it regularly and model it for others.

▶ **ADVOCACY, INCLUSION, AND SOLIDARITY:** We must expect nothing less, and we must find ways to keep lifting up these values and commitments. As the word solidarity suggests, we cannot do it alone. Coalition building is hard work and takes time. But it is worth the effort to be part of the messy work of creating the more just world we want to see. Our workplaces provide an important vehicle for that work.

▶ **ENTREPRENEURSHIP:** Women are often socialized towards humility and towards accepting the roles that we're taught to be "lucky" enough to occupy. But we must take charge of our own careers and keep looking for ways to create new opportunities for our projects, dreams and values, even when we're working in institutions we didn't create. Entrepreneurs dare and dream, and this is part of the work.

▶ **RECOGNIZE CYCLES:** The intellectual and emotional work of reflection is part of self-compassion and context awareness. When you feel disempowered and unbalanced, lean on your own story to remember times when this was not true, and embrace what you can learn from that awareness. Learn to recognize and enjoy the ride of generative moments in your career and accept with grace times when you need to step back, take a rest, set boundaries, and regroup.

▶ **TAKE THE LONG VIEW:** You are a long-term investment, and you need to treat yourself that way. The work that you're passionate about, the values that animate you--these are also long-term investments. While you can and should seize moments of urgency, light a spark, and be disruptive when it makes sense, you can also remind yourself that change-making takes time. Social transformation and career empowerment are marathons, not sprints.

▶ **NURTURE HABITS OF SELF-REFLECTION:** Learn to sit with the deeper questions, about meaning, feedback, values alignment, and relationships. Ask what is shifting, growing, and receding in your work life, and what the possibilities of the moment are. These are powerful self-reflective habits. They provide clarity, held within the container of self-compassion and ever-growing wisdom as we move through our work and life journeys.

While I have emphasized throughlines across an entire values-driven career, I hope this book has also helped you think about the developmental tasks of the career stage in which you find yourself. I hope you are able to find new ways to connect with others through the lens of a career journey arc. We never know what is going on in other people's lives unless we develop relationships, ask questions, and hold space with humility. *Leading With Courage* reminds us that we can create more opportunities to develop these connections by understanding career stage situations and generational experiences, as well as by growing an understanding of privilege and inequality.

I also hope you have broadened your understanding of what it means to lead at every level. Asking questions is leading. Raising your voice is leading. Caregiving and holding a team together, whether you're a manager or not, this is leading. Managing a complex life, practicing and modeling some balance and some variation in how you show up, this too is leading and role modeling. Mentoring is leading. Practicing mindful self-advocacy and negotiation are leadership skills. Advocacy and allyship, especially when you have some positional power, this is transformational leadership.

Supporting leaders at every level when they show courage, compassion, and collaboration, this is leading. We can offer that support individually and advocate for that support systemically. A theme that emerged again and again in my research and experience is how much direct supervisors matter. Middle managers are actually some of the most squeezed employees, but they're on the front lines and expected to be heroes. We can support them better (though we can also ask more of them).

High-level leaders need to find ways to empower middle managers as learners, carers, relationship builders, and advocates for their people. The research on women's leadership reminds us that we can often learn a lot from diverse women leaders in all these areas, particularly women of color. Organizations looking to offer more manager training should tap into the wisdom that already exists in their organizations, while acknowledging and rewarding that wisdom. Look for places where transformational, relationship-based, systems-aware leadership is happening, and build from there. This is leadership.

Listening, attending thoughtfully to feedback, adapting to change, using whatever power you have to improve systems towards more diversity, equity, and inclusion, this is leading. Bringing people into decision-making processes, learning how to build coalitions and communication matrices, this is leading. Making brave and hard decisions in a hostile environment is leading. Holding formal leaders accountable in a spirit of hope and with humanity, this is leading. Challenging hierarchies that separate leaders from the rest of us, this is leading.

If you're reading this book, you are no doubt an admirer of change-making as leadership. Like you, I'm impatient for change every single day, and I've spent decades of my life working for it. The stories of women in these professional workplaces offer us some additional insight into the processes of changemaking. I hope you can see how change-making fits into life stories and identities. How even as we are trying to be activists, we are sometimes struggling to stay afloat and keep our lives together, or we're surviving hostility and marginalization at work. Other times, we are in the right place and the right time to thrive, challenge, contribute, and build new and beautiful things. No one can hold it all together over a whole lifespan or working lifespan. This is why we're stronger together, stronger when we know one another as people, and offer grace to ourselves and others.

WHAT WILL YOU DO NEXT?

Start with self-reflection and branch out. Work with others!

FOR YOURSELF:

Hopefully you alternated between inspiration and hope and the necessary frustration we feel when reading about systemic problems.

▶ What themes, patterns, and emotions came up for you as you read this book? If you picked up this book, it's probably because you were looking for some guidance for your own situation. What did you find that resonated and/or offered the potential for new strategies and directions?

▶ Are you in a generative and energetic place?

▶ Are you in a moment where you need to reassess?

▶ How much do you have to offer and where are you able and willing to put your energy now, especially for the conversations, projects, and initiatives that will require significant energy?

▶ Do you have the social support at work and in your life in general to do what you'd like to do next?

▶ How will you empower yourself and who will help you in your next iteration of that self-empowerment project?

▶ What kinds of personal reflections or group conversations do you need to have to take your next step?

▶ Will you talk with your manager or supervisor, a trusted mentor, an EAP adviser or other counselor or coach?

▶ Begin to think about the larger meaning and possibilities and challenges of your work at this moment by beginning with yourself, with those habits of self-reflection.

IN BROADER CIRCLES

Can you examine and challenge workplace norms and policies in your organization? For example, unwritten rules or gaps in policies that...

▶ Penalize caregivers

▶ Exploit caregiving and other teambuilding at work that can be overlooked as the real leadership it is

▶ Perpetuate norms of whiteness and normative (or even toxic) masculinity or insider access to advancement opportunities that marginalize so many people

▶ Obscure the leadership value of people who challenge those norms

▶ Create environments where microaggressions, bullying or harassment can go unaccounted for

▶ Perpetuate ageism by marginalizing older people, especially women who are not positional leaders, and younger people whose challenging voices can provide the disruption and creative vision our workplaces need

WHO CAN YOU TEAM UP WITH TO...

▶ Create new spaces at work for critical conversations about all of the above

▶ Spark your own conversations that generate learning, humility, and awareness of people's stories, struggles, and wisdom?

▶ Challenge racism, sexism, homophobia, transphobia, ableism, Islamophobia, anti-Semitism, and all the other isms that divide and marginalize

▶ Empower women, trans, nonbinary all LGBTQ+ people and BIPOC people/people of the global majority. This includes learning about the leadership wisdom of these groups while remembering that everyone is an individual with their own story and experience.

▶ Build coalitions to create processes in which pro-social, justice and equity-centered values are infused into decision-making in your organization

▶ Challenge the arbitrary boundaries of the workplace and the community in order to expand the resources of your workplace into your community, and create learning opportunities in relation to your community, with an eye towards justice.

Thank you for taking yourself out of the present moment, news cycles, and quick-fix soundbites on women's career empowerment to delve into the stories of resilient women over generations. I hope these stories inspire you to lead from anywhere with your values, honor your questions, nurture your vision for a better world, and keep finding ways to learn from the stories and wisdom of the women in your life.

AUTHOR BIO

DR. JODI VANDENBERG - DAVES is a leadership strategist, coach, and consultant with
extensive experience in higher education and
nonprofit leadership. With a dedication to
empowering transformational leaders and
creating more inclusive workplaces, Jodi fa-
cilitates career journeys for individuals at all
stages of their professional lives. She also

advises organizations on talent retention and development. She specializes
in strengthening diverse women's leadership across all levels, emphasizing
values and social impact.

As a former professor and academic leader, Jodi is deeply committed
to mentorship and applies research-based strategies to her work. Through
professional development courses, facilitation, and keynote speaking, she
empowers individuals and organizations to achieve workplace transformation, promoting cultures of inclusive leadership.

Holding a doctorate in History, Jodi has taught and held leadership
roles at the University of Wisconsin-La Crosse, focusing on systems of
privilege, inequality, and social change. Her expertise includes women's
history, gender, race, and leadership. Her nonprofit experience includes directing her community's Diversity Council, where she expanded the organization's capacity and advanced its mission of building inclusive workplaces and communities.

Jodi is the author of several works, including *Modern Motherhood: An American History* (Rutgers University Press, 2014), and has contributed research and popular articles on intersectional gender issues, along with a book of poems, *Poems in the Mother Tongue*. As a writer and editor, she is also passionate about helping other authors bring their voices to the forefront.

VISIT HER WEBSITE:

https://www.jodivandenberg-daves.com/ to learn more about Jodi's speaking, coaching, online courses, and other services.

ACKNOWLEDGEMENTS

First and foremost, I extend my heartfelt thanks to the women interviewed for this book. You shared your journeys with honesty and insight: your challenges and triumphs, your vulnerability and wisdom—all the ingredients of learning and practicing empowered, courageous leadership. Your stories have been a gift for me personally, and now they are a gift to the world.

Second, a special thanks to three friends with whom I talked and thought about leadership more than anyone else: Dr. Christine Hippert, Dr. Keely Rees, and Sanna Yoder. Through early morning tea dates and long runs by the river, we processed the challenges and opportunities of leadership in the reality of imperfect systems. We taught one another how to think more expansively. We served as mentors and ballasts for one another in our commitments to meaningful professional journeys in the midst of rich personal lives. Thank you, also, Christine, for an important early read of a version of the manuscript that set me off in the direction I needed to go.

My former academic department, named Women's, Gender, and Sexuality Studies (WGSS) at the time this book was launched, has always been peopled with incredibly supportive humans and powerful, courageous leadership. Thank you for the heartfelt championing of this project from my WGSS colleagues, especially Dr. Mahruq Khan, Dr. Deb Hoskins, Dr. Terry Glenn Lilley, Andrea Hansen, Laura Garves, Dr. Sara Docan-Morgan (WGSS affiliate and interim department chair while I launched this book), and my steadfast friend over the decades, Elise Denlinger. WGSS support not only inspired me but helped me secure the sabbatical I needed to get the book started. I am grateful to the College of Arts, Social Sciences, and Humanities of the University of Wisconsin-La Crosse for funding that sabbatical.

This book was greatly strengthened by the developmental editing work and wisdom of Megan Pugh, who provided critical mid-stage feedback on the manuscript. Later stage editorial help includes wise writing advice from my friend Dr. Sharon Jessee, and excellent timely feedback from my beta readers, Teri Holford, Abby Wenger, Taylor Wheeler, and Jess Witkins. I also appreciate the publishing logistics expertise from Amanda Zieba and the proofreading and formatting work of Amy Savoy. The beautiful cover art was expertly created by Alex Pinto Designs.

This book grew alongside my business, JVD Consulting, LLC. My business mentors helped me to see and develop the interconnectedness of these endeavors. My mom, Charlene Vandenberg, is an ambitious realtor, practicing for over 45 years. She has been an inspiration and source of great ideas on my entrepreneurial and author journey–and every other leg of the journey! Special thanks as well to Sarah Arendt-Beyer, Maryann Baldwin, Jordan Degree, Dr. Erica Srinivasan, and the ever visionary, always-in-my-corner Mary Zimmermann. And--for shining the light in so many ways, just when I needed it most--special thanks to Dr. Carolyn Colleen Bostrack.

For opportunities to hone the ideas of the book through speaking engagements, training, and coaching, special shout outs to: coaching clients and the participants in my Unlocking Your Leadership Potential course; the Greater La Crosse Area Diversity Council; University of Wisconsin-Madison Center for Research on College-Workforce Transitions; University of Wisconsin Madison Continuing Studies, especially the participants in my online course on mentoring course. Also, to the incomparable Amanda Goodenough of Goodenough Consulting, whose collaborations with me have helped me grow, and whose thought leadership always expands my understanding of justice.

Other key players in that regard include my generations of college students, especially the recent ones—Millennial and Gen Z—who yearn for justice and meaning in their lives, and who raise the hard and beautiful questions. And my now grown children, of those same generations, who have stretched me with their expansive social, moral, and political imaginations.

Thank you as well to my many friends, more numerous than I can name. Your patience and encouragement lifted me up all along the writing journey. Friends make life beautiful and always remind me I'm more than what I produce or do in the world.

And thanks to my family, also too numerous to name. By Vandenbergs and Daves alike, I've always been so well supported in fulfilling my life aspirations, including this one. My parents, Les and Charlene Vandenberg, were the original teachers about solidarity, a lesson I keep trying to live throughout my life. The already mentioned Vandenberg-Daves children, Allison, Sylvia, and Brad, support me and provide me with hope, vision, and love. John Vandenberg-Daves has listened endlessly to every drama, machination, and hope related to this book and all my other projects. I am so fortunate to have his love and encouragement over more than 35 years, helping me realize my dreams.

ENDNOTES

INTRODUCTION

[1] "What the Statistics Say About Generation Z," The Annie E. Casey Foundation, Jan. 25, 2025. https://www.aecf.org/blog/generation-z-statistics

[2] "The Deloitte Global 2022 Gen Z and Millennial Survey." Deloitte, 2022. https://www2.deloitte.com/content/dam/Deloitte/global/Documents/About-Deloitte/about-deloitte-global-report-full-version-2020.pdf
Jennifer Miller, "For Younger Job Seekers, Diversity and Inclusion in the Workplace Aren't a Preference. They're a Requirement." *The Washington Post,* February 18, 2021. https://www.washingtonpost.com/business/2021/02/18/Millennial-genz-workplace-diversity-equity-inclusion/
Jacob, Charmaine. "Young People Are Increasingly Overwhelmed at Work, Survey Shows." CNBC. CNBC, February 1, 2022. https://www.cnbc.com/2022/02/01/young-people-are-increasingly-overwhelmed-at-work-bain-co-survey.html.

[3] "The Deteriorating Social Self in Younger Generations," Sapiens Lab, in *Rapid Report Mental Health Million Project,* May 2022. https://sapienlabs.org/wp-content/uploads/2022/05/Rapid-Report-The-Deteriorating-Social-Self-in-Younger-Generations.pdf

[4] "Failure is not an option for Black women: Effects of organizational performance on leaders with single versus dual-subordinate identities," Ashleigh Shelby Rosette, *Journal of Experimental Social Psychology* 48 no. 5 (2012): 1162-1167.

[5] "Women in the Workplace 2024: 10th Annual Report," Lean In, 2024. https://leanin.org/women-in-the-workplace?gad_source=1&gad_campaignid=21710962798&gbraid=0AAAAADdFP-I6QQjKTl3AU22uR5yT9TbDV&gclid=CjwKCAjwgb_CBhBMEiwA0p3oOA2yloBA1BOoDrkYVXaOkmGqAUHXev7_CJyLn5gJ3Bx-lioOXcTBGhoCFW0QAvD_BwE

[6] "More Than 80% of Transgender Employees in the US Have Experienced Discrimination or Harassment at Work," UCLA School of Law Williams Institute, Nov., 2024. https://williamsinstitute.law.ucla.edu/press/trans-workplace-press-release/

[7] Harts, Minda, *The Memo What Women of Color Need to Know to Secure a Seat at the Table* (New York, NY: Seal Press), 2020.

[8] Courtney L. McCluney et al, "To Be or Not to Be...Black: The Effects of Racial Codeswitching on Perceived Professionalism in the Workplace," *Journal of Experimental Social Psychology* 97 (Nov. 2021).

[9] Caroline Castrillon, "Why Women-Led Companies are Better for Employees" Caroline Castrillon, *Forbes*, March 24, 2019. https://www.forbes.com/sites/carolinecastrillon/2019/03/24/why-women-led-companies-are-better-for-employees/

[10] Julia Boorstin, *When Women Lead: What They Achieve, Why They Succeed, and How We Can Learn From Them* (Avid Reader Press, 2022)

[11] Harts, Minda. *The Memo What Women of Color Need to Know to Secure a Seat at the Table.* (Seal Press, 2020).

[12] Dave Hemprich-Bennet, Dani Rabiotti, and Emma Kennedy, "Beware survivorship bias in advice on science careers," *Nature,* Sept. 2021. https://www.nature.com/articles/d41586-021-02634-z

[13] Today, too many college degree holders spend extensive time in service jobs (where they may be wielding disproportionate impact as union organizers in places like Starbucks, now that many no longer see service work as a short-term gig). In addition, we tend to think of direct services jobs like waitressing and retail cashiering as having limited opportunity for upward mobility, and as part of waged labor rather than salaried professionalism. But entry level professional type jobs that are overwhelmingly staffed by women—disability resource work, employment services, community health worker jobs, or work in domestic violence shelters—are often waged jobs too, often requiring direct service, and often providing few opportunities for advancement. In addition, the rise of the gig economy contributes to fluctuating identities for today's "professional class." Much more needs to be written about the shifting contours of the professional workplace. "The Revolt of the College Educated Working Class," *New York Times*, April 29, 2022. https://www.nytimes.com/2022/04/28/business/college-workers-starbucks-amazon-unions.html

Yao Yao, "One Foot in the Online Gig Economy: Coping with a Splitting Professional Identity," *Journal of Professions and Organization* 9 no. 3 (2022): 273-290.

[14] Barbara Annis and Keith Merron, *Gender Intelligence: Breakthrough Strategies for Increasing Diversity and Improving Your Bottom Line* (Harper Business, 2014), 33.

[15] Quoctrung Bui and Claire Cain Miller, "The Age That Women Have Babies: How a Gap Divides America," *New York Times*, Aug. 4, 2018. https://www.nytimes.com/interactive/2018/08/04/upshot/up-birth-age-gap.html

CHAPTER 1

[16] Adrienne Rich, Lies, Secrets, and Silence: Selected Prose, 1966-1978. (W.W. Norton, 1979.)

[17] Mary Anne Wishrosky, "The Secretary: Invisible Labor in the Work worlds of Women," Human Organization 53, no. 1 (1994): 33-49.

[18] Stefanie K. Johnson and Juan M. Madera, "Sexual Harassment Is Pervasive in the Restaurant Industry. Here's What Needs to Change," Harvard Business Review, January 18, 2018. https://hbr.org/2018/01/sexual-harassment-is-pervasive-in-the-restaurant-industry-heres-what-needs-to-change

[19] Michael Lynn and Tony Simons, "Predictors of Male and Female Servers' Average Tip Earnings," Journal of Applied Psychology 30, no. 2 (2000): 24-252.

[20] Gallup, "What Are Teens Doing After School?" *Gallup News*, accessed December 3, 2024, https://news.gallup.com/poll/15943/what-teens-doing-after-school.aspx.

[21] National Center for Education Statistics, "College Student Employment," *Condition of Education*, accessed December 3, 2024. https://nces.ed.gov/programs/coe/indicator/ssa/college-student-employment#:~:text=The%20percentage%20of%20full%2Dtime,in%202015%20(78%20percent).

[22] Pew Research Center. "What's Behind the Growing Gap Between Men and Women in College Completion?" Last modified November 8, 2021. Accessed December 3, 2024https://www.pewresearch.org/short-reads/2021/11/08/whats-behind-the-growing-gap-between-men-and-women-in-college-completion/

[23] "Is College Worth the Price?" *The New York Times Magazine*, September 5, 2023. Accessed December 3, 2024.https://www.nytimes.com/2023/09/05/magazine/college-worth-price.html

[24] C. Neill Epperson, Pooja Shah, and Theodore D. Satterthwaite. "Toward a Lifespan Neurobiology of Depression: Insights from Developmental Studies." *Journal of Neuroscience* 39, no. 42 (2019): 8207–8215.

[25] National Academies of Sciences, Engineering, and Medicine, "Sexual Harassment of Women: Climate, Culture, and Consequences in Academic Sciences, Engineering, and Medicine," Washington, DC: The National Academies Press. (2018.) doi: https:// doi.org/10.17226/24994.

[26] Marta Tienda, "Diversity ≠ Inclusion: Promoting Integration in Higher Education. Educ Res. 42 no. 9 (2013): 467-475. doi: 10.3102/0013189X13516164. https://www.ncbi.nlm.nih.gov/pmc/articles/PMC4530621/

[27] Michelle M. Tokarczyk, *Working-Class Women in the Academy: Laborers in the Knowledge Factory* (Boston: University of Massachusetts Press, 1993.)

[28] Alcino Donadel, "Stikes and Unions: Graduate Students Marshall Their Forces Nationwide," *UB University Business*, Feb. 2023. https://universitybusiness.com/strikes-and-unions-graduate-students-marshal-their-forces-nationwide/

[29] Terry Nguyen, "Student Activists Want Change: And They're Starting in the Classroom," *Vox*, July 29, 2020. https://www.vox.com/identities/2020/7/29/21345114/students-diversify-curriculum-change-antiracist

[30] "Profile: Social Workers," Data USA. 2025. https://datausa.io/profile/soc/social-workers

[31] National Assn. of Social Workers, "NASW Opposes Association of Social Work Boards (ASWB) Exams," Feb. 3, 2023.https://www.socialworkers.org/News/News-Releases/ID/2611/NASW-Opposes-Association-of-Social-Work-Boards-ASWB-Exams

CHAPTER 2

[32] The Nation's Report Card, "NAEP Report: Mathematics," 2025. https://www.nationsreportcard.gov/mathematics/nation/groups/?grade=8

[33] Julia Files et al, "Speaker Introductions at Internal Medicine Grand Rounds: Forms of Address Reveal Gender Bias," *Journal of Women's Health* 26, no. 5 (2017), 413-419 doi: 10.1089/jwh.2016.6044.

[34] Bennett, Jessica. *Feminist Fight Club: A Survival Manual for a Sexist Workplace* (New York: HarperCollins, 2016.); Catalyst, "How to Break Barriers for Women in STEM, Tech, and Trades," Nov. 13,

2024.https://www.catalyst.org/research/women-in-male-dominated-industries-and-occupations/

[35] Jennifer L. Berdahl, Peter Glick, and Marianne Cooper. "How Masculinity Contests Undermine Organizations, and What to Do About It." *Harvard Business Review*, November 2, 2018. https://hbr.org/2018/11/how-masculinity-contests-undermine-organizations-and-what-to-do-about-it

[36] Audrey Babic and Isabelle Hansez, "The Glass Ceiling for Women Managers: Antecedents and Consequences for Work-Family Interface and Well-Being at Work," *Frontiers in Psychology 12* (2021).

[37] Jenny Vazquez-Newsum, *Untapped Leadership: Harnessing the Power of Underrepresented Leaders* (Lanham, MD: Prometheus, 2023), 139

[38] Tema Okun, "White Supremacy Culture" Website. https://www.whitesupremacyculture.info/

[39] Ruchika T. Malhotra, "The Psychological Toll of Being the Only Woman of Color at Work," Harvard Business Review, Sept. 20, 2022. https://hbr.org/2022/09/the-psychological-toll-of-being-the-only-woman-of-color-at-work

[40] American Association of University Women, "Broken Ladders: Barriers to Representation in Nonprofit Leadership," May 2018. https://www.aauw.org/app/uploads/2020/03/women-in-leadership.pdf

[41] Baines, Donna, Sara Charlesworth, Ian Cunningham, and Janet Dassinger. "Self-Monitoring, Self-Blaming, Self-Sacrificing Workers: Gendered Managerialism in the Non-Profit Sector." *Women's Studies International Forum* 35, no. 5 (2012): 362–371.

[42] Faith Mitchell, "Nonprofit Leadership is Out of Step with America's Changing Demographics," Urban Institute, Dec. 9, 2021. https://www.urban.org/urban-wire/nonprofit-leadership-out-step-americas-changing-demographics

[43] Jessica Mendieta and Amy Silver O'Leary, "How (and Why_ Nonprofits are Supporting the Mental Health of Their Employees," National Council of Nonprofits, May 11, 2022. https://www.councilofnonprofits.org/articles/how-and-why-nonprofits-are-supporting-mental-health-their-employees

[44] McKinsey, Women in the Workplace 2024: The 10th Anniversary Report," Sept. 17, 2024. https://www.mckinsey.com/featured-insights/diversity-and-inclusion/women-in-the-workplace

[45] Olga Khazan, "Why Are There So Many Women in Public Relations?" The Atlantic, Aug. 8, 2014 https://www.theatlantic.com/business/archive/2014/08/why-are-there-so-many-women-in-pr/375693/. Scholarly research in Germany on

women in PR agencies also revealed the perks of organizational cultures for women employees. Frolich, Romy, and Sonja B. Peters, "PR Bunnies Caught in the Agency Ghetto? Gender Stereotypes, Organizational Factors, and Women's Careers in PR Agencies," *Journal of Public Relations Research* 19 n. 3 (2007), 229-254.

CHAPTER 3

[46] Jenny Vazquez-Newsum, *Untapped Leadership: Harnessing the Power of Underrepresented Leaders* (Prometheus, 2023), 54.

[47] Caitlin Mullen, "This is When Confidence at Work Peaks for Women," *The Business Journals*, Aug. 8, 2019. https://www.bizjournals.com/bizwomen/news/latest-news/2019/08/this-is-when-confidence-at-work-peaks-for-women.html

CHAPTER 4

[48] "Mentoring Women in the Workplace: A Global Study" Report. DDI Consulting, 2019. https://www.ddiworld.com/research/mentoring-women-in-the-workplace

CHAPTER 5

[49] McKinsey, Women in the Workplace, 2022. https://leanin.org/women-in-the-workplace?gad_source=1&gad_campaignid=21710962798&gbraid=0AAAAADdFP-K9B1Zt_yFFcHakqCoucTABu&gclid=CjwKCAjwkvbEBhApEiwAKUz6--vzU_26HNQwVVt0UZ5z6vWaMMkQ5iyHY_tdmZ4EYbtoTO5OzHxjMhoCKpgQAvD_BwE

[50] Dnika, J. Travis, Jennifer Thorpe-Moscon, and Courtney McCluney, Emotional Tax: How Black Women and Men Pay More at Work and How Leaders Can Take Action (Catalyst, 2016)

[51] This has been especially studied in the academic world. See Yolanda Flores Niemann, Gabriella Gutierrez y Muhs, & Carmen G. Gonzalez, Eds. Presumed Incompetent: Race, Class, Power, and Resistance of Women in Academia (Utah State University Press, 2012)

[52] "Equality Rising: LGBTQ Workers and the Road Ahead," HRC Foundation, 2023 https://www.hrc.org/resources/a-workplace-divided-understanding-the-climate-for-lgbtq-workers-nationwide

[53] Courtney L. McCluney et al, "To Be or Not to Be...Black: The Effects of Racial Codeswitching on Perceived Professionalism in the Workplace," Journal of Experimental Social Psychology 97 (Nov. 2021); Claire Damken Brown and Audrey Nelson, Code Switching: How to Talk So Men Will Listen (Penguin, 2009.)

[54] "Wears Jump Suite. Sensible Shoes. Uses Husband's Last Name," New York Times, June 20, 1993. https://www.nytimes.com/1993/06/20/magazine/wears-jump-suit-sensible-shoes-uses-husbands-last-name.html

[55] Joan C. Williams, "The Five Biases Pushing Women Out of STEM," Harvard Business Review, March 24, 2015. https://hbr.org/2015/03/the-5-biases-pushing-women-out-of-stem

[56] Janice Gassam Asare, "How Hair Discrimination Affects Black Women at Work," Harvard Business Review, May 10, 2023. https://hbr.org/2023/05/how-hair-discrimination-affects-black-women-at-work

[57] "Equality Rising: LGBTQ Workers and the Road Ahead," HRC Foundation, 2023 https://www.hrc.org/resources/a-workplace-divided-understanding-the-climate-for-lgbtq-workers-nationwide

[58] "Women in the Workplace 2024: 10th Annual Report," Lean In, 2024. https://leanin.org/women-in-the-workplace?gclid=CjwKCAjw69moBhBgEiwAUFCx2DprFzCQtIEAtX63exqm5pobW4qVLHzHDpv3s1NcoOQjppZqRI_rYRoC_mUQAvD_BwE

[59] "Equality Rising: LGBTQ Workers and the Road Ahead," HRC Foundation, 2023 https://www.hrc.org/resources/a-workplace-divided-understanding-the-climate-for-lgbtq-workers-nationwide

[60] Employment Characteristics of Families 2024," Bureau of Labor Statistics News Release, April 2025. https://www.bls.gov/news.release/pdf/famee.pdf

[61] "Pandemic 'Will Take Our Women Back 10 Years Back' in The Workplace," New York Times, June 29, 2021. https://www.nytimes.com/2020/09/26/world/COVID-women-childcare-equality.html#:~:text=Substantial%20research%20has%20shown%20that,for%20children%20and%20the%20family.

[62] Deborah Rhode, Women and Leadership, (Oxford University Press, 2017).

[63] Vazquez-Newsum, Untapped Leadership, 27.

[64] Colleen Ammerman and Boris Groysberg, "3 Workplace Biases That Derail Mid-Career Women," Harvard Business Review, Sept. 16, 2022. https://hbr.org/2022/09/3-workplace-biases-that-derail-mid-career-women

[65] Colleen Ammerman and Boris Groysberg, "3 Workplace Biases That Derail Mid-Career Women," Harvard Business Review, Sept. 16, 2022. https://hbr.org/2022/09/3-workplace-biases-that-derail-mid-career-women

66 Sheryl Sandberg, *Lean In: Women, Work and the Will to Lead* (Alfred A. Knopf, 2013.)

67 "Commit to Mentoring Women: Not Harassing Women is Not Enough," Lean In, 2020. https://leanin.org/mentor-her

68 See Deborah Rhode, *Women and Leadership* (Oxford Univ. Press, 2017), for further discussion. Also, •Alice H. Eagly & Linda L. Carli, *Through the Labyrinth: The Truth about How Women Become Leaders* (Harvard Business School, 2007).

69 Michelle K. Ryan and S. Alexander Haslam, "The Glass Cliff: Exploring the Dynamics Surrounding the Appointment of Women to Precarious Leadership Positions," *The Academy of Management Review* 32 no. 2 (2007): 549-572. Alison Cook and Christy Glass, "Glass Cliffs and Organizational Saviors: Barriers to Minority Leadership in Work Organizations?" *Social Problems*, 60 no 2 (2013): 168-187

70 Marguerite Ward, "The Glass Cliff is a Serious Problem for Women in Corporate America: Here's How to Dismantle It," *Business Insider*, March 2, 2022. https://www.businessinsider.com/women-and-people-of-color-face-glass-cliff-us-2020-7

71 Deborah Rhode, *Women and Leadership* (Oxford University Press, 2017)

72 "Workplace Sexual Harassment, " US GAO, Report to Congressional Requesters, 2020. https://www.gao.gov/assets/gao-20-564.pdf

73 Chloe Reichel, "Sexual Harassment: Who Suffers and How," *The Journalist's Resource*, October 25, 2017 https://journalistsresource.org/economics/sexual-harassment-assault-health-discrimination-race/

74 Maria L. Ontiveros, "Three Perspectives on Workplace Harassment of Women of Color," *Golden Gate University Law Review 23 no. 3* (1993): 817-828

75 Kristina Davis, "Poll: Sex Harassment Caused 41 Percent of Victims to Leave Their Jobs," *The San Diego Union Tribune*, Dec. 24, 2017. https://www.sandiegouniontribune.com/business/economy/sd-me-harassment-survey-20171220-story.html

76 Frank Dobbin and Alexander Kalev, "Why Sexual Harassment Programs Backfire, " *Harvard Business Review*, May-June 2020 https://hbr.org/2020/05/why-sexual-harassment-programs-backfire

77 "Limiting Our Livelihoods: The Cumulative Impact of Sexual Harassment on Women's Careers, 2019" American Association of University Women, 2019. https://www.aauw.org/resources/research/limiting-our-livelihoods/

78 "Women in the Workplace 2024: 10th Annual Report," Lean In, 2024. BhCeARIsAGxWtUyJLNZouszMlBbPu9GKZFCXknusFtMgg9yN1A09t9 wSvAjLLreZ3HkaAtA7EALw_wcB

[79] Monique Valcour, "Beating Burnout," *Harvard Business Review*, Nov. 2016. https://hbr.org/2016/11/beating-burnout#:~:text=Three%20Components,%2C%20and%20inefficacy%E2%80%94in%20turn.

[80] "Women in the Workplace 2024: 10th Annual Report," Lean In, 2024. BhCeARIsAGxWtUyJLNZouszMlBbPu9GKZFCXknusFtMgg9yN1A09t9wSvAjLLreZ3HkaAtA7EALw_wcB

[81] TIffany Burns et al, "Women Do More to Fight Burnout–And It's Burning Them Out," *Harvard Business Review*, Oct. 22, 2021. https://hbr.org/2021/10/women-do-more-to-fight-burnout-and-its-burning-them-out

[82] Sources: U.S. Equal Employment Opportunity Commission. (2016). *Report of the co-chairs of the EEOC Select Task Force on the Study of Harassment in the Workplace* (Executive Summary & Recommendations). https://www.eeoc.gov/select-task-force-study-harassment-workplace MR Tuckey, et al. "Workplace bullying as an organizational problem: Spotlight on people Management Practices. *Journal of Occupational Health Psychology* 27 no. 6 (2022): 544-565.

CHAPTER 6

[83] Kim Parker, "Women More than Men Adjust Their Careers for Family Lives," Pew Research, Oct. 1, 2015. https://www.pewresearch.org/short-reads/2015/10/01/women-more-than-men-adjust-their-careers-for-family-life

[84] Ben Wigert and Heather Barrett, "The Manager Squeeze: How the New Workplace is Testing Team Leaders," *Gallup Workplace*, Sept. 6, 2023.

[85] "Women in the Workplace 2024: 10th Annual Report," Lean In, 2024. https://leanin.org/women-in-the-workplace?gclid=CjwKCAjw69moBhBgEiwAUFCx2DprFzCQtIEAtX63exqm5pobW4qVLHzHDpv3s1NcoOQjppZqRI_rYRoC_mUQAvD_BwE

CHAPTER 7

[86] Sarah Wells, Go Ask Your Mothers: One Simple Step for Managers to Support Working Mothers for Team Success (Matt Holt, 2024)

[87] See, for example, Rose Hackman: Emotional Labor: The Invisible Work Shaping Our Lives and How to Claim Our Power (New York: Macmillan, 2023).

[88] Natalie Kitroeff and Jessica Silver-Greenberg, "Pregnancy Discrimination Is Rampant Inside America's Biggest Companies," *The New York Times*, June 15, 2018,

https://www.nytimes.com/interactive/2018/06/15/business/pregnancy-discrimination.html

[89] The "motherhood mandate" is a fundamental concept in the study of motherhood and gender historically. Margaret Marsh and Wanda Ronner fleshed out the idea well in their book, *The Empty Cradle: Infertility in America from Colonial Times to the Present* (Johns Hopkins University Press, 1996).

[90] Juliana Menasce Horowitz, "Despite challenges at home and at work, most working moms and dads say being employed is what's best for them," Pew Research Study, Sept. 12, 2019. https://www.pewresearch.org/short-reads/2019/09/12/despite-challenges-at-home-and-work-most-working-moms-and-dads-say-being-employed-is-whats-best-for-them/

[91] Lila Schochet, "The Childcare Crisis is Keeping Women Out of the Workforce," Center for American Progress, March 28, 2019. https://www.americanprogress.org/article/child-care-crisis-keeping-women-workforce/

[92] Liana Fox, "Moms, Work, and the Pandemic," *U.S. Census Bureau*, March 2021, https://www.census.gov/library/stories/2021/03/moms-work-and-the-pandemic.html

[93] Hope Kirwan, "The Erasure of 40 Years Progress: How the Pandemic Is Affecting Working Women in Wisconsin," *Wisconsin Public Radio*, Oct. 12, 2020. https://www.wpr.org/economy/erasure-40-years-progress-how-pandemic-affecting-working-women-wisconsin.

[94] Elaine Povich, "As Women Return to Jobs, Remote Work Could Lock in Gains," *Stateline*, May 3, 2022 https://stateline.org/2022/05/03/as-women-return-to-jobs-remote-work-could-lock-in-gains/.

[95] Claire Cain Miller, "The Household Work Men and Women Do, and Why," *The New York Times*, February 12, 2020 https://www.nytimes.com/2020/02/12/us/the-household-work-men-and-women-do-and-why.html

[96] Avivah Wittenberg-Cox, "To Keep Women in the Workforce, Men Need to Do More at Home," *Harvard Business Review*, April 2021 https://hbr.org/2021/04/to-keep-women-in-the-workforce-men-need-to-do-more-at-home.

[97] *Caregiving in the United States*, American Association of Retired Peresons Report, May 2020, https://www.aarp.org/content/dam/aarp/ppi/2020/05/full-report-caregiving-in-the-united-states.doi.10.26419-2Fppi.00103.001.pdf

[98] Amy Friedrich, "Kids Are Facing a Mental Health Crisis: What Can Employers Do to Help?" *BenefitsPRO*, May 24, 2022, https://www.benefitspro.com/2022/05/24/kids-are-facing-a-mental-health-crisis-what-can-employers-do-to-help/

[99] SHRM, "SHRM Releases 2022 Employee Benefits Survey," June 2022, https://www.shrm.org/about-shrm/press-room/press-releases/pages/shrm-releases-2022-employee-benefits-survey--healthcare-retirement-savings-and-leave-benefits-emerge-as-the-top-ranked-be.aspx

[100] U.S. Department of Labor, "Who Is Eligible for FMLA?," August 2020, https://www.dol.gov/sites/dolgov/files/OASP/evaluation/pdf/WHD_FMLA 2018PB1WhoIsEligible_StudyBrief_Aug2020.pdf

[101] National Partnership for Women and Families, "Paid Leave Is Essential for Families," May, 2021, https://nationalpartnership.org/report/paid-leave-is-essential-for/

[102] Deborah L. Rhode, *Women and Leadership* (New York: Oxford University Press, 2014), 34.

[103] McKinsey & Company, "Women in the Workplace," 2024. https://www.mckinsey.com/featured-insights/diversity-and-inclusion/women-in-the-workplace

[104] Sylvia Ann Hewlett, "The Power of Out," *Harvard Business Review*, June 2013, https://hbr.org/2013/06/the-power-of-out

[105] Arlie Russell Hochschild, *The Managed Heart: Commercialization of Human Feeling* (University of California Press, 1983)

[106] Rose Hackman, Emotional Labor: The Invisible Work Shaping Our Lives and How to Reclaim Our Power (Flatiron Books, 2024)

[107] Kate Aronoff, "Emotional Labor and Gender Bias in the Workplace," *The Guardian*, March 27, 2023. https://www.theguardian.com/society/2023/mar/27/emotional-labor-work-women-career-gender.

[108] "How to Create a Leave Donation Program," Society for Human Resource Managers, Dec. 14, 2023. https://www.shrm.org/resourcesandtools/tools-and-samples/how-to-guides/pages/howtocreatealeavedonationprogram.aspx.

[109] "Inside the Employee Volunteer Programs of 5 B Corporations," SOCAP Globak, June 2017, https://socapglobal.com/2017/06/inside-the-employee-volunteer-programs-of-5-b-corps/

[110] "Parents Are Time-Squeezed: These Policies Can Help," Brookings Institution, August 13, 2021, https://www.brookings.edu/blog/up-front/2021/08/13/parents-are-time-squeezed-these-policies-can-help/

[111] Eugene Scalia and William W. Beach, "Leave Benefits: Access, All Civilian Workers, March 2020," in *National Compensation Survey: Employee Benefits in the United States*, Bureau of Labor Statistics, March 2020, https://www.bls.gov/ncs/ebs/benefits/2020/employee-benefits-in-the-united-states-march-2020.pdf. These statistics include parental and caregiving leave

but not leave to care for one's own health. Paid leave availability has increased and is likely to continue to increase: "New SHRM Research Shows Employers Offering Paid Leave Has Increased," Society for Human Resource Managment Sept. 15, 2020, https://www.shrm.org/about-shrm/press-room/press-releases/pages/new-shrm-research-shows-employers-offering-paid-leave-has-increased.aspx

[112] Asha Banerjee et al., "Unions Are Not Only Good for Workers. They're Good for Communities and for Democracy," *Economic Policy Institute*, December 15, 2021, https://www.epi.org/publication/unions-and-well-being/

CHAPTER 8

[113] Lean In, "Women in the Workplace 2024," https://leanin.org/women-in-the-workplace?gclid=CjwKCAjw69moBhBgEiwAUFCx2DprFzCQtIEAtX63ex qm5pobW4qVLHzHDpv3s1NcoOQjppZqRI_rYRoC_mUQAvD_BwE.

[114] Carla McCann and Donald Komaskavic-Devey, "Pregnancy Discrimination in the Workplace," University of Massachusetts Center for Employment Equity, May 2021.

[115] Shiu-Yik Aku, Andreanne Tremblay, and Leyuan You, "Times Up: Does Female Leadership Reduce Workplace Sexual Harassment?" Academy of Management, July 29, 2020, https://journals.aom.org/doi/10.5465/AMBPP.2020.21007abstract.

[116] Jenny Vazquez-Newsum, *Untapped Leadership: Harnessing the Power of Underrepresented Leaders* (Prometheus, 2023), 72, 76.

[117] Rita Sever, Leading for Justice: Supervision, HR, and Culture (SheWrites Press, 2021).

CHAPTER 9

[118] Aviva Wittenberg-Cox, "Women's Career Trajectories Can Be a Model for an Aging Workforce," *Harvard Business Review*, Oct. 7, 2020. https://hbr.org/2020/10/womens-career-trajectories-can-be-a-model-for-an-aging-workforce

[119] "Employment Projections, 2023-2033," Bureau of Labor Statistics, Aug. 29, 2024. https://www.bls.gov/news.release/pdf/ecopro.pdf

[120] Richard Fry and Dana Braga, "Older Workers Are Growing in Number and Earning Higher Wages," Pew Research, Dec. 14, 2023.

[121] "Earnings Peak at Different Ages for Different Demographic Groups," Payscale, 2020. https://www.payscale.com/research-and-insights/peak-earnings/#overall

[122] Richard Fry and Dana Braga, "The Growth of the Older Workforce," Pew Research, Dec. 14, 2023. https://www.pewresearch.org/social-trends/2023/12/14/the-growth-of-the-older-workforce/

[123] Sarah Lawrence-Lightfoot: The Third Chapter: Passion, Risk, and Adventure in the 25 Years After 50 (Sarah Crichton Books, 2009.)

[124] Josh Bersin and Tomas Chamorro-Premuzic, "The Case for Hiring Older Workers," *Harvard Business Review,* Sept. 26, 2019. https://hbr.org/2019/09/the-case-for-hiring-older-workers

[125] Amy Diehl, Leanne M. Dzubinski and Amber L. Stephenson, "Women in Leadership Face Ageism at Every Age," *Harvard Business Review,* June 16, 2023. https://hbr.org/2023/06/women-in-leadership-face-ageism-at-every-age

[126] Ibid.

[127] "Women in the Workplace 2024: 10th Annual Report," Lean In, 2024. https://leanin.org/women-in-the-workplace?gclid=CjwKCAjw69moBhBgEiwAUFCx2DprFzCQtIEAtX63ex qm5pobW4qVLHzHDpv3s1NcoOQjppZqRI_rYRoC_mUQAvD_BwE

CHAPTER 10

[128] Ken Dychtwald, Robert Morison and Katy Terveer, "Redesigning Retirement," *Harvard Business Review,* March-April 2024. https://hbr.org/2024/03/redesigning-retirement

[129] Aviva Wittenberg-Cox, "Women's Career Trajectories Can Be a Model for an Aging Workforce," *Harvard Business Review,* Oct. 7, 2020. https://hbr.org/2020/10/womens-career-trajectories-can-be-a-model-for-an-aging-workforce

[130] Aviva Wittenberg-Cox, "What Work Looks Like for Women in Their 50s," Harvard Business Review, April 22, 2016. https://hbr.org/2016/04/what-work-looks-like-for-women-in-their-50s

[131] Aviva Wittenberg-Cox, "4 Phases of Women's Careers–Copin with the Crisis and the 30s," Forbes, May 10, 2020. https://www.forbes.com/sites/avivahwittenbergcox/2020/05/10/4-phases-of-womens-careers--coping-with-the-crisis--the-30s/

[132] Jaywon Lee et al, "Purpose and meaning in life and job satisfaction among the aged," International Journal of Aging & Human Development, 85 no. 4 (2017): 377–402

[133] Lona Choi-Allum, "High on Priority List for Older Workers: Meaningful Employment and Flexibility," American Association of Retired Persons, Jan. 18, 2023. https://www.aarp.org/pri/topics/work-finances-retirement/employers-workforce/multicultural-work-jobs-study-2023/

[134] Ken Dychtwald, Robert Morison and Katy Terveer, "Redesigning Retirement," Harvard Business Review, March-April 2024. https://hbr.org/2024/03/redesigning-retirement

[135] One recent study found Native Americans and people of Middle Eastern descent had the most positive views of the elderly. Raqota Berger, "Aging in America: Ageism and General Attitudes toward Growing Old and the Elderly," *Open Journal of Social Sciences* 5 no. 8 (2017).

[136] David S. Wong and Debrasree Das Gupta "Age-race-ethnicity Segregation in the United States: Where do Minority Older Adults Stand?" *Wiley Online Library*, Jan. 14, 2023. https://doi.org/10.1002/psp.2642

[137] "News Platform Fact Sheet, Pew Research, 2024. https://www.pewresearch.org/journalism/fact-sheet/news-platform-fact-sheet/#:~:text=For%20example%2C%20Americans%20ages%2050,like%20social%20media%20or%20podcasts.

www.ingramcontent.com/pod-product-compliance
Lightning Source LLC
Chambersburg PA
CBHW071718120626
46550CB00001B/293